A Note from the Publisher

As the authors wrote this book they made every attempt to choose children's literature titles which were in print or which were commonly available in a number of libraries they checked. The publishing industry at this time is undergoing great change due mostly to takeovers and mergers. This situation creates havoc in keeping children's literature in print. What is in print today, may be out of print tomorrow; and what is out of print today, may be back in print tomorrow. We checked the in-print status of the books included in this guide twice within three months and found major differences. Printed here is a list of all of the books mentioned and their in-print status as of December 2, 1993. We feel certain that many of the out-of-print titles listed here will eventually be back in print if you send orders to your favorite distributor and then query the publishers. Many publishers respond by putting the titles back into print. For example, *How Much Is a Million?* and *The Magic School Bus at the Waterworks* are such popular titles that they are due to come back into print at any moment. Have your library media specialist notify publishers of your wants. We are notifying publishers also and will encourage them to keep all the titles from this book in print.

In Print as of December 2, 1993

A, My Name Is Alice (Bayer), p. 176

Alexander, Who Used to Be Rich Last Sunday (Viorst), p. 51

Angelina's Birthday Surprise (Holabird), p. 43 alternate activity

Annie's Pet (Brenner), p. 152 alternate activity

Anno's Math Games II (Anno), p. 102 alternate activity

Anno's Math Games III (Anno), p. 68

Anno's Mysterious Multiplying Jar (Anno and Anno), p. 52

Archimedes (Lafferty), p. 102 alternate activity

Arthur's Funny Money (Hoban), p. 155

Benjy in Business (Van Leeuwen), p. 165 alternate activity

Berenstain Bears' Trouble with Money (Berenstain/Berenstain), p. 152 alternate activity

Binary Numbers (Watson), p. 33 alternate activity

Bringing the Rain to Kapiti Plain (Aardema), p. 134 alternate activity

Bunches and Bunches of Bunnies (Mathews), p. 45

Business Is Looking Up (Aiello), p. 165 alternate activity

Code Busters! (Burton), p. 181 alternate activity

Codebreaker Kids, The (Stanley), p. 181 alternate activity

Counting Wildflowers (McMillan), p. 39

Devil Storm (Nelson), p. 134 alternate activity

Dinah for President (Mills), p. 133 alternate activity

Do You Wanna Bet? (Cushman), p. 136

Dollars and Cents for Harriet (Maestro and Maestro), p. 150

Doorbell Rang, The (Hutchins), p. 47

Esio Trot (Dahl), p. 109 alternate activity

Flat Stanley (Brown), p. 67

Get Rich Mitch! (Sharmat), p. 144 alternate activity

Getting Elected: The Diary of a Campaign (Hewett), p. 133 alternate activity

Grandfather Tang's Story (Tompert), p. 72

Grouchy Ladybug, The (Carle), p. 98

Harriet's Halloween Candy (Carlson), p. 23

Hot Fudge (Howe), p. 157 alternate activity

How Big Is a Foot? (Myller), p. 99

How Did Numbers Begin? (Sitomer and Sitomer), p. 21

How Many Snails? (Giganti), p. 15

How Many Ways Can You Cut a Pie? (Moncure), p. 149 alternate activity

I Can Be an Architect (Clinton), p. 87 alternate activity

I Hate Mathematics! Book, The (Burns), p. 66 alternate activity

If You Made a Million (Schwartz), p. 163

Julia Morgan, Architect of Dreams (Wadsworth), p. 87 alternate activity

Kid Who Ran for President, The (Morris), p. 133 alternate activity

Magic School Bus Inside the Earth, The (Cole), p. 112

Magic School Bus Inside the Human Body, The (Cole), p. 114

Magic School Bus Lost in the Solar System, The (Cole), p. 56

Math Fun with Tricky Lines and Shapes (Wyler/Elting), p. 88 alternate activity

Math Games (Anno), p. 88 alternate activity

Moira's Birthday (Munsch), p. 127

Noah's Ark (Lorimer), p. 17 alternate activity

On Monday When It Rained (Kachenmeister), p. 105 alternate activity

One Monday Morning (Sulevitz), p. 105 alternate activity

One That Got Away, The (Everett), p. 14 alternate activity

One Watermelon Seed (Lottridge), p. 16

One Wide River to Cross (Emberley), p. 17

Paper John (Small), p. 76

Popcorn (Asch), p. 48

Purse, The (Caple), p. 152 alternate activity

Roman Numerals (Adler), p. 22

Sam Johnson and the Blue Ribbon Quilt (Ernst), p. 179

Science Book of Numbers (Challoner), p. 33 alternate activity

Sea Squares (Hulme), p. 178 alternate activity
Sea Witches (Robertson and Gal), p. 185
Senefer (Lumpkin), p. 33 alternate activity
Seven Eggs (Hooper), p. 105 alternate activity
Shape of Me and Other Stuff, The (Dr. Seuss), p. 64
Shapes and Strctures and Their Influence on Our World
    (Knapp), p. 83 alternate activity
Shapes Game, The (Rogers), p. 65
So Many Cats (de Regniers), p. 40
Some Things Go Together (Zolotow), p. 175
Statistics (Srivastava), p. 125
Structures and Materials (Taylor), p. 83 alternate activity
Summer Wheels (Bunting), p. 43 alternate activity

10 Bears in My Bed (Mack), p. 12
Ten Little Mice (Dunbar), p. 42 alternate activity
13th Clue, The (Jonas), p. 181 alternate activity
Time for Horatio (Paine), p. 110
Tom Fox and the Apple Pie (Watson), p. 149 alternate activity
Too Hot to Hoot (Terban), p. 183
Toothpaste Millionaire, The (Merrill), p. 57
Turtle Street Trading Co., The (Klevin), p. 167
Two By Two (Hewitt), p. 17 alternate activity
Weight and Balance (Taylor), p. 103 alternate activity
What's Cooking, Jenny Archer? (Conford), p. 161
Wheels (Hughes), p. 43 alternate activity
Zero! Is It Something? Is It Nothing? (Zaslavsky), p. 19

Out of Print as of December 2, 1993

Alice and the Boa Constrictor (Adams and Coudert), p. 159
Annie's One to Ten (Owen), p. 41
Around the World in Eighty Days (Verne), p. 116
Averages (Srivastava), p. 129
Base Five (Adler), p. 33 alternate activity
Boy with Square Eyes, The (Snape and Snape), p. 77
Case of the Stolen Code Book, The (Rinkoff), p. 181
Clue in Code, A (Singer), p. 195
Day That Monday Ran Away, The (Heit), p. 105
Diary of a Church Mouse (Oakley), p. 108
8,000 Stones (Wolkstein), p. 109
Fractions Are Parts of Things (Dennis), p. 151
Gator Pie (Mathews), p. 149
Great Take-Away, The (Mathews), p. 42
Harold & Chester in Hot Fudge (Howe), p. 157
Harriet Goes to the Circus (Maestro and Maestro), p. 13
Heavy Is a Hippopotamus (Schlein), p. 103
Henry's Pennies (McNamara), p. 152
How Much Is a Million? (Schwartz), p. 53
How to Count Like a Martian (St. John), p. 33
Jason and the Money Tree (Levitin), p. 165
Job for Jenny Archer, A (Conford), p. 165 alternate activity
Less Than Nothing Is Really Something (Froman), p. 28
Life of Numbers, The (Krahn and de la Luz Krahn), p. 14
Magic School Bus at the Waterworks, The (Cole), p. 169
Matt's Mitt and Fleet-Footed Florence, p. 126 alternate activity
Million Dollar Jeans (Roy), p. 144

Miss Pickerell and the Weather Satellite (MacGregor and
    Pantell), p. 134
Mr. Badger's Birthday Pie (MacDonald), p. 149 alternate
    activity
Number Families (Srivastava), p. 31
Number Ideas Through Pictures (Charosh), p. 178
Numblers (MacDonald), p. 14 alternate activity
Odds and Evens (O'Brien), p. 178 alternate activity
Penelope Gets Wheels (Peterson), p. 43
Pezzettino (Lionni), p. 101
Probability (Linn), p. 131
Rubber Bands, Baseballs, and Doughnuts (Froman), p. 88
Shape: The Purpose of Forms (Laithwaite), p. 83
Socrates and the Three Little Pigs (Mori), p. 145
Solomon Grundy (Hogett), p.189 alternate activity
Solomon Grundy, Born on Oneday (Weiss), p. 189
Space, Shapes, and Sizes (Srivastava), p. 102
Spirals (Sitomer and Sitomer), p. 82
This Is 4: The Idea of a Number (Razzell and Watts), p. 24
Visual Magic (Thomson), p. 190
What Can She Be? An Architect (Goldreich and Goldreich), p.
    87
What Do You Mean by "Average"? (James and Barkin), p. 133
What Is Symmetry? (Sitomer and Sitomer), p. 66
World of Wonders (Ockenga), p. 14 alternate activity

MATH THROUGH CHILDREN'S LITERATURE
Making the NCTM Standards Come Alive

Kathryn L. Braddon
Nancy J. Hall
Dale Taylor

1993
TEACHER IDEAS PRESS
A Division of
Libraries Unlimited, Inc.
Englewood, Colorado

TEACHER IDEAS PRESS
A Division of Libraries Unlimited, Inc.
P.O. Box 6633
Englewood, CO 80155-6633
1-800-237-6124

Library of Congress Cataloging-in-Publication Data

Braddon, Kathryn L.
    Math through children's literature : making the NCTM Standards
  come alive / Kathryn L. Braddon, Nancy J. Hall, and Dale Taylor.
    xviii, 218 p. 22x28 cm.
    Includes index.
    ISBN 0-87287-932-1
    1. Reading. 2. Children's literature. 3. Mathematics--Study and
  teaching (Elementary) I. Taylor, Dale, 1942- . II. Hall, Nancy J.
  III. Title.
  QA135.5.B678 1993   91-34286
  372.7'044--dc20   CIP

To my husband, three children, and the students and staff at Manchester-Shortsville Central School.

—Kathryn L. Braddon

To my husband, who is still my best friend, even after all this.

—Nancy J. Hall

To my wife and two sons, Greg and Brent Taylor.

—Dale Taylor

Contents

Preface xiii

Acknowledgments xv

How to Use This Book xvii

Part I
THE MATHEMATICS CURRICULUM

1 – An Overview of Mathematics Education 1
Historical Perspective 1
The Essentials of Education 2
The Role of Reading 2
Change 3
Rote Learning of Mathematics Basic Facts 3
The Breadth of Mathematics 4
Why Study Mathematics? – Integration 5
Calculators in the Mathematics Classroom 6
Notes 6

Part II
THE PROCESS COMPONENTS

2 – An Overview of Math Standards 1 Through 5 7
Standard 1 Mathematics as Problem Solving 7
Standard 2 Mathematics as Communication 8
Standard 3 Mathematics as Reasoning 8
Standard 4 Mathematical Connections 9
Standard 5 Estimation 9

Part III
THE CONTENT COMPONENTS

3 – Standard 6: Number Sense and Numeration 11
Books for Grades K-3 11
Mathematical Content Vocabulary 11
10 Bears in My Bed (Mack) 12
Harriet Goes to the Circus (Maestro and Maestro) 13

3 — Standard 6: Number Sense and Numeration — *Continued*

  The Life of Numbers (Krahn and de la Luz Krahn)...................................14

  How Many Snails? (Giganti)...................................15

  One Watermelon Seed (Lottridge)...................................16

  One Wide River to Cross (Emberley)...................................17

  Zero. Is It Something? Is It Nothing? (Zaslavsky)...................................19

 Books for Grades 4-6...................................21

  Mathematical Content Vocabulary...................................21

  How Did Numbers Begin? (Sitomer and Sitomer)...................................21

  Roman Numerals (Adler)...................................22

  Harriet's Halloween Candy (Carlson)...................................23

  This Is 4: The Idea of a Number (Razzell and Watts)...................................24

  Less Than Nothing Is Really Something (Froman)...................................28

  Number Families (Srivastava)...................................31

  How to Count Like a Martian (St. John)...................................33

 Related Books and References...................................34

  Counting...................................34

  Large Numbers and Infinity...................................35

  Number Concepts...................................36

  Numerals and Art...................................36

  Ordinals...................................36

  Other Base Systems...................................36

  Zeros and Negative Numbers...................................36

  Miscellaneous...................................37

  Adult References...................................37

4 — Standard 7: Concepts of Whole-Number Operations and Standard 8: Whole-Number Computation...................................38

 Books for Grades K-3...................................39

  Mathematical Content Vocabulary...................................39

  Counting Wildflowers (McMillan)...................................39

  So Many Cats (de Regniers)...................................40

  Annie's One to Ten (Owen)...................................41

  The Great Take-Away (Mathews)...................................42

  Penelope Gets Wheels (Peterson)...................................43

  Bunches and Bunches of Bunnies (Mathews)...................................45

  The Doorbell Rang (Hutchins)...................................47

 Books for Grades 4-6...................................48

  Mathematical Content Vocabulary...................................48

  Popcorn (Asch)...................................48

  Alexander, Who Used to Be Rich Last Sunday (Viorst)...................................51

  Anno's Mysterious Multiplying Jar (Anno and Anno)...................................52

  How Much Is a Million? (Schwartz)...................................53

  The Magic School Bus Lost in the Solar System (Cole)...................................56

  The Toothpaste Millionaire (Merrill)...................................57

Related Books and References...60
  Addition and Subtraction..60
  Calculators 61
  Multiplication and Division...61
  Miscellaneous 61
  Adult References 62

5 — Standard 9: Geometry and Spatial Sense...................................63
  Books for Grades K-3...63
    Mathematical Content Vocabulary...63
    The Shape of Me and Other Stuff (Dr. Seuss) 64
    The Shapes Game (Rogers)..65
    What Is Symmetry? (Sitomer and Sitomer) 66
    Flat Stanley (Brown)...67
    Anno's Math Games III (Anno)...68
    Grandfather Tang's Story (Tompert)..72
  Books for Grades 4-6...76
    Mathematical Content Vocabulary...76
    Paper John (Small)..76
    The Boy with Square Eyes (Snape and Snape)..............................77
    Spirals (Sitomer and Sitomer)..82
    Shape: The Purpose of Forms (Laithwaite)..................................83
    What Can She Be? An Architect (Goldreich and Goldreich) 87
    Rubber Bands, Baseballs, and Doughnuts (Froman).......................88
  Related Books and References...91
    Architecture..91
    Dimensionality...91
    Drawing and Computer Graphics...91
    Geometric Shapes and Concepts...92
    Miscellaneous 93
    Non-Geometric Shapes..93
    Paper-Folding and Paper-Cutting Geometry/Symmetry.....................94
    Proportionality..94
    Quilting 95
    Shadows and Reflections..95
    Topology...96
    Adult References 96

6 — Standard 10: Measurement..97
  Books for Grades K-3...97
    Mathematical Content Vocabulary...97
    The Grouchy Ladybug (Carle)...98
    How Big Is a Foot? (Myller)..99
    Pezzettino (Lionni)..101
    Space, Shapes, and Sizes (Srivastava).......................................102
    Heavy Is a Hippopotamus (Schlein)...103
    The Day That Monday Ran Away (Heit)......................................105

6—Standard 10: Measurement—*Continued*
Books for Grades 4-6...108
  Mathematical Content Vocabulary..108
  Diary of a Church Mouse (Oakley)...108
  8,000 Stones (Wolkstein)..109
  Time for Horatio (Paine)...110
  The Magic School Bus Inside the Earth (Cole)................................112
  The Magic School Bus Inside the Human Body (Cole)..........................114
  Around the World in Eighty Days (Verne).....................................116
Related Books and References..118
  Area...118
  Calendar...118
  Days of the Week...118
  Linear Measurement...119
  Miscellaneous Measurement..120
  Temperature..121
  Time...121
  Volume and Capacity..122
  Weight and Mass..123
  Adult References...123

7—Standard 11: Statistics and Probability..................................124
Books for Grades K-3..124
  Mathematical Content Vocabulary..124
  Statistics (Srivastava)..125
  Fleet-Footed Florence (Sachs)..126
  Moira's Birthday (Munsch)..127
  Averages (Srivastava)..129
  Probability (Linn)...131
Books for Grades 4-6..132
  Mathematical Content Vocabulary..132
  What Do You Mean by "Average"? (James and Barkin)............................133
  Miss Pickerell and the Weather Satellite (MacGregor and Pantell)............134
  Do You Wanna Bet? (Cushman)..136
  Million Dollar Jeans (Roy)...144
  Socrates and the Three Little Pigs (Mori)...................................145
Related Books and References..146
  Probability and Statistics...146
  Weather..146
  Adult References...147

8—Standard 12: Fractions and Decimals......................................148
Books for Grades K-3..148
  Mathematical Content Vocabulary..148
  Gator Pie (Mathews)..149
  Dollars and Cents for Harriet (Maestro and Maestro).........................150
  Fractions Are Parts of Things (Dennis)......................................151
  Henry's Pennies (McNamara)...152

Arthur's Funny Money (Hoban)..155
Harold & Chester in Hot Fudge (Howe)..............................157
Books for Grades 4-6..158
Mathematical Content Vocabulary...158
Alice and the Boa Constrictor (Adams and Coudert).........159
What's Cooking, Jenny Archer? (Conford).........................161
If You Made a Million (Schwartz).......................................163
Jason and the Money Tree (Levitin)....................................165
The Turtle Street Trading Co. (Klevin)..............................167
The Magic School Bus at the Waterworks (Cole)...............169
Related Books and References..171
Fractions—Cooking...171
Fractions—Music...172
Fractions—Pies and Pizzas/Food..172
Fractions—Miscellaneous..172
Decimals...172
Money—Miscellaneous..173
Money-Making Ideas for Kids...173

9—**Standard 13: Patterns and Relationships**.....................175
Books for Grades K-3...175
Mathematical Content Vocabulary...175
Some Things Go Together (Zolotow).....................................175
A, My Name Is Alice (Bayer)...176
Number Ideas Through Pictures (Charosh)..........................178
Sam Johnson and the Blue Ribbon Quilt (Ernst).................179
The Case of the Stolen Code Book (Rinkoff).......................181
Books for Grades 4-6...182
Mathematical Content Vocabulary...182
Too Hot to Hoot (Terban)..183
Sea Witches (Robertson and Gal)..185
Solomon Grundy, Born on Oneday (Weiss).........................189
Visual Magic (Thomson)..190
A Clue in Code (Singer)...195
Related Books and References..197
Pattern Books...197
Poetry Patterns..198
Secret Codes...198
Visual Patterns...198
Miscellaneous...199
Adult References..199

Appendix—Traditional Patterns of Teaching Mathematics with Changes Suggested by the NCTM Standards...201

Incorporating the Standards into the Traditional Mathematics Scope and Sequence...201

Content Traditionally Covered in Grades K-6 and Suggested Changes.............202

Index..211

About the Authors..218

Preface

Elementary students who love good literature are often the same children who dislike completing worksheets filled with math problems or who struggle with those troublesome word problems. With the whole language philosophy and literature-based language arts becoming more prevalent, it became evident that integrating math and literature would be not only an exciting, but also a logical union.

Math Through Children's Literature was undertaken to recognize and apply the conventional wisdom that children learn by being actively involved in the learning process, rather than by filling out another set of exercises on worksheets. By integrating math and literature, word problems can use familiar stories to allow students to address the mathematical functions rather than struggle needlessly with unfamiliar vocabulary. Mathematical activities that are stimulated by literature inspire students to explore and investigate concepts. And the marriage of math with quality literature fosters the realization that math is all around us.

Math Through Children's Literature utilizes the National Council of Teachers of Mathematics (NCTM) Standards as a base for the math activities and features quality children's literature that is readily available through school or public libraries. Part I gives an overview of mathematics education. Part II provides an overview of math standards 1 through 5. The balance of *Math Through Children's Literature* explores books and related math activities for grades K-3 and 4-6 for standards 6 through 13. Related books and references are suggested for further exploration.

Teachers using this book may want to enhance the math yearbook by integrating a beloved book such as *10 Bears in My Bed*. Others may find that using a book such as *Gator Pie* to introduce fractions helps the students understand textbook material more fully. Some teachers may decide to replace a math textbook unit, such as measurement, with a series of books and activities. No matter how you choose to use *Math Through Children's Literature*, it is hoped that you will investigate further possibilities for exploring math in all aspects of your program, truly making the NCTM Standards come alive!

In *Math Through Children's Literature* every effort has been made to use resource books that are now readily accessible to educators. Most are available through your local bookstore or through public or school libraries. Inquire about titles in print with your local bookstore or book wholesaler. If you have trouble locating a particular title, ask your librarian to assist you with interlibrary loans or advise you regarding similar titles that will also work.

Acknowledgments

Grateful acknowledgment is made to Michelle Klein and Doug Morrow for their graphics in this book; John Lennon and Arthur Lowenthal for their computer assistance; Mary Ferris and the others at Wood Library; Griff at Village Green for finding books; and friends and relatives for their moral support and interest. Grateful acknowledgment is also made for permission to use illustrations and material from the following copyrighted books: pp. 84, 88, and 89 reprinted with the permission of Macmillan Publishing Company from *Loads of Codes and Secret Ciphers* by Paul B. Janeczko, text copyright © 1984 Paul B. Janeczko; pp. 13 and 15 from *More Codes for Kids*, copyright © 1979 by Burton Albert, Jr., reprinted by permission of McIntosh and Otis, Inc., published by Albert Whitman and Company; p. 265 from *Mathematics Their Way* by Mary Baratta-Lorton, copyright © 1976, Addison-Wesley Publishing Company; the illustrations by M. C. Escher, copyright © M. C. Escher/Cordon Art— Baarn—Holland, all rights reserved; pp. 58 and 91 from *The I Hate Mathematics! Book* by Marilyn Burns, copyright © 1975 by the Yolla Bolly Press, by permission of Little, Brown and Company; pp. 35 and 54 from *Anno's Math Games III* by Mitsumasa Anno, copyright © 1982 by Kuso-Kobo, © 1992 by Philomel Books, reprinted by permission of Philomel Books; pp. 40 and 41 from *Off and Running: The Computer Offline Activities Book* by Tim Erickson, copyright © 1986 Regents, University of California, EQUALS, Lawrence Hall of Science; pp. 14-15 from *Paper Folding Fun* by Robert Harbin, copyright © 1960, reprinted by permission of the Trustees of the British Origami Society; p. 18 from *Do You Wanna Bet?* by Jean Cushman. Text copyright © 1991 by Jean Cushman. Reprinted by permission of Clarion Books/Houghton Mifflin Co. All rights reserved.

How to Use This Book

As a teacher, my first reaction to teaching mathematics through literature was dismissive. Mathematics, after all, particularly at the elementary level, should be taught through the use of manipulatives. If math were to be integrated with another subject, it would be science, not language arts. Fortunately, it is sometimes possible to teach an old dog new tricks.

I've learned that teaching mathematics through literature isn't such a crazy idea after all. While mathematics is perhaps the most difficult subject to integrate with reading and language arts, many more literature books lend themselves to this type of integration than I had initially suspected. It's also true that approaching mathematics through literature is often more palatable to many students and teachers who have found earlier experiences with mathematics unpleasant. In addition, stories can show students how math is applied in the "real world" in ways that textbooks rarely do. Finally, the use of literature and the use of manipulatives are not, by any means, mutually exclusive.

This book is organized according to the National Council of Teachers of Mathematics (NCTM) Standards for the elementary level.* These standards reflect the latest in research and successful practices developed by the people who have the greatest expertise in this area. Because the standards advocate an approach to teaching mathematics that may be somewhat different from the way many textbooks are organized, and different from the practices most familiar to teachers, a correlation between the standards and a more conventional scope and sequence is included in the appendix.

The first five elementary mathematical standards can be thought of as components that permeate the entire mathematics curriculum. Problem solving, communication, reasoning, connections, and estimation are the major processes to be woven through the mathematics concepts found in the remaining eight standards. It is sometimes difficult to isolate these processes, and therefore, no books or activities for standards 1 through 5 have been included.

Standards 6 through 13 are considered the content components and the books and activities highlighted in a specific chapter focus primarily on the concepts included in that standard. However, there is a considerable amount of overlap, and standards often build on one another. For example, when adding a deposit to a checking account, you would be dealing with both standard 8—Whole Number Computation and standard 12—Fractions and Decimals. Therefore, you will find cross-referencing among the content standards. Because standards 1 through 5 address processes and permeate so many of the activities, cross-referencing does not include these standards.

The books chosen for each of the content standards can be used to introduce or reinforce the specific mathematical concepts addressed by that particular standard. These books and activities are

---

*The NCTM Standards are divided into three levels: Kindergarten through fourth grade, fifth grade through eighth grade, and ninth grade through twelfth grade. This division doesn't completely match a book designed to be used by teachers in grades K-6, but we feel we have successfully addressed the concepts important for intermediate grades.

not meant to encompass your entire mathematics curriculum. However, they can generate student interest, illustrate the application of specific concepts, and demonstrate the pervasiveness of mathematics in everyday life.

In addition to being organized according to NCTM Standards, the books have been categorized as either most appropriate for students in grades K-3 or for students in grades 4-6. Within each section is a list of content vocabulary that may be new to the students, and the featured books are presented in order of increasing difficulty. Obviously, student abilities vary a great deal even within a specific grade level. You are the best judge of your students' abilities, and you will need to evaluate which books and activities will be best suited to your students. You can, of course, choose other books from the Related Books and References section listed at the end of each chapter, or adapt activities to the particular needs of your students.

The subtitle to this book is *Making the NCTM Standards Come Alive.* The books highlighted in each chapter were chosen not only for their applicability to the concepts, but also to stimulate student interest. Your enthusiasm to explore the literature and activities with your students is essential and will motivate them even further. Enjoy your adventures!

1—An Overview of Mathematics Education

HISTORICAL PERSPECTIVE

Mathematics is a process for communicating data and a study of pattern and order. A special role is reserved for mathematics in education because of its universal applicability.

The study of mathematics has existed at least as long as recorded history. Mathematics has changed over the centuries, and its effect on culture has been profound and complex. During the last few centuries mathematics has progressed from its status as a somewhat static field of study to its current dynamic status. In fact, mathematics education as a separate field of scholarly endeavor is essentially a middle-twentieth-century phenomenon.

To understand why mathematics reform today is in debate, we must review our recent history. The present mathematics curriculum was designed to prepare shopkeepers, farmers, and factory workers for the 1940s. Some of those skills are still useful today. However, in the 1990s the requirements of society ask all its citizens, male and female, and all its cultures and backgrounds to be well prepared in the area of mathematics, and this need far exceeds basic computational skills.

The pendulum in educational thought seems to be in constant motion. In mathematics opinions on how and what should be learned shift quite rapidly. A quick review of just the last thirty-five years indicates how ideas in the field of mathematics have developed and changed:

- In the late 1950s, the Sputnik space shot by the Soviets caused the United States to expend a large amount of effort and spend a lot of money on developing mathematics curriculum revisions.

- During the early 1960s, sometimes called the modern math era due to learning-style changes from more traditional approaches, mathematicians developed the assumption that mathematical understanding could best be developed by precision and rigor.

- The late 1960s saw a backlash to these "modern math" textbooks. This period, often called the transition period because of the change from exact, rote learning of math facts and algorithms to a process-driven, hands-on approach, was affected by the writings of such people as Jean Piaget.

- The beginning of the 1970s became known as the laboratory mathematics period because of the extensive use of manipulative teaching materials. With the broadening acceptance of Piaget's ideas, the mathematics curriculum began to include manipulative materials, lab materials, and hands-on activities.

- The end of the 1970s reflected a back to the basics attitude. Unfortunately, no one could agree on what the basics actually were in mathematics. However, two issues did come to the forefront during this time. The first was an understanding that equal access to mathematics education must be available to all people if this country is to remain a world leader or even stay competitive with the rest of the world. The second issue was that technological developments were making many former basic mathematics skills almost obsolete.

- Early in the 1980s came the publication *An Agenda for Action*, published by the National Council of Teachers of Mathematics.[1] Its primary focus suggested that problem solving be given a greater effort in the 1980s. However, problem solving was found to be more difficult and complicated to teach than anyone had imagined.

- The second half of the 1980s was called the era of realization because of the need for reforms in mathematics education due to the large amount of research supporting this view. Writings such as *Everybody Counts, Curriculum and Evaluation Standards for School Mathematics*, and *Reshaping School Mathematics* set the direction for mathematics in the 1990s.[2] These writings designated criteria for the K-12 mathematics curriculum as well as a focus on how students come to understand mathematics.

THE ESSENTIALS OF EDUCATION

The public has a valid concern about the basic skills and knowledge of our students, and it should reject simplistic solutions to these problems. The three *R*s we have traditionally spoken about are limited in scope when one views the complex, highly technological society we live in. Also, expecting the historic testing methods and evaluation systems teachers used in the past to measure what is now considered essential is not possible given the large limitations on these instruments and today's expanded needs.

The primary goal of education at this time is to develop informed, thinking individuals able to participate in today's complex society. Skills and abilities do not grow in isolation from other content areas; rather, all subjects using language and symbol systems, the development of reason, and the experiences that lead to emotional and social maturity must grow in concert.

Preparing students to meet the needs of the twenty-first century requires all disciplines to join together and acknowledge their interdependence. Also, all segments of society—legislators, parents, educators, and the business community—must work together to identify what is truly essential for students to know.

THE ROLE OF READING

Reading is a process in which the reader's knowledge and textual information act together to produce meaning. Good readers skillfully integrate information in the text with what they already know. Skilled readers are flexible. How they read depends upon the complexity of the text, their familiarity with the topic, and their purpose for reading.

As proficiency develops reading should be thought of not so much as a separate subject in school, but as integral to learning mathematics, literature, social studies, and science. When connections among these subject areas develop, students are better able to understand motive and action, form and function, or cause and effect. The idea that reading instruction and subject-matter instruction should be integrated is an old one in education, but there is little indication that such integration often occurs in practice.

One primary characteristic that distinguishes an effective classroom from an ineffective one is the teacher's commitment to the belief that all children can learn to read and be successful students.

Becoming a Nation of Readers: The Report of the Commission on Reading[3] emphasizes why it is important to integrate the school's subject areas. Mathematics is a communication tool that works directly with the skill of reading and allows the student to use and understand data found in all school subjects and to interpret the logic and patterns found in those subjects. Reading and mathematics skills must go hand in hand for the student to become a successful learner.

CHANGE

Much has been and will be written about the adjustments necessary in mathematics education. The primary reason to write this book is to demonstrate how teachers and parents can begin effecting this change for students.

HOW DO THE NCTM CURRICULUM AND EVALUATION STANDARDS DIFFER FROM WHAT IS BEING DONE TODAY?

The standards emphasize

- applying mathematics over mathematics computation;

- spending less time on rote drill and more time on problem solving;

- using computers and calculators as "fast pencils" during the course of problem solving;

- seeing mathematics as an integrated whole rather than as a series of isolated topics;

- learning the *meaning* of operations such as addition and multiplication, as well as simply learning the operations.

The greatest difference for today's elementary-age students can be achieved by changing two attitudes. First, rote learning of basic mathematics facts (adding, subtracting, multiplying, and dividing skills) is still of vital importance. However, rote learning of basic facts is better taught after the student has acquired purpose for these facts, not before students are allowed to do mathematics, which is traditionally what has happened in the United States. Second, the breadth of mathematics should be taught as soon as students have usefulness for this information in relating to their world.

ROTE LEARNING OF MATHEMATICS BASIC FACTS

In the United States a tradition was begun that is quite different from most other parts of the world. Parents and teachers believe that once a child begins school the memorization of the basic math facts must be accomplished prior to the student doing mathematics. In fact, teachers and parents have been so successful at presenting this idea that many people believe that the computational skill is mathematics rather than a vehicle to do mathematics.

Certainly rote learning of math facts and processes is of value to today's students. These skills help students understand much about our number system. Rote learning of math facts and processes also provides students a necessary and efficient method to perform computational functions.

There are real difficulties, however, with teaching rote learning of mathematics facts prior to developing a need for these skills. People do not remember unrelated facts very well. Many who teach memorization skills recognize this problem and have become successful helping people memorize facts by teaching them to tie known facts to new information. Teachers know the many hours they spend almost entirely on math facts and basic computational procedures in grades kindergarten through sixth and how little long-term retention of these skills their students have had.

Teachers can improve the rote learning of math facts by delaying this instruction until students understand the number system and have need for this skill. An example of this is when a kindergarten teacher begins the school year by having play money—pennies, nickels, dimes, and quarters—available to students. Whenever students need a pencil, paper, crayon, or work sheet, they must buy it with play money. Initially the teacher must help a few sellers make the correct change. After several days enough students have learned the procedure so that peer help is all that is needed. Shortly after the first month of school nearly all students in the room are able to make the correct change up to twenty-five cents. At this time the teacher may begin teaching adding and subtracting facts through 25. Kindergartners, with very few exceptions, are able to quickly rote learn their adding and subtracting math facts through 25. Note that the teaching of the math facts was not greatly delayed. In fact, these kindergarten students will learn their math facts much quicker than is the norm in this country. Even if this activity is delayed until first grade, the students are still far ahead of what is considered normal.

The withholding of mathematics power is the other major loss students have suffered because of the traditional expectations required in rote learning. Students who solve problems that are real and valuable to them want to do it again and again. Teachers and parents should therefore have as a goal an environment that is rich in real-life problem-solving situations for children, and they should provide the efficient tools that the children can effectively use to help them solve these problems. This means students should have access to calculators, computers, paper and pencil, and memorization abilities necessary to solve their problems as soon as they need and can be taught to use each of these skills.

THE BREADTH OF MATHEMATICS

Parents and teachers have observed children doing mathematics prior to their school years.

Young children work with number sense and numeration when they begin counting and grouping objects.

Preschoolers work with whole number operations when they count how old they are and show the results on their fingers. Children at this age can also quickly tell who received more or less candy, Christmas gifts, and so on.

Before students start to school they often use whole-number computation. They not only can say who received more candy, Christmas presents, or pennies, but they can say how many more.

Often overlooked is the geometry and spatial sense preschoolers have developed. Remember how they draw shapes, play with fitting shapes into balls and puzzles, and how these skills help them to better understand their own world.

Certainly measurement plays a big part in very young children's learning to relate to their world. Remember how they always want to compare their physical size with that of other children and adults.

Collecting and analyzing data is a big part of a preschooler's life. Statistics and probability are regularly used by children to determine whether they have their fair share.

Certainly before the age of five, children enjoy and want to use fractions and decimals. Remember how they always want the bigger half.

Preschoolers spend a great deal of time discovering patterns and relationships. Consider how many times a young child looks at things to discover how they go together or how they are alike or different.

WHY STUDY MATHEMATICS? — INTEGRATION

The integration of mathematics into language arts and science through useful and creative problem-solving activities almost always raises the level of learning. Help in understanding the integration process may be found in the rather broad definitions of these three major areas of learning. Language arts may be considered as the curriculum area devoted to the study of the communication skills of speech, writing, hearing, reading, and sometimes touch. Science may be considered the curriculum area for the study and understanding of any and all fact and the development of a variety of learning processes. Mathematics may be considered the curriculum area devoted to the study of the communication skills of gathering and comparing data as well as to the study of patterns and order. The communication skills necessary for language arts and math allow us to both receive and share information. Consider the difference that occurs when we attempt to develop our communication skills in math and language arts in isolation, versus when those skills are practiced performing activities we see as important to our lives.

Integration is a buzzword in education today, but too often the meaning seems to suggest that if the teacher throws any two subject areas together, something better will happen. With a little more purposeful thought, teachers can easily raise the interest, complexity, and success of some of their favorite activities.

Some of the learning taxonomies one finds today suggest there are different levels of learning and that teachers and parents should strive to help students achieve more complex learning skills. It has been suggested that learning complexity follows the pattern outlined below.

- restatement of fact

- restatement of facts in child's own words

- showing or doing, using information

- breaking a whole into parts

- building a new whole from parts

- making judgments from the facts

By considering how teachers have traditionally taught each subject area in isolation, one can understand how activities with students have stayed largely at the lower levels of these taxonomies. In fact, many believe that at least 90 to 95 percent of classroom instruction time has traditionally been spent in the first two steps. However, when a teacher attempts to teach language-arts and mathematics skills for the purpose of understanding science, most activities involved in this integration are seen to cause the students to work at least at the fourth level or higher.

CALCULATORS IN THE MATHEMATICS CLASSROOM

Groups such as the NCTM now recommend the integration of the calculator into the school mathematics program at all grade levels (K-12) in classwork, homework, and evaluation. Calculators have been used much less frequently in the classroom than in the rest of society. The goal is to allow all students to develop skills in mental, paper-and-pencil, and calculator computation so that they learn to select the most efficient method for each situation they encounter. Some of the time that students currently use for practicing computation could be more efficiently spent helping students understand mathematics, develop reasoning and problem-solving strategies, as well as to simply use and apply mathematics.

Students must be taught how and when to use the calculator. To be an effective user of a calculator students of all grade levels must be able to estimate and judge the reasonableness of a problem. An understanding and knowledge of the basic facts and processes are as important as ever. The evaluation of students' mathematical understanding of concepts and their applications on criterion-referenced tests and standardized tests is being designed to measure the students' effectiveness with a calculator as well as mental math and paper-and-pencil methods.

Some people believe that students will not learn the basic math facts if they use a calculator. Studies indicate just the opposite. In fact, the calculator enhances the students' ability to learn mathematics. Young as well as older students are often able to use a calculator to perform mathematics beyond the level of their computational skill level, thus freeing their minds for greater and more stimulating education.

NOTES

[1]National Council of Teachers of Mathematics, *An Agenda for Action: Recommendations for School Mathematics of the 1980s* (Reston, Va.: NCTM, 1980).

[2]Board on Mathematical Sciences and Mathematical Sciences Education Board, *Everybody Counts: A Report to the Nation on the Future of Mathematics Education* (Washington, D.C.: National Academy Press, 1989); National Council of Teachers of Mathematics, *Curriculum and Evaluation Standards for School Mathematics* (Reston, Va.: NCTM, 1989); Mathematical Sciences Education Board, National Research Council, *Reshaping School Mathematics* (Washington, D.C.: National Research Council, 1990).

[3]National Institute of Education, *Becoming a Nation of Readers: The Report of the Commission on Reading* (Washington, D.C.: Government Printing Office, 1984).

2—An Overview of Math Standards 1 Through 5

Teachers instructing at the elementary school level may consider the first five math standards as processes that permeate the mathematics curriculum. Problem solving, communication, reasoning, connections, and estimation are the major processes to be woven through the mathematics concepts found in the remaining eight elementary standards.*

STANDARD 1
MATHEMATICS AS PROBLEM SOLVING

Problem solving provides the basic framework for learning most of the mathematical concepts and skills. The primary reason for choosing to write this book in this format came from the understanding that many of the best problem-solving situations grow naturally from the students' own background, which is developed through being aware of the world that surrounds them and through their reading. A variety of strategies may be used to help students develop this skill for solving open-ended problems. An environment that encourages questions, investigations, speculations, and explorations is encouraged.

The study of mathematics should emphasize problem solving so that students can

- use problem-solving approaches to investigate and understand mathematical content,

- formulate problems from everyday and mathematical situations,

- develop and apply strategies to solve a wide variety of problems,

- verify and interpret results with respect to the original problem, and

- acquire confidence in using mathematics meaningfully.

---

*The thirteen standards in this book are reprinted with permission of the National Council of Teachers of Mathematics from *Curriculum and Evaluation Standards for School Mathematics* (Reston, Va.: The Council, 1989).

STANDARD 2
MATHEMATICS AS COMMUNICATION

Mathematics is a language that can help students construct links between their informal, intuitive notions and the abstract languages and symbolism of mathematics. Much of the sense that children make of their world comes from their relations with other people. Communicating helps children to clarify their thinking. Representing (translating a problem or an idea into a new form), talking, listening, writing, and reading are key communication skills and should be viewed as important parts of any mathematics curriculum. Cooperative-learning groups are a good way to teach students communication techniques for sharing their thoughts with other people. In addition, concept-mapping activities (simple visual devices that allow students to relate major concepts from one source to another) help children to better comprehend if they can find cross-links or relationships in the material presented to them. Concept maps help children to center on key ideas and to focus on what is necessary to complete a task.

The study of mathematics should include numerous opportunities for communication so that students can

- relate physical materials, pictures, and diagrams to mathematical ideas;

- reflect on and clarify their thinking about mathematical ideas and situations;

- relate their everyday language to mathematical language and symbols; and

- realize that representing, discussing, reading, writing, and listening to mathematics are vital parts of learning and using mathematics.

STANDARD 3
MATHEMATICS AS REASONING

Children and teachers need to understand that being able to explain thinking is as important as the answer. Critical thinking and establishing a spirit of inquiry are important in all mathematics classroom environments. Students who have learned to show their concepts through mathematics and students who are comfortable with analysis, synthesis, and evaluation techniques are preparing for their future in the twenty-first century.

The study of mathematics should emphasize reasoning so that students can

- draw logical conclusions about mathematics;

- use models, known facts, properties, and relationships to explain their thinking;

- justify their answers and solution processes;

- use patterns and relationships to analyze mathematical situations; and

- believe that mathematics makes sense.

STANDARD 4
MATHEMATICAL CONNECTIONS

Ideas and activities children work with must flow easily from one task to the next. Students must recognize the relationship between mathematics and the other subjects with which they are working. Extended exposure to integrated topics gives students a better chance of retaining the concepts and skills taught.

The study of mathematics should include opportunities to make connections so that the students can

- link conceptual and procedural knowledge;

- relate various representations of concepts or procedures to one another;

- recognize relationships among different topics in mathematics;

- use mathematics in other curriculum areas; and

- use mathematics in their daily lives.

STANDARD 5
ESTIMATION

Estimation skills and understanding enhance the abilities of students to deal with everyday quantitative situations. Estimation illustrates that mathematics does not always involve exactness. Most early children's mathematics involve estimation skills, and they prove to be effective—as they can be for everyone.

The curriculum should include estimation so that students can

- explore estimation strategies;

- recognize when an estimate is appropriate;

- determine the reasonableness of results; and

- apply estimation in working with quantities, measurement, computation, and problem solving.

3—Standard 6: Number Sense and Numeration

The mathematics curriculum should include whole-number concepts and skills so that students can

- construct number meanings through real world experiences and the use of physical materials;

- understand the numeration system by relating counting, grouping, and place value concepts;

- develop number sense; and

- interpret the multiple uses of numbers encountered in the real world.

Number sense is generally considered to have five components:

1. Developing number meanings, cardinal and ordinal;

2. Exploring number relations with manipulatives;

3. Understanding relative sizes of numbers;

4. Developing feelings about the relative effect of using numbers;

5. Developing measurement skills of common objects and situations.

BOOKS FOR GRADES K-3

MATHEMATICAL CONTENT VOCABULARY

average	how many	order	sixth
base systems	hundred	ordinals	smallest
cost	infinity	pint	symbol
countdown	largest	position	ten
eight	measure	pound	tenth
eighth	nine	quart	thermometer
fifth	ninth	rounding	third
first	notation	second	three
five	number	sequence	two
four	numeral	seven	zero
fourth	odometer	seventh	
googol	one	six	

10 Bears in My Bed
Stan Mack
(New York: Pantheon Books, 1974)

A little boy goes to his bedroom to go to sleep and finds ten bears in his bed. He tells them to roll over and one by one they leave by way of the window. Finally, all the bears are gone, and the little boy has the bed all to himself. This is a delightful goodnight countdown from 10 to 1.

Activities

1. When the little boy goes to bed, he finds 10 bears in his bed. There are four bears in the first row, four bears behind them, and two more behind them. Using Xs to represent bears, have the children show how many different ways the bears could theoretically be positioned.

   Example: X X X X X   or   X X X X X X X

             X X X X X   X X

                                X

2. If ten bears are in the bed, how many feet are in the bed? How many toes? (They may want to draw pictures in order to count.)

3. Have the children find out how much a bear weighs. Using their calculators, have them figure out how much ten bears weigh. What else weighs that much? Do they think the bed would have broken with the weight of ten bears on it? (Standard 10)

4. Have the children measure their beds at home and bring in the results. Pick one, or have each child use his/her measurements, and cut out the same size piece of butcher paper. Have the children lie down and see how many of them can fit onto the bed at one time. Would ten fit? (Standard 10)

5. Have the children find out how wide a bear is. Transfer the measurements to butcher paper, and cut the paper. You may want to make ten bears. Place the paper bear on the paper bed to discover how many bears would fit onto the bed. Would ten bears fit? How big would the bed have to be to accommodate ten bears? Have the children measure this on paper, and cut it out. (Standard 10)

6. Have the children measure a classroom window (or find out how big bedroom windows usually are). Would a bear fit through this size window as it does in the book? (Standard 10)

7. Have the children count how long it would take before the little boy could get into bed if it took each bear two minutes to leave. (Standard 7)

Harriet Goes to the Circus
Betsy Maestro and Giulio Maestro
(New York: Crown, 1989)

Harriet the elephant wakes up early to go to the circus because she wants to be first in line in order to get the best seat. She is the first one there, and one-by-one her animal friends line up behind her. But, much to Harriet's dismay, the entrance to the circus tent is at the other end of the line. Everyone turns around, and Harriet is now the last in line. However, it turns out the chairs are in a circle inside the tent, and everyone gets a front seat.

This is a good introduction to ordinal numbers.

Activities

1. On the first page of *Harriet Goes to the Circus*, Harriet is waking up. Ask the children what they think she will do first. Second? Third? What is the last thing she will do before she leaves her house?

    Ask the children to make a list of what they do in the morning before they come to school. Then have them put these activities in the proper sequence.

2. Utilizing ordinal names, ask the children questions about the story. For example: What is Harriet doing on the fourth page?

3. Give each child a large strip of oaktag with guide lines for printing. Have each child choose one sentence (there are 29 in the story) to write on each strip. (If this is too hard for the students to do themselves, you or an aide can do it beforehand.) Then have the students put the strips in the story's correct order. Children can work on this by themselves at other times as well.

4. Get a jar of peanut butter, a jar of jelly, a loaf of bread, and a butter knife. Have the children give you directions on how to make a peanut butter and jelly sandwich. Have them tell you what to do first, second, and so on. Follow their instructions verbatim.

5. Have children brainstorm situations in which ordinals are used.

Positions	Orders
in line	book pages
in the first paragraph	birth order (first child)
contests/prizes	activities (which is first?)
directions (take second left)	

6. Tell the students that when the animals are standing in line for the circus,

    The mouse is next to the duck.
    The duck is not first.
    Harriet is next to the mouse.
    Harriet is first in line.
    Then ask, "In which position is the mouse?"

Later the animals discover that the entrance to the tent is located at the other end of the line, and everyone turns around.

The owl used to be last or tenth in line;
now the owl is first in line.
The dog used to be eighth in line;
now the dog is third in line.
The monkey used to be fourth in line.
In which position is the monkey now?

7. Have the children take on the roles of the different animals and act out the story.

8. Have the children write a pattern book based on the story *Harriet Goes to the Circus*.

The Life of Numbers
Fernando Krahn and Maria de la Luz Krahn
(New York: Simon & Schuster, 1970)

Number One is bored living alone, so he decides to look for a friend to play with. He meets up with Zero first, but doesn't want to play with him because he's nothing. He finds the rest of the numerals, Two through Nine, but for various reasons they can't or won't play with number One. On his way home he again meets Zero, and together they become Ten.

SPECIAL NOTE: Most activities can be done without the book. Substitutes include: Everett, Percival. *The One That Got Away*. NY: Clarion Books, 1992; MacDonald, Suse. *Numblers*. NY: Dial Books for Young Readers, 1988; Ockenga, Starr. *World of Wonders*. Boston: Houghton Mifflin, 1988. (Activity 4)

Activities

1. In the book *The Life of Numbers*, numerals are shown in unusual places. Have the children make up stories about these numerals.

2. Have the children research how numerals have looked in the past and how they look in other cultures. Leonard Fisher's *Number Art* is a good reference for this.

3. Discuss with the children how they think about different numbers and numerals. (Explain the difference between a number and a numeral.) Have the children make up new symbols for numbers. They might also want to write stories about the personalities of numbers/numerals.

4. Have children brainstorm phrases, songs, movies, etc. that use numbers. For example:

At sixes and sevens	Dressed to the nines
We're #1	When you're #2, you try harder
Seventh heaven	Walking on cloud nine
Eight is enough	Five alive
7-Up	7-11
Tea for two	Fourscore and seven years ago
I 1 a skunk	Three-ring circus
I 2 a skunk	One-man band
I 3 a skunk	Three Musketeers bar
I 4 a skunk	*The Three Bears*
I 5 a skunk	Engine, engine, number nine
I 6 a skunk	Cat-o'-nine-tails
I 7 a skunk	Hang ten
I 8 a skunk! You did!	Ten-penny nails

5. Discuss with the children how putting numerals in different positions can represent different numbers.

6. At the end of the book, One and Zero get together. Ask the children to see how many numbers they can come up with using only one and zero. What is the largest number they can make? What is the smallest number they can make?

7. Tell the children they can use all the numerals in the book (0-9) only once. What is the largest number they can make? What is the smallest? Using all the numerals as many times as they want, how many numbers can they make? This is one way to introduce the concept of infinity.

How Many Snails?
Paul Giganti
(New York: Greenwillow Books, 1988)

In this book, the author takes a walk to various places such as the meadow, the lake, the garden, the beach, the park, the library, the bakery, and the toy store. He wonders about the things he sees in each place and their different characteristics.

Activities

These activities can be done by the whole class, or you can divide the students into ten groups and have each group investigate a set of questions. (The activities for this book also reflect Standard 10.)

1. In the book, the author wonders how many clouds there are. Ask students if they can find out how many clouds there are. How many types of clouds are there? What are they? What size are clouds? How high up in the air are clouds?

2. On another page, the author wonders how many flowers there are. Ask students to investigate how many types of flowers exist and their names. What is the smallest flower in the world? The largest? How many seeds do flowers have? How many petals? What different colors do flowers come in? (Students might want to graph this information to show if one color is prevalent.)

3. When he goes to the lake, the author wonders, "How many fish are there?" Have students research how many different kinds of fish exist and their names. What is the smallest fish in the world? How small is it? What is the largest? How many fins do fish have? How much do fish eat?

4. Walking in the garden, he wonders how many snails there are. Have students find out how many different types of snails there are and their names. What is the largest snail ever found? How big was it? What is the smallest? How fast do snails travel? How long do they live?

5. At the beach, he wonders how many starfish there are. Have students determine how many kinds of starfish oceanologists have discovered and their names. How many different colors do starfish come in? What is the largest starfish ever found? How large was it? What is the size of the smallest? How many "arms" do starfish have? How deep under water do starfish live?

6. When the author walks in the park, he wonders how many dogs there are. Have students research how many types of dogs exist and the names of some of them. What is the size of the smallest? What is the size of the largest? How many teeth do dogs have? How much do they eat? How much do they weigh? How fast do they run? How loud do they bark?

7. At the library, the author wonders how many books there are. Ask the children to investigate how many books are in your school library. In the public library. In their home. If it is not considered an invasion of privacy, students may want to survey other students to find out how many books they have in their homes. They can also find out how many books are in local bookstores. Students could graph the number of books in these various places. How many books are in print? How many categories of books are there? How many pages do most picture books have? What different sizes of books are there? What is the largest book ever published? The longest? The smallest? The shortest? Why are there numbers on the spines of books in the library?

8. Walking to the bakery, the author wonders how many cupcakes there are. Have students look up how many types and flavors of cupcakes there could be. How many cupcakes are in a dozen? In a baker's dozen? How long do cupcakes take to bake? How much icing is used for each one? How many calories are in a cupcake? How much do cupcakes cost?

9. In the toy store, the author wonders how many toys exist. Have students try to find out how many toys are sold in the United States in one year. How many toys are there in various stores? In catalogs? In their homes? How many toys are made in the United States in one year? How much do toys cost? How long do they last?

10. At the end of the book, the author goes walking at night and wonders how many stars there are. This is a good opportunity to talk about large numbers or even introduce the concept of infinity. Have students research how many different types of stars there are and their names. What is the size of the largest star? The smallest? What is the temperature of the hottest star? How heavy is the heaviest star? How far away is the sun? How far away is the next closest star? How long would it take to get there? How many stars are in a constellation?

One Watermelon Seed
Celia Barker Lottridge
(Toronto: Oxford University Press, 1986)

Max and Josephine planted a garden with several different seeds and young plants. Then they weeded and watered and waited. Finally, one day they had plenty of fruits and vegetables to pick. This is a counting book that not only gives children the opportunity to count from 1 to 10, but also from 10 to 100.

Activities

1. In the book, Max and Josephine planted a garden. They planted 1 watermelon seed, 2 pumpkin seeds, 3 eggplant seeds, 4 pepper seeds, 5 tomato plants, 6 blueberry bushes, 7 strawberry plants, 8 bean seeds, 9 seed potatoes, and 10 corn seeds. Divide the children into ten groups and have each group choose a plant to research. Have each group answer the following questions about its plant: (Standard 10)

    a.   How long is the growing season for this plant?

    b.   How much rainfall does this plant need?

    c.   What is the largest and smallest specimen of this plant ever recorded?

    d.   How many fruits or vegetables usually grow on one of these plants? What does the book say this fruit or vegetable yielded? Is this accurate?

    e.   How much do the seeds or small plants of this fruit or vegetable cost?

    f.   How are these fruits or vegetables usually sold in the grocery store? By the pint? By the pound?

    g.   How much does this item cost in the grocery store?

    h.   How many recipes can you find for this plant?

2.   Have children do a survey among their classmates or other students in the school to find out which one of these foods is most popular. Have them graph their results. (Standard 11)

3.   Have children research how many kernels are on an ear of corn. Ask if Max and Josephine picked 100 ears of corn, how many kernels would they have? (Use calculators if necessary.) Would they really have had "hundreds and thousands of big white crunchy puffs" as it says in the book? (Standard 7)

4.   The children may want to do further research on popcorn. Do all kernels pop? Have them count the number of kernels in one-half cup of popcorn. Pop the popcorn. Count the number of unpopped kernels and/or the pieces of popped popcorn. Do some brands really have fewer unpopped kernels? Have the children record the name of the brand popped. More advanced students can devise a ratio or percentage for this. (Standard 11)

5.   Strawberries and blueberries are usually sold by the pint or the quart. Have the children count the number of strawberries in a pint. Is it always the same number? Why or why not? How many blueberries are in a pint? Is the number of blueberries in a pint the same as the number of strawberries in a pint? Why or why not? (Standard 10)

One Wide River to Cross
Barbara Emberley
(Englewood Cliffs, N.J.: Prentice-Hall, 1976)

In this rhyming book the animals come to the ark that old Noah built. They come, one by one, two by two, three by three, and so on, all the way to ten by ten. Then it rains so much that the ark ends up on Mount Ararat.

SPECIAL NOTE: The 1992 paperback edition is available. Substitutes include: Hewitt, Kathryn. *Two By Two: The Untold Story*. NY: Harcourt Brace Jovanovich, 1984; Lorimer, Lawrence T., reteller. *Noah's Ark*. NY: Random House, 1978.

Activities

1.   This can be used as a jumping off point to have children count, for example, by 2s and 3s and so on. Using manipulatives may make this easier. Using nickels and dimes for counting by 5s and 10s is usually more familiar for children. Duplicate the Hundred Chart in figure 3.1 and have the children color in every second number or every fourth number to help them count by 2s and 4s. Instead of coloring, the children could place beans on the numbers.

Fig. 3.1. Hundred Chart.

Hundred Chart

1	2	3	4	5	6	7	8	9	10
11	12	13	14	15	16	17	18	19	20
21	22	23	24	25	26	27	28	29	30
31	32	33	34	35	36	37	38	39	40
41	42	43	44	45	46	47	48	49	50
51	52	53	54	55	56	57	58	59	60
61	62	63	64	65	66	67	68	69	70
71	72	73	74	75	76	77	78	79	80
81	82	83	84	85	86	87	88	89	90
91	92	93	94	95	96	97	98	99	100

2. In the book, the different animals are drawn in rows or groups of 2 up to groups of 10. These illustrations could be used to explain the concept of multiplication. (Standard 7)

   Example: 2 groups of 2 = 4

   10 groups of 10 = 100

3. Have the children practice counting by 10s using objects in rows and objects in stacks (such as pennies or cubes).

4. Counting by 10s is a good introduction to place value. Have the children make bean sticks (glue 10 pinto beans to a tongue depressor) and practice counting by 10s. Then have them use the sticks and single beans to represent different numbers.

   Example: 23 is 2 bean sticks and 3 single beans.

5. For an additional challenge, begin introducing the children to other base systems.

6. In the book, it rained for 40 days and 40 nights. Have the children figure out how many weeks this is equal to. How many months?

7. Have the children calculate how much rain had accumulated at the end of forty days if it rained one inch per day. Have them measure how high or deep this is. How does this compare with their own height? What else is that high or deep? Considering what they have read about the flood, how many total inches of rain do they think fell? How many inches would that equal per day? If it rained one inch per day for 365 days, how high or deep would the water be? (Standards 8 and 10)

8. Have the children use the *Guinness Book of World Records* or the *World Almanac* to discover the greatest and least amount of rainfall that has ever been recorded in an hour/day/year. (Standard 11)

9. Using the *World Almanac*, have the children find out the average amount of rainfall for their area of the country. What is the average amount of rainfall in a desert or a tropical rain forest? (Standard 11)

10. There is a musical score in the back of the book. While learning the song, you can explain to the children how counting is used in music. Show them the notation for whole notes, half notes, quarter notes, and eighth notes, and explain how long each note is held. Have them count the number of beats in a measure.

Zero. Is It Something? Is It Nothing?
Claudia Zaslavsky
(New York: Franklin Watts, 1987)

The author discusses the meaning and mathematical possibilities of the number 0, ranging from the history of 0 to riddles about 0.

Activities

1. Have students brainstorm places where they would find 0. For example:

odometer	ruler
thermometer	timer
space countdown	tennis score
license plate	tic-tac-toe game
house address	football score

2. In the book, the author gives instructions for making an odometer on pp. 15-17. Make these with the children. (Standard 10)

3. On pp. 28-31 of the book, the author has included riddles about 0s. Have the children solve these and then make up their own.

4. Have the students make paper or cardboard rulers to help them understand the 0 as a beginning point. (Standard 10)

5. Bake cookies with the students, pointing out the significance of the 0 on a timer, on a measuring cup, and on the oven temperature knob. The number 0 marks a beginning point in these cases as well, even when it does not appear explicitly. (Standard 10)

6. Have the students write a story about the adventures of Zero.

7. Using yarn, make three circles in a row on the floor. Give each student a handful of beans. Have the children form a line and walk past the circles. As the first child passes the circle on the far right, have her place a bean in the circle. As the children do this, be sure to write the correct numeral on the board representing the number of beans in each circle. Have the next child do the same until there are nine beans in the circle. Then remove the beans from the circle and instruct the next child to put his bean in the adjacent circle. This can continue as long as you like, illustrating the process that some historians believe was used in Madagascar to count warriors, and resulting in the use of 0 for place value.

    Children may wish to use this method to count their school's student population as it enters the building in the morning. (Standard 11)

8. In the book, the author writes that sometimes 0 means something. Have children explain what the 0 means in numbers such as 10 and 20.

9. Introduce the children to the googol—a number that consists of a 1 with one hundred 0s following it.

10. Divide the children into pairs. Give each pair a plain piece of paper and instruct them to draw a line down the middle from the top to the bottom, dividing the sheet in two. Have each one write her name on one side of the line. Each child will take turns rolling a die. Each can choose to take the number shown on the die or 10 times that number. Each player gets seven rolls.

    Whoever has the score closest to 100 without exceeding it wins. (Standard 8)

11. On pp. 10-11 the author discusses round numbers. Have the children count the number of boys and girls in the class. Using a number line, have them round that number to the nearest 10. Write the answer on the board. Have them practice rounding with other numbers as well. Ask the children why they think these are called round numbers.

BOOKS FOR GRADES 4-6

MATHEMATICAL CONTENT VOCABULARY

abacus	factors	parallelogram	square
average	graph	prime numbers	square numbers
base system	Hindu-Arabic	products	survey
binary system	multiples	quadrilateral	symbol
calorie	multiplication	rectangle	tangram
common multiple	negative numbers	rectangular solid	trapezoid
coordinates	number	rhombus	triangular numbers
cube	numeral	Roman numerals	weigh
equivalent	order	sequence	

How Did Numbers Begin?
Mindel Sitomer and Harry Sitomer
(New York: Thomas Y. Crowell, 1976)

This book helps students think about how prevalent numbers are in our lives and how the use of numbers probably developed. It delineates several concepts that are central to our concept of number.

Activities

1. Have students brainstorm situations in which they use numbers.

counting	calendars	clocks
game scores	ages	addresses
library books	money	clothes sizes
phones	page numbers	radio stations
room numbers	prices	measuring
sewing	speedometer	gas pumps
temperature	TV channels	milk/lunch count

2. In groups or individually, have students write a story about a day without numbers. (You may want to refer to *The Day the Numbers Disappeared* by Leonard Simon and Jeanne Bendick.)

3. Try going through a day without using numbers in school. For example, cover the clock, have students hide their watches, and find other ways to represent things without numbers. (Standard 4)

4. Make cookies without using the numbers found on the recipe card, nor for the oven temperature. (Standard 10)

5. Have students think of ways to keep track of things without using numbers.

6. Historically, people have used body parts to help them count. In parts of China, the word for two is the same as the word for eyes. In Tibet, the word for two is the same as the word for ears. You might say I saw as many people as I have eyes, or I killed as many sabertooth tigers as there are suns. Have students make up other expressions like this.

7. Have students think about how they could use their fingers to count. Do we have enough fingers to count most things we want to keep track of? How can we use our fingers to count more than 10?

Teach students how to use fingermath.

Roman Numerals
David A. Adler
(New York: Thomas Y. Crowell, 1977)

The development and use of Roman numerals are examined in this introductory book. The book also includes an activity to help students translate Hindu-Arabic numerals into Roman numerals.

Activities

1. Before reading the book, have students brainstorm where they might see Roman numerals today.

2. Tell students the symbol for 1 in Roman numerals is I and 5 is V. Ask them what they think the symbols for 2, 3, and 4 are. If they don't answer IV on their own, tell them the correct answer and ask them why they think IV would mean 4. Why wouldn't 3 be IIV?

3. Tell students that the Roman symbol for 10 is two 5s, one on top the other. Have them figure out the symbols for 6, 7, 8, and 9. Discuss their answers. Then have them try 11 through 20. Discuss the importance of order or sequence. (There can never be more than three of the same symbol in a row.)

4. On pp. 16-17, the book gives instructions to cut out eight pieces of paper or cardboard. Have the students cut out three pieces that are 2 inches square, one 1½ inch square, and four that are 1 inch square. Then write 10 on the largest, 5 on the middle-sized one, and 1 on the smallest square. On the back, write the Roman numeral equivalent. Make sure the 10s, 5s, and 1s are showing.

   Have the students make the number 27 using the largest card first, then the middle-sized, and the smallest (10, 10, 5, 1, 1). Then have them turn their cards over to see the Roman numerals. Next have them make 31 (10, 10, 10, 1).

   Using the cards, have them write all the numbers from 1 to 39 in Roman numerals. Be sure to check for three of the same symbol in a row.

5. Tell the students that L = 50, C = 100, and D = 500. Then have them write 59, 65, 145, 199, and 550 in Roman numerals.

6. Have students practice using Roman numerals by writing their ages in Roman numerals, their room numbers, the lunch count, their addresses, the speed limits, recipes, etc. Have them make a clock or a ruler using Roman numerals.

7. Give students several examples of Roman numerals and have them translate them into Hindu-Arabic numerals.

8. Spend a day only using Roman numerals.

9. Give students math problems using Roman numerals. (Standard 8)

Example:	V	L	X	XX
	+ V	+ L	− III	− XII
	____	____	____	____

10. Discuss with students why, in most cases, we don't use Roman numerals anymore. How are Roman numerals different from Hindu-Arabic numerals?

Harriet's Halloween Candy
Nancy Carlson
(Minneapolis, Minn.: Carolrhoda Books, 1982)

Harriet goes trick-or-treating and gets a big bag of candy. When she gets home, she pours it out on the floor and organizes it according to color, size, and finally by her favorites.

Every time Harriet eats some of her candy, she hides what is left in different places. When she runs out of hiding places, she decides to eat up the rest.

Activities

1. In the book *Harriet's Halloween Candy*, Harriet organizes her candy by color, size, and by her favorites. Divide the students into groups and give each group a bag of wrapped candy. Have each group come up with as many ways as they can to sort this candy. Share answers.

2. The book does not reveal how many pieces of candy were in Harriet's loot, but you can poll the students in the class to find out how many treats each one collected trick-or-treating. Have students count the total number of treats collected by the class. (Standards 7 and 11)

   If students are ready, explain to them the concept of average and have them calculate the average number of treats collected by members of the class. (Standards 8 and 11)

3. Discuss with students the types of candy they receive when trick-or-treating. Help them develop a survey form to use to research the types of treats received by other students in the school. Graph this information and determine which treat was passed out most often. The class might also want to take a survey to discover which treat is most popular with students and publish the results in the local newspaper as a guide for those handing out treats. (Standard 11)

4. If Harriet received three pieces of candy at each house, to how many houses would she have to go to get 100 pieces of candy? Have students explain how they figured this out. Ask them how many treats they usually receive at each house. (Standard 7 or 8)

5. If Harriet did collect 100 pieces of candy, and she ate two each day, how many days would it take her to finish all the candy? What date would it be? If she ate one piece every hour, how many days would it take her to finish 100 treats? How long would it take her to finish the candy if she ate two each day, and gave her brother two each day as well? (Standard 7 or 8)

6. Bring into class different kinds of treats, divide the class into groups, then have each group weigh samples of each type. Do pieces of the same type weigh the same? Do different types have different weights? Using an average, or deciding to choose just one type, how much would 100 pieces of candy weigh? What other things weigh about the same amount? (Standard 10)

7. Harriet spent a lot of time trying to hide her candy. Have the students figure out how much space each treat takes up. Using this information, have them determine how much space 100 pieces would take up and what kind of spaces or places Harriet could have used to hide her treats. Have students figure out how many pieces would fit in a 6" x 6" bag. (Standard 10)

8. Have the students find out the approximate cost of each piece of candy. Using this information, have students determine the total cost of 100 pieces of candy. (Standard 8)

9. Harriet is not a skinny dog. Have students find out how many calories are in a typical treat. If Harriet eats 100 pieces of candy, how many calories will she consume? Have students find out how much exercise it takes to work off one calorie. Using this information, how many hours will Harriet have to exercise to use up all the calories from her treats? (Standard 8)

This Is 4: The Idea of a Number
Arthur G. Razzell and K. G. O. Watts
(Garden City, NY: Doubleday, 1967)

This book looks at the concept of 4 in many ways. It starts with sets of 4 and names for sets of 4, moving to various quadrilaterals. It also covers square numbers, area in square units, magic squares, and introduces a game based on squares called "Nine Men's Morris." It deals with the geometry of tangrams, and rectangular solids, and finishes with examples of how 4 appears in history, nature, art, science, and literature.

Activities

1. The book shows how several ancient civilizations represented the number 4. Have students research how other cultures represent the number 4 today.

2. The Latin word for four is quattuor. Many English words use part of this word (usually quad) to indicate four. The book gives the examples, quadrille, quadrireme and quadrangle. Have students brainstorm or research others.

3. A quadrilateral is an enclosed shape with four straight lines as sides. In small groups, have students make a list of examples of quadrilaterals found in the classroom, at home, outdoors, and in everyday life. (Standard 9)

4. There are several special types of quadrilaterals. Have students research definitions for trapezoids, squares, rectangles, parallelograms, and rhombuses. Then have students see how many different shapes they can draw for each one while still fitting the definition. (Standard 9)

5. Make a reproduction of the picture on pp. 20-21. Have students find the squares, rectangles, parallelograms, trapezoids, and rhombuses. Then have them make their own drawing using these shapes. Or have them cut these shapes out of construction paper and glue them on a larger piece of paper to make a design. (Standard 9)

6. Square numbers are discussed on pp. 22-23. Once students understand that square numbers actually form a square, have them determine the first consecutive square numbers. Then have students subtract the first square number from the second and write down the answer. Subtract the second from the third, and so on. Ask the students if they perceive a pattern. Can they predict the next square number from the pattern? (Standard 13)

7. Have students cut out 24 one-inch square pieces of paper. Have them manipulate the squares to create any shape they want, making sure the squares do not overlap. Then have them color in the design on graph paper. Have them repeat the process to discover how many different configurations all have the area of 24 square inches. From this, ask them if they can think of a formula for determining the area of a square. (Standard 10)

8. Have students cut a square foot out of construction paper. Using the Area Measurement Data Collection Sheet (see fig. 3.2) have them record their estimates of the area (in square feet) of various objects in the classroom. Then have them use their paper square foot to measure and record the actual area. (Standard 10)

9. On pp. 32-33, the authors discuss magic squares. In a magic square, the numbers in each row, each column, and each diagonal add up to the same sum. (For example, see fig. 3.3.) Have students finish the magic squares on p. 33. (Standard 8)

   Have students make their own magic squares. First write numerals on small circle labels. Affix these to wooden cubes or plastic poker chips. Have students manipulate the cubes or chips to create a magic square. Remember, a magic square can be more than three by three. (Standard 8)

10. Have the students practice the number tricks shown on pp. 34-35.

11. Many games are based on the square. Have the students brainstorm as many of these as they can. Then play Nine Men's Morris as explained in the book on p. 37.

12. In the diagram on p. 38 of the book, 12 counters are arranged on the board with no more than 2 counters in any row, up, down, or diagonally. Show the students the position of the counters and have them find as many other ways as they can to arrange the counters with no more than 2 counters in any row, up, down, or diagonally.

13. Tangrams are also covered in this book. There are several activities in chapter 5 on geometry and spatial sense that could be used here as well. (Standard 9)

Fig. 3.2. Area Measurement Data Collection Sheet.

Object	Estimate	Actual Measurement

Fig. 3.3. Magic Square.

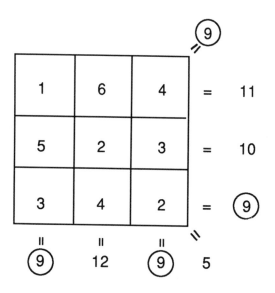

Total score 9 + 9 + 9 + 9 = 36

14. A cube is a three-dimensional square. Have students make a cube from the pattern below. (Standard 9)

Fig. 3.4.

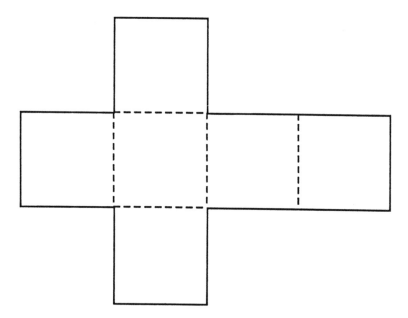

15. As is discussed at the end of the book, the concept of four shows up in many places—quarters, quadrillon, four-in-hand, four-poster bed, and so on. Have students brainstorm as many of these examples as they can and make a classroom list with illustrations. Do this for other numbers as well.

Less Than Nothing Is Really Something
Robert Froman
(New York: Thomas Y. Crowell, 1973)

This book illustrates numerous everyday applications of negative numbers, and includes a game for students to play.

Activities

1. Have students brainstorm occasions when negative numbers are used. For example:

   space countdown   diving underwater
   subzero temperatures   timelines before 1 A.D.
   financial debits (checkbooks)   coordinate graphing

2. Divide students into small groups. Have each group make a number line on the classroom floor or on a sidewalk outside the school. Have them make 0 the midpoint and number from 1 to 10 to the right and left of the 0. Be sure to have them put the minus sign in front of each numeral to the left of the 0. Then, have one student make up a math problem for another student to walk on the line. Switch roles until every student gets a turn. (Standard 7)

   Example: The student starts at 0. Her classmate gives her the problem $3 - 5$. The first student walks three steps forward and five steps backward, ending up on -2.

3. The book gives directions for making and playing a game called "P.A.M." (Plus and Minus). In pairs, have the students make and play this game. (Standard 7)

4. Reproduce the checkbook register in figure 3.5. Have students begin with a balance of $100. Then make up some expenses and have the students start deducting until the amount is in negative numbers. Students may use calculators. For example:

beginning balance	$100.00
buy Nintendo game	-60.00
	40.00
rent three videos	-3.00
	37.00
buy new sneakers	-49.95
	-12.95
buy pizza	-9.95
	-22.90

Fig. 3.5. Check Register.

Number	Date	Description of Transaction	Payment/Debit (-)		Deposit/Credit (+)		Balance Forward		
		To _____					Pay't or Dep		
		For _____					Bal.		
		To _____					Pay't or Dep		
		For _____					Bal.		
		To _____					Pay't or Dep		
		For _____					Bal.		
		To _____					Pay't or Dep		
		For _____					Bal.		
		To _____					Pay't or Dep		
		For _____					Bal.		
		To _____					Pay't or Dep		
		For _____					Bal.		
		To _____					Pay't or Dep		
		For _____					Bal.		
		To _____					Pay't or Dep		
		For _____					Bal.		
		To _____					Pay't or Dep		
		For _____					Bal.		
		To _____					Pay't or Dep		
		For _____					Bal.		
		To _____					Pay't or Dep		
		For _____					Bal.		
		To _____					Pay't or Dep		
		For _____					Bal.		
		To _____					Pay't or Dep		
		For _____					Bal.		
		To _____					Pay't or Dep		
		For _____					Bal.		
		To _____					Pay't or Dep		
		For _____					Bal.		
		To _____					Pay't or Dep		
		For _____					Bal.		
		To _____					Pay't or Dep		
		For _____					Bal.		

5. Have students play a game similar to Battleship. One student marks an X in one of the four quadrants. The student's partner tries to determine where the X is by guessing a coordinate pair. The first student marks down the guesses on a piece of paper and charts each one on his graph with a circle. The game continues until the X is found. Switch roles. Reproduce figure 3.6.

Fig. 3.6. Coordinate Graphing.

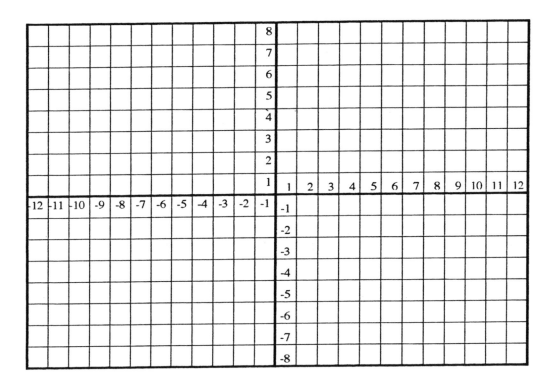

Number Families
Jane Jonas Srivastava
(New York: Thomas Y. Crowell, 1979)

Members of a family always have at least one thing in common. The same is true for numbers. This book discusses odd and even numbers, numeral shapes, multiplication, multiples, factors, and prime numbers, as well as square and triangular numbers. The author guides the reader through hands-on activities that make all these concepts seem simple.

Activities

1. The book states that all members of human families have at least one thing in common. It claims that the same is true for number families. It shows number families that are written using straight lines or families that are all even numbers or can all be divided by three, etc. Have students work in pairs to write down a group of numbers that has at least one thing in common. Have pairs exchange papers and try to figure out what those numbers have in common, or what makes them a family. (Standard 13)

2. Tell students that one way to determine if a number is odd or even is to put the objects in two rows and see if they match up. If they do, the number is even; if not, the number is odd. Ask students to think of another way to figure this out. (Divide by 2.) Therefore, besides the family of even numbers, to what other family do all even numbers belong? (two times) (Standard 7)

3. The book points out that some numbers belong to different times families. Some belong to the "two times" family, some belong to the "three times" family, some belong to the "four times" family, and so on.

   a. Divide students into six groups and assign a times family to each one, starting with "two times" up to "seven times." Using calculators, have them come up with all the members of that times family up to 100, or as many members of the family as they can in 15 minutes. Give each group a different color marker, and be sure to have students list the equations largely and legibly on a piece of paper.

   Example: $2 \times 2 = 4$
   $2 \times 3 = 6$
   $2 \times 4 = 8$

   After they are finished, if the students are not already familiar with the terminology, explain to them the meaning of the terms factor and multiple.

   b. Now combine two groups of students into one—the twos with the threes, the fours with the fives, and the sixes with the sevens. Explain that some numbers belong to more than one times family and have the students search for those numbers on their sheets. Instruct them to use their markers to circle those products that appear on both sheets.

   Example: $2 \times 8 = 16$ and $4 \times 4 = 16$

   So both products would be circled.

Explain to the students that the numbers they have circled are all common multiples of the two numbers they started with. Give each group a large piece of paper. Have them title it Common Multiples of _____ and _____, and then list the numbers they have in common.

c. Next combine the twos and fours, the threes and sixes, and the fives and sevens. Once again, instruct students to look for numbers that belong to both families and circle these products. Then have them make a sheet delineating the common multiples for these groups.

d. Recombine groups, this time putting together twos and fives, threes and sevens, and fours and sixes. Repeat the procedures from above.

e. This time, combine the twos and sixes, the fives and threes, and the fours and sevens. Repeat previous procedures.

f. Finally, combine the twos and sevens, the threes and fours, and the fives and sixes. Repeat previous procedures.

g. At this point, most of the numbers will be circled at least once, and some in several colors, but there should be a few that are not. Have the groups report which numbers are not circled and write these on the board. Ask the students what they notice about these numbers. Explain that some numbers only belong to two different number families, and they are called prime numbers.

Have students figure which numbers between 1 and 20 are prime. Ask them if they can discern a pattern that will help them predict the next few prime numbers.

4. Some numbers belong to a family known as triangular numbers. If objects representing the number can be formed into a triangular shape, it is a triangular number. Using manipulatives, have students figure out and write down the first six consecutive triangular numbers (3, 6, 10, 15, 21, 28). (One is sometimes considered a triangular number as well.) Ask students to look for a pattern that might help them predict the next few triangular numbers. Ask them to try writing a formula for this pattern. (Standard 13)

5. Other numbers belong to a family known as square numbers. If objects representing the number can be formed into a square, it is a square number. Using manipulatives, have students figure out and list which numbers between 1 and 25 are square numbers (4, 9, 16, 25). Have them look for a pattern that would enable them to predict other square numbers. Have them try to write a formula for this pattern. Then ask students to see if they can determine any relationship between square numbers and triangular numbers. (Adding two consecutive triangular numbers gives you a square number. For example: 3 + 6 = 9) (Standard 13)

Show students how to represent a square number using scientific notation. Have them brainstorm situations in which square numbers are used.

How to Count Like a Martian
Glory St. John
(New York: Henry Z. Walck, 1975)

The author shows how the ancient Egyptians, Babylonians, Mayas, Greeks, Chinese, and Hindus counted, in addition to showing what symbols they used. She explains how to count using an abacus and a computer and challenges readers to decode the "Martian" system. This is a great introduction to other symbolic representation systems and other base systems.

SPECIAL NOTE: Most activities can be done without the book. Substitutes include: Watson, Clyde. *Binary Numbers*. NY: Thomas Y. Crowell, 1977; Adler, David. *Base Five*. NY: Thomas Y. Crowell, 1975; Challoner, Jack. *The Science Book of Numbers*. NY: Harcourt Brace Jovanovich, 1992; Lumpkin, Beatrice. *Senefer*. Trenton, NJ: Africa World Press, 1992.

Activities

1. In the beginning of the book, a message comes in from Mars, probably in some sort of mathematical rather than linguistic code. The listening radio astronomer (the reader) decides to explore how other cultures communicate mathematically in order to decode the message. Divide the class into five groups. Have each group research one of the following groups: Ancient Egyptians, Babylonians, Mayas, ancient Greeks, and the ancient Chinese. Have them answer the following:

    a. What are the symbols for 1 through 9?

    b. Do they have a symbol for 0?

    c. What is their symbol for 10?

    d. At what point do the symbols start repeating? How many repeating symbols are there?

    e. What are the important symbols to know in order to count to 100 in this system?

    f. Is the sequence of symbols important in this system?

    g. Does this system help you figure out the Martian code on pp. 1-3?

    Tell the students in each group to be ready to teach the other groups how to count using their system.

2. In chapter 7, the author discusses counting using an abacus. If possible, get an abacus for each group and have students practice using one. If not, use pictures such as those shown in the book to illustrate the concept. Have students use the abacus, or pictures, to show the numbers 1, 10, 16, 101, 150, 1,204, and 59,030. Be sure to label each place in the abacus.

3. In chapter 8, the Hindu-Arabic numeral system is discussed. Compare this system to the others studied by the different groups. Have the groups show how many symbols it takes to write 289 using their systems. Talk about the importance of only using 10 symbols and the concept of place.

4. Chapter 9 explains how to count like a computer using the binary system. Tell students that in the binary system or base two, there are only two symbols used, and 0 = 0, 10 = 2, 11 = 3, 100 = 4, and 1000 = 8. Challenge them to figure out how the system works and what 111111 is equal to. At some point, you may want to change the labels on the abacus.

5. Go to pp. 60-61 in the book and put the Martian signals on the blackboard, or have them copied onto paper, for students to examine. Ask them how many different symbols the Martians are using. From that information, ask them what base system they think the Martians are using. If bee-beep = 0, beep = 1, beep-beep = 2, and beep-beep-beep = 3, have students set up the abacus for base four and write the Martian equivalent of 10, 25, 100, and 1,046. (They may wish to use the symbols on p. 62.) Finally, have students decode the Martian signals. (Standard 13)

6. Have students make up their own numerical symbols and experiment with other base systems. Each group could make up their own system and challenge other groups to decipher it. (Standard 13)

RELATED BOOKS AND REFERENCES

COUNTING

Allbright, Viv. *Ten Go Hopping*. London: Faber & Faber, 1985. (K-3)

Anno, Mitsumasa. *Anno's Counting Book*. New York: Thomas Y. Crowell, 1975. (K-3)

_____. *Anno's Counting House*. New York: Philomel Books, 1982. (K-3)

Archambault, John. *Counting Sheep*. New York: Henry Holt, 1989. (K-3)

Bang, Molly. *Ten, Nine, Eight*. New York: Greenwillow Books, 1983. (K-3)

Bayley, Nicola. *One Old Oxford Ox*. New York: Atheneum, 1977. (K-3)

Blumenthal, Nancy. *Count-A-Saurus*. New York: Four Winds Press, 1989. (K-3)

Carle, Eric. *Rooster's Off to See the World*. Saxonville, Mass.: Picture Book Studio, 1972. (K-3)

Conover, Chris. *Six Little Ducks*. New York: Thomas Y. Crowell, 1976. (K-3)

Ehlert, Lois. *Fish Eyes, a Book You Can Count On*. New York: Harcourt Brace Jovanovich, 1990. (K-3)

Elkin, Benjamin. *Six Foolish Fishermen*. New York: Children's Press, 1957. (K-3)

Feelings, Muriel. *Moja Means One: The Swahili Counting Book*. New York: Dial Press, 1971. (K-3)

Haskins, Jim. *Count Your Way Through the Arab World*. Minneapolis, Minn.: Carolrhoda Books, 1987. (K-3)

_____. *Count Your Way Through China*. Minneapolis, Minn.: Carolrhoda Books, 1987. (K-3)

Hoban, Tana. *Count and See*. New York: Macmillan, 1974. (K-3)

Hutchins, Pat. *1 Hunter*. New York: Greenwillow Books, 1982. (K-3)

Keats, Ezra Jack. *Over in the Meadow.* New York: Four Winds Press, 1971. (K-3)

Kirn, Ann. *Nine in a Line.* New York: Grossett & Dunlap, 1966. (K-3)

Leodhas, Sorche Nic. *All in the Morning Early.* New York: Holt, Rinehart & Winston, 1963. (K-3)

McLeod, Emilie Warren. *One Snail and Me.* New York: Atlantic Monthly Press, 1961. (K-3)

Merriam, Eve. *Project 1-2-3.* New York: McGraw-Hill, 1971. (K-3)

Ockenga, Starr, and Eileen Doolittle. *World of Wonders—A Trip Through Numbers.* Boston: Houghton Mifflin, 1988. (K-6)

O'Keefe, Susan Heyboer. *One Hungry Monster.* Boston: Little, Brown, 1989. (K-3)

Owen, Annie. *Annie's One to Ten.* New York: Alfred A. Knopf, 1988. (K-3)

Pomerantz, Charlotte. *One Duck, Another Duck.* New York: Greenwillow Books, 1984. (K-3)

Sendak, Maurice. *One Was Johnny.* New York: Harper & Row, 1962. (K-3)

Testa, Fulvio. *If You Take a Pencil.* New York: Dial Press, 1982. (K-3)

Trinca, Rod, and Kerry Argent. *One Woolly Wombat.* Brooklyn, N.Y.: Kane/Miller, 1985. (K-3)

Wildsmith, Brian. *The Twelve Days of Christmas.* New York: Franklin Watts, 1972. (K-3)

Yeoman, John, and Quentin Blake. *Sixes and Sevens.* New York: Macmillan, 1971. (K-3)

Yolen, Jane. *An Invitation to the Butterfly Ball.* New York: Parents Magazine Press, 1976. (K-3)

Zavlasky, Claudia. *Count On Your Fingers African Style.* New York: Thomas Y. Crowell, 1980. (K-3)

LARGE NUMBERS AND INFINITY

Ekker, Ernst A. *What Is Beyond the Hill?* New York: J. B. Lippincott, 1985. (K-3)

Gág, Wanda. *Millions of Cats.* New York: Coward-McCann, 1928. (K-3)

Modell, Frank. *One Zillion Valentines.* New York: Greenwillow Books, 1981. (K-3)

Schwartz, David M. *How Much Is a Million?* New York: Lothrop, Lee & Shepard, 1985. (4-6)

———. *If You Made a Million.* New York: Lothrop, Lee & Shepard, 1989. (4-6)

NUMBER CONCEPTS

Bendick, Jeanne. *Names, Sets and Numbers.* New York: Franklin Watts, 1971. (K-3)

Charosh, Mannis. *Number Ideas through Pictures.* New York: Thomas Y. Crowell, 1974. (K-3)

Leighton, Ralph, and Carl Feynman. *How to Count Sheep Without Falling Asleep.* Englewood Cliffs, N.J.: Prentice-Hall, 1976. (4-6)

Robinson, Shari. *Numbers, Signs and Pictures.* New York: Platt & Munk, 1975. (K-3)

Simon, Leonard, and Jeanne Bendick. *The Day the Numbers Disappeared.* New York: Whittlesey, 1963. (K-6)

NUMERALS AND ART

Fisher, Leonard Everett. *Number Art.* New York: Four Winds Press, 1982. (K-3)

MacDonald, Suse, and Bill Oakes. *Numblers.* New York: Dial Books for Young Readers, 1988. (K-3)

_____. *Puzzlers.* New York: Dial Books for Young Readers, 1989. (K-3)

ORDINALS

Bishop, Clare Hutchet. *Five Chinese Brothers.* New York: Coward-McCann, 1938. (K-3)

Lasker, Joe. *Lentil Soup.* Chicago: Albert Whitman, 1977. (K-3)

Martin, Bill, Jr. *Monday, Monday, I Like Monday.* New York: Holt, Rinehart & Winston, 1970. (K-3)

Mathews, Louise. *Cluck One.* New York: Dodd, Mead, 1982. (K-3)

OTHER BASE SYSTEMS

Adler, David A. *Base Five.* New York: Thomas Y. Crowell, 1975. (4-6)

Watson, Clyde. *Binary Numbers.* New York: Thomas Y. Crowell, 1977. (K-6)

ZEROS AND NEGATIVE NUMBERS

Munsch, Robert, and Michael Martchenko. *50 Below Zero.* Toronto: Annick Press, 1987. (K-3)

Sitomer, Mindel, and Harry Sitomer. *Zero Is Not Nothing.* New York: Thomas Y. Crowell, 1978. (4-6)

MISCELLANEOUS

Anno, Mitsumasa. *Anno's Math Games.* New York: Philomel Books, 1987. (K-3)

_____. *Anno's Math Games II.* New York: Philomel Books, 1989. (K-3)

Hayes, Cyril, and Dympna Hayes. *Number Mysteries.* Milwaukee, Wis.: Penworthy, 1987. (K-6)

Neve, Margaret. *More and Better.* Englewood Cliffs, N.J.: Prentice-Hall, 1977. (K-3)

O'Brien, Thomas C. *Odds and Evens.* New York: Thomas Y. Crowell, 1971. (K-3)

ADULT REFERENCES

Bunch, Bryan H. *Fun with Math.* New York: World Book Encyclopedia, 1983.

Ifrah, George. *From One to Zero — A Universal History of Numbers.* New York: Penguin Books, 1985.

Lieberthal, Edwin M. *Chisanbop Finger Calculation Method.* New York: Van Nostrand Reinhold, 1978.

_____. *The Complete Book of Fingermath.* New York: McGraw-Hill, 1979.

Paulos, John Allen. *Innumeracy: Mathematical Illiteracy and Its Consequences*, 1st ed. New York: Vintage Books, 1990.

Stenmark, Jean Kerr, et al. *Family Math.* Berkeley, Calif.: the Regents, University of California, 1986.

4—Standard 7: Concepts of Whole-Number Operations and Standard 8: Whole-Number Computation

STANDARD 7

The mathematics curriculum should include concepts of addition, subtraction, multiplication, and division of whole numbers so that students can

- develop meaning for the operations by modeling and discussing a rich variety of problem situations;

- relate the mathematical language and symbolism of operations to problem situations and informal language;

- recognize that a wide variety of problem structures can be represented by a single operation; and

- develop operation sense.

Consider these four points under the concept of whole-number operations:

1. Children should learn to trust their insight and intuition when determining the correct operation to solve problems.

2. The value of word problems is determined if children correctly use them to increase their recognition of the relationships between a single operation and problems with different structures.

3. The language of operations is important to learn: *addend, factor, multiple, product, quotient, sum difference* and so on.

4. Children should understand the properties of operations including the relationships between operations, between numbers, and within equations.

STANDARD 8

The mathematics curriculum should develop whole-number computation so that students can

- model, explain, and develop reasonable proficiency with basic facts and algorithms;

- use a variety of mental computation and estimation techniques;

- use calculators in appropriate computational situations; and

- select and use computational techniques appropriate to specific problems and determine whether the results are reasonable.

This standard addresses the variety of methods a person should be able to use to compute. Many situations require mental computation for exactness or estimation. A student should be able to use paper-and-pencil algorithms and the calculator to find the correct answer and to estimate an answer. Good conceptual approaches help to strengthen the development of computational skills. Having students learn computation skills through their own real-world problem solving is also helpful.

BOOKS FOR GRADES K-3

MATHEMATICAL CONTENT VOCABULARY

addition	eleven	maximum	revolution
average	equally	minus	seventeen
bills	equation	money	sixteen
coins	estimate	more	subtraction
combinations	fewer	multiplication	take away
difference	fifteen	nineteen	ten
dimes	fourteen	number sentence	thirteen
divide	gallons	pictograph	twelve
dollars	group	price	twenty
dozen	how many	quarters	weight
eighteen	less	rate	

Counting Wildflowers
Bruce McMillan
(New York: Lothrop, Lee & Shepard, 1986)

This book uses beautiful photographs of wildflowers to illustrate the concepts of addition and subtraction up to 20.

Activities

1. Point out to the children that at the bottom of the first page there is a row of 10 circles. The Fragrant Water Lily is represented by a white circle. Ask the children how many circles are green. On the board, write the equation $1 + 9 = 10$. Continue to discuss the circles with the children as you read each page.

2. At the bottom of p. 11, there are 20 circles. Covering up the red circles that represent the Maltese cross blossoms, ask the children how many circles are left. Have them write an equation for this.

3. On p. 17, there are 17 circles representing the black-eyed Susans in the picture. Ask the children how many more black-eyed Susans would have to be in the picture in order to have 20.

4. Ask children, "If there were 10 chickweed blossoms in the garden, and you picked 2, how many would be left?" Ask them to write an equation showing this.

5. Ask the children to figure out how many flower blossoms are shown in the whole book. They may want to use circles or counters to represent the flowers.

6. In the book, there are photographs of bee bain as well as mullein pink. Ask the children which photograph shows more blossoms. How many more? Ask the children how many more mullein pink blossoms would have to be in the picture to equal the number of bee bains shown.

7. There is a photograph of common tansies. Ask children how many blossoms they would have to pick in order to have an equal number of blossoms shown in the photograph of forget-me-nots.

8. Have the children use the book to make up their own math problems.

So Many Cats
Beatrice Schenk de Regniers
(New York: Clarion Books, 1985)

This is a story of a family with one lonely cat. However, the cat doesn't stay lonely for long.

Activities

1. In the book, the family starts out with just one lonely cat. Have the students write an equation using the names of the cats to show what happened in the story. Then have the children replace the names with numbers.

2. Have the children work in groups to write out as many other combinations of cats as they can think of that would equal 12.

3. The family ends up with a dozen cats. Have children brainstorm what other things come in dozens. Explain that a baker's dozen is equal to 13, not 12. (Standard 6)

4. Have the children survey their classmates to find out what kinds of pets people have. By cutting pictures out of magazines or by drawing their own, have them make a pictograph to represent this information.

5. Remind the children that we know of three children in the family. If an equal number of cats sat on each child's lap, how many cats would be on each lap?

6. Caring for so many cats can become expensive. Have the children use calculators, if necessary, to figure out the following: (Standards 8 and 12)

    a. How much does cat food cost?

    b. If each cat eats one can of cat food each day, how many cans of cat food will the family need to buy for one week?

c. How much will the cat food cost for one week?

d. How many cans of cat food will they need to buy in one year?

e. How much will the cat food cost them for one year?

7. Fluffy, Muffy, and Smoke are kittens. Ask the children to use counters or a diagram to figure out how many cats would be in the house if the rest of the cats in the house had four kittens each.

8. For an extra challenge, ask the children to use their calculators to solve these problems.

If each cat brings home another cat every day, how many cats would there be on day 2? On day 5?

How many days would it be before there were one million cats?

Annie's One to Ten
Annie Owen
(New York: Alfred A. Knopf, 1988)

The illustrations in this book show all the different combinations of objects that can be grouped together to equal 10.

Activities

1. Have the children write addition and subtraction number sentences for each page.

Example: One rainbow and nine clouds is $1 + 9 = 10$.

2. In groups, have children list all the different ways they can think of to write 10.

Example: $10 \times 1 = 10$

$12 - 2 = 10$

$5 + 4 + 1 = 10$

3. Have the children make up word problems for the pictures.

Example: There are two spoons and eight pitchers. How many more spoons are needed for each pitcher to have a spoon?

4. Have the children make up a pattern story for the whole book or for just one part. (Standard 13)

Example: What's the story behind the seven pineapples and the three pears?

5. Use the illustrations to explain the concept of multiplication.

    Example: Ten rabbits each have two ears. How many rabbit ears are there altogether?
    (10 x 2 = 20)

However, the illustration of nine planets and their moons won't work. Ask the students why this doesn't work.

The Great Take-Away
Louise Mathews
(New York: Dodd, Mead, 1980)

A group of pigs are all industrious except for one lazy hog who decides to steal from the others. He wears a black cloak over a minus sign on his chest. He proceeds to rob baby rattles, party gifts, necklaces, and pocketbooks until he is caught robbing the Piggy Bank.

Using rhyme and colorful illustrations, this book shows examples of subtraction in everyday life. Subtraction word problems are stated throughout the book as the pig robs each victim.

SPECIAL NOTE: The activities are specific to the text. To illustrate the concept of subtraction, consult the bibliography and the following: Dunbar, Joyce. *Ten Little Mice*. NY: Harcourt Brace Jovanovich, 1990.

Activities

1. The robber pig went to the nursery school and stole some of the rattles. When the police arrive, they are told that there had been seven rattles and only three are left. Have the children set up and solve an equation that will reveal how many rattles were stolen.

2. Next the robber pig gave a magic show at a birthday party. There were originally nine gifts, but by the time the pig left, there were only four. Ask the children to determine how many were taken away in the theft.

    In the first picture of the party, there are 17 balloons tied to the trees. The robber pig uses nine to make his escape. How many should still be left at the party?

    When we next see the robber pig by the fence, he has seven balloons. Ask the children to write and solve an equation that shows how many balloons have been lost or broken in the getaway.

3. At the masquerade party, there were 10 ladies wearing necklaces. After the robber pig left, only two necklaces remained. How many necklaces did the pig steal?

    Reports of the robberies began appearing in the newspapers. In the picture of the newspaper stand, we can count 23 papers hanging from the stand and on the counter. It looks as if nine pigs have bought or are getting ready to buy a paper. Assuming there are no other papers to account for, have students set up an equation to show how many papers the newsstand had initially.

4. At the circus, there are 12 people with pocketbooks. After the robber pig disappears, there is only one left. How many pocketbooks were stolen?

    When we see the picture at the beginning of the circus show, there are 36 pigs watching the acrobats. After the show, there appear to be 13 visitors left. Have the children write and solve an equation to indicate how many spectators left.

5. There are eight customers at the bank when the robber pig comes in. After he is arrested, we see four pigs jumping for joy. How many fewer pigs is this?

6. When the robber pig is captured, the police find 1 half-eaten cake, 4 rattles, 5 gifts, 8 necklaces, 11 pocketbooks, and 10 bags of money in his cloak. How many items did the robber pig have in his cloak?

   During each robbery, the pig left some items behind. Ask the children to explain how they would figure out how many items were not stolen in each robbery. How many were left behind in all the robberies put together?

7. Have the children estimate the weight of a real pig. Then have them find out the average weight of a pig. Have them do the same thing for all the items the pig stole. Then estimate how much the pig weighed when he was wearing his cloak full of the stolen items. Finally, using calculators, have the children figure out his weight with the loaded cloak. (Standard 10)

8. Have the children make up other escapades for the take-away pig. They may even want to write them in rhyme.

9. The take-away pig said that subtracting was what he did best. Have the children brainstorm situations in which it is good to take away things.

trash	tooth fairy	losing weight
take-out food	goodwill	purchases

   Then have the children write poems or stories about a job the take-away pig could start when he gets out of jail so he can still take things away, but not be stealing. Maybe he works in a math book publishing company training minuses, or becomes a tooth fairy pig.

Penelope Gets Wheels
Esther Allen Peterson
(New York: Crown, 1981)

Penelope wants to buy wheels with her birthday money so that she will not have to walk anymore. Penelope knows that she is not rich enough or old enough for a car, so she goes shopping for a bike. The bikes are too expensive, so she looks around the store and decides to buy roller skates. The next day when everyone is going to the ballpark, Penelope puts on her skates and skates to the game. She does not get any traffic tickets; she arrives at the park before her friend, Jim, who has to find a place to lock his bike; and she beats Mr. Smith, who has to park his car. Penelope decides that "roller skates are the best wheels a kid can have."

SPECIAL NOTE: Activities can be done without the book. Substitutes include: Hughes, Shirley. *Wheels*. NY: Lothrop, Lee & Shepard, 1991; Holabird, Katharine. *Angelina's Birthday Surprise*. NY: Clarkson N. Potter, 1989; Bunting, Eve. *Summer Wheels*. NY: Harcourt Brace Jovanovich, 1992.

Activities

1. Penelope receives 10 one dollar bills, 4 quarters, and 5 dimes for her birthday. Have the children figure out how much money she received.

2. Have the children list other combinations of coins and bills that would equal $11.50.

3. Penelope tells her mother that she is older now and doesn't want to walk anymore—she wants wheels.

   a. Penelope would like a car, but she realizes that she isn't old enough or rich enough to buy one. Have the children research how much their favorite car costs. (Standard 6)

   b. When Penelope arrives at the store, she sees a silver racing bike that she wants. The saleslady tells her it costs $119.00. How much more money does Penelope need to buy the racing bike?

   c. If Penelope receives $11.50 each year on her birthday, how many years will it take her to buy the bike if the price doesn't increase?

   d. Have students research how much a racing bike might cost in your community. (Standard 6)

   e. When Penelope realizes she can't buy the racing bike, she looks at a smaller bike. It costs $79.95. How much is she short this time? (Standard 12)

   f. What is the difference in price between the racing bike and the smaller bike? (Standard 12)

   g. Penelope settles on a pair of roller skates for $9.95. With tax, they cost $10.45. How much tax does she have to pay? (Standard 12)

   h. After paying for the roller skates, how much money does Penelope have left? (Standard 12)

   i. Have students research what Penelope can buy with the $1.05 she has left. (Standard 6)

4. The people listed in the chart below have crossed the United States on wheels. Using the *Guiness Book of World Records*, have the students find out what means of travel each person used, how many miles they traveled, the number of days it took them to accomplish the feat, and what their rate of speed was. (Standards 6 and 11)

   Fig. 4.1.

Across the United States on Wheels				
Name	Means of Travel	Miles	Number of Days	Speed
Paul Cornish				
Clinton Shaw				
John Lees				
Charles Creighton & James Hargis				
David Ryder & Floyd S. Rood				

5. Collect a variety of wheels in different sizes and have children measure the number of revolutions each makes in one yard. Compare. (Standard 10)

    Make a colored mark at one spot on each wheel. Then have students measure the number of revolutions each wheel makes in one minute. Compare. (Standard 10)

    Ask the students to find out why anyone would want to know that information about wheels.

Bunches and Bunches of Bunnies
Louise Mathews
(New York: Scholastic, 1978)

Through rhyming text and colorful pictures of bunnies, the multiplication facts of 1 x 1 up to 12 x 12 are explored.

Activities

1. At the birthday party in the story there are 16 bunnies. Four cut the cake, four shake the gifts, four drink ginger ale, and four pin the tail on the rabbit. This can be expressed by the equation 4 x 4 = 16. This is not the only equation which yields a product of 16. Demonstrate, using counters to represent the bunnies, how the bunnies could be in two groups of eight. Make up a rhyme for the bunnies at the birthday party using that equation. Have children work in cooperative groups, and do the same for the following:

    a. bunnies at the magic show, 6 x 6 = 36;

    b. bunnies at the parade, 7 x 7 = 49;

    c. bunnies at the beach, 8 x 8 = 64;

    d. bunnies at the school, 9 x 9 = 81;

    e. bunnies at the auction, 10 x 10 = 100; and

    f. bunnies at the family reunion, 12 x 12 = 144.

2. In the beginning of the book, we see two proud bunny parents each holding one baby bunny. Rabbits are notorious for having lots of baby bunnies. A female rabbit, or doe, can have four to eight litters per year with three to nine bunnies in each. Have the children figure out the following.

    a. If the doe in the picture has six bunnies in each litter and has six litters in a year, how many bunnies will she have in one year?

    b. There is another bunny in the picture. If his wife has the same number of litters with the same number of bunnies in each litter as the first doe, how many baby bunnies will they both have at the end of the year?

c.   If the first doe has only four litters with three bunnies in each, how many baby rabbits will there be?

d.   If she has eight litters with nine bunnies in each, how many baby rabbits will there be?

e.   If the first doe continues to have six baby bunnies in each litter and six litters each year, how long will it be before there are 144 bunnies in the family as we saw at the family reunion?

f.   For more of a challenge, have the students assume that the first doe continues to have 36 bunnies each year. Assume that half of these are female. Each bunny is able to start reproducing at six months of age. If each female bunny also has 36 baby bunnies each year, how many bunnies will there be altogether in five years?

3.   There are 25 bunnies shown at the ball. Four are in the band. If the rest are all dancing, how many are dancing?

If the band played a waltz, and everyone decided to dance, how many couples would there be?

4.   There are 36 bunnies at a magic show. We don't know all the tricks the bunnies saw, but this might have been one. Begin with a large double sheet of newspaper. Fold it in half once and then fold it in half again. Then tell the children that you will give $1 million to the first one who can fold it in half eight more times. After they have tried, show them the math involved.

Fold the paper in half the first time	1 x 2 = 2
Fold it again	2 thicknesses x 2 = 4
Fold it again	4 x 2 = 8
Fold it a fourth time	8 x 2 = 16
Fold it in half again	16 x 2 = 32
Fold it in half a sixth time	32 x 2 = 64
Fold it in half a seventh time	64 x 2 = 128
Fold it in half the eighth time	128 x 2 = 256
Fold it in half the ninth time	256 x 2 = 512
Fold it in half the last time	512 x 2 = 1024

5.   In a parade, the marching bands usually march in rows. In the picture of the parade, there are 28 spectators. If the rest of the bunnies were all in the band, and there were the same number of bunnies in each row, how many rows would there be? How many bunnies would be in each row?

6.   At the beach, the book states that eight bunnies find shells. If each of these bunnies finds four shells, how many seashells are found altogether by these bunnies?

Rather than counting bunnies in the water, the lifeguard at the beach has decided to count the ears and divide by 2. If there are 28 bunnies in the water, how many ears should she be able to count? What could be a problem with this approach?

7. The book shows 81 bunnies in one classroom at school. That's a lot. Have the children explain how these bunnies could be split into smaller classes.

8. At the track meet, there appear to be 46 rabbits in the bleachers. The average rabbit weighs about three pounds. Have the students use their calculators to find out how much weight is on the bleachers. (Standard 10)

9. When all the bunnies gathered together at the family reunion, there are 144 bunnies. One pound of rabbit pellets will feed approximately three bunnies each day. How many pounds of rabbit pellets would be necessary to feed all 144 bunnies?

The Doorbell Rang
Pat Hutchins
(New York: Greenwillow Books, 1986)

Mother makes a dozen cookies for Victoria and Sam to share. The doorbell rings and Tom and Hannah from next door come in. Victoria and Sam share their cookies. The doorbell rings again. This time it is Peter and his little brother. Now six children have to share the cookies. The doorbell rings again. It is Joy and Simon and their four cousins. The children divide the cookies. When the doorbell rings again, they think about eating their cookies quickly before answering it, but decide to wait. To their relief, it is Grandma at the door with an enormous tray of freshly baked cookies.

Activities

1. Have the children solve the following problems based on *The Doorbell Rang*.

    a. Mom gives Sam and Victoria a plate of cookies. She tells them that she made plenty, and they should share the cookies. Sam and Victoria say, "That's six each." How many cookies did Mom bake?

    b. Before Sam and Victoria can eat their six cookies, the doorbell rings. It is Tom and Hannah from next door. Since they decide to share the cookies equally, how many will each child get?

    c. Before they divide the cookies, the doorbell rings again. This time it is Peter and his little brother. Now how many cookies will each child get?

    d. The doorbell rings once again. Joy and Simon and their four cousins come in. Are there still enough cookies for everyone to share? How many will each child get?

    e. Just as they are ready to eat, the doorbell rings. To their relief, it is Grandma with an enormous tray full of more cookies. In the picture, it looks like there may be approximately five dozen cookies on the tray. If the children split all of Grandma's cookies among themselves, how many more cookies would they get apiece?

2. *The Doorbell Rang* tells the story of children and cookies with words. Have the children use equations to tell the story in numbers.

3. There are eight chairs at Sam and Victoria's kitchen table. Have the children explain how all the children in the story could fit around the table.

4. If each child in the story had one cup of milk with the cookies, how many gallons of milk would they drink altogether? (Standard 10)

5. Have the children plan to make chocolate chip cookies. The recipe on the back of Nestle's semi-sweet morsels says that it makes five dozen cookies. Assuming that is true, have students determine how many cookies each one of them will get to eat. Try making cookies and see. (Standard 10)

BOOKS FOR GRADES 4-6

MATHEMATICAL CONTENT VOCABULARY

advertising	equation	minimum	ratio
allowance	equivalent	money	revolution
average	estimates	nickels	scale
barter	expanded notation	number systems	scientific notation
billion	exponents	ones	service
budget	factorials	ounces	stock
bulk savings	gallon	pennies	stock market
calories	googol	percent	teaspoon
consumer	gross	pound	temperature
cups	hundreds	product	tens
dimensions	light-year	profit	tons
dimes	loan	proportion	trillion
displacement	markup	quarters	weight
dollars	million	quarts	

Popcorn
Frank Asch
(New York: Parents Magazine Press, 1976)

Sam's parents go out to a Halloween party and leave Sam alone. Sam decides to throw an impromptu party for his friends. He asks them each to bring a snack. Every guest brings popcorn. Later, they pop all of the popcorn. They pop so much that it fills the whole house. Sam and his guests feel sick after they finish eating it all. When Sam's parents arrive home, they have a surprise for him—a box of popcorn.

Activities

1. Explain that in the book *Popcorn*, Sam's friends brought 12 cans of popcorn to the party. The popcorn cans held 3 ounces of unpopped corn each. Using a calculator, have the students determine how many ounces of unpopped corn the guests brought altogether.

Tell the students that eight boys and five girls were at Sam's party, including Sam. There were 12 cans of unpopped corn. Tell students that ½ cup of unpopped corn makes 16 cups of popped corn. Assuming that each can held ½ cup of unpopped corn, have the students estimate how many cups of popped corn were made. If each party guest ate the same amount, estimate how much each boy and each girl ate. Have them use their calculators to check their estimates. (Standard 12)

2. Have the students find out at what temperature popcorn pops. They might also want to investigate why popcorn pops and sweet corn doesn't. (Standard 10)

3. In the story, Sam and his friends eat all the popcorn. Have students brainstorm other things they might have been able to do with the popcorn if they'd had more time to get rid of it. If students don't identify it in the brainstorming, tell them that popcorn is sometimes used for packing material. Have them research the cost of popcorn used as packing material versus the cost of styrofoam peanuts. If you are doing this around the holiday season, your students may wish to promote and sell popcorn for packing material.

4. Have the students calculate the costs of making popcorn. Be sure to have them include the cost of cooking oil, if used, and the cost of adding butter and salt. They may wish to sell popcorn as a fundraiser. Have them calculate the costs of popcorn at local movie theaters. Without considering bulk savings, how much profit is made? (Standard 12)

   Currently, a can that holds 24 ounces of popped corn is sold in many stores for $7.95. Using calculators, have the students figure out how much the popped corn costs per ounce. If a 16-ounce package of unpopped corn costs $.79, how much profit is made when it is sold popped in a 24-ounce can? (Standard 12)

5. Have students investigate how many calories are in one cup of popped popcorn without salt or butter. How many are in one cup of popcorn with salt only? How many are in one cup of popcorn with butter only? How many are in one cup of popcorn with salt and butter? How does this compare with other snacks? The U.S. Department of Agriculture's Human Nutrition Information Service has designed a handbook that tallies the fat, calories, and nutrients in munchies. It lists the number of calories for a cup of the following snacks:

corn chips, 230	cheese puffs or twists, 236
cornnuts, 372	popcorn, oil popped, 55
pretzels, 162	popcorn, air popped, 31
almonds, 810	potato chips, 152
cashews, 748	tortilla chips, 178
peanuts, 837	trail mix, 693
pistachios, 776	

6. Have the class collect popcorn recipes. They may wish to compile the recipes into a book and sell it. They can figure out the publication costs such as copying, binding, etc., to set a price. (Standard 12)

7. Buy a one-pound package of popcorn for the following activities.

   a. Have each student estimate how many kernels are in the package. Then divide the students into groups and have each group count a portion of the kernels. Using the calculator, add these together to determine the actual number of kernels.

b. Measure ½ cup of the unpopped corn. Pop it in an electric corn popper. Measure the popped corn. Write a ratio showing unpopped corn to popped corn.

c. Have students determine how much space one pound of popped popcorn would take up. Have them figure out how much popped popcorn it would take to fill up the classroom. (Standard 10)

d. Have students devise at least two ways to determine how far one million pieces of popped popcorn would reach if lined up. Use calculators to find the distance.

e. In the book, Sam and his friends eat all the popcorn before Sam's parents get back. Have the students time how long it takes them to eat one-half cup of popped popcorn. Using this information and the information obtained in the activity above, have the students figure out how long it would take them to eat a classroom full of popcorn. (Standard 10)

f. Weigh one cup of unpopped popcorn. Weigh one cup of popped popcorn. Which is heavier? What's the proportion? (Standard 10)

8. Make popcorn balls with your class using the following recipe:

4 cups granulated sugar   1 tsp. salt
2 cups water   1 cup light corn syrup
2 tsp. vinegar   2 tsp. vanilla
10 quarts popped corn

Directions:

Butter the sides of a saucepan. Combine sugar, water, salt, syrup, and vinegar in the pan. Cook to hard ball stage (250°F on a candy thermometer). Stir in vanilla. Slowly pour over popped corn, stirring to mix well. Have students butter hands lightly before shaping into balls. Recipe makes 30 to 40 popcorn balls. (Standard 10)

9. During the party, four of Sam's friends sat on the sofa. Read the clues to your students and ask them to figure out the order in which Sam's friends were sitting on the sofa. (Drawing pictures may help them solve the problem.)

Betty is next to Billy.
She is not at an end.

Billy is to the right of Betty.
He is not at an end.

Bernie is at one end.
He is not next to Billy.

Bonny is at one end.
She is not next to Betty.

Alexander, Who Used to Be Rich Last Sunday
Judith Viorst
(New York: Atheneum, 1978)

Alexander's brothers, Nicholas and Anthony, both have money, but all he has are bus tokens. Then Alexander receives one dollar from his grandparents. He wants to save it for a walkie-talkie, but he spends it quickly and ends up with—bus tokens.

Activities

1. Tell students that Alexander has two brothers who have money saved up. Have them solve the following problems. (Students may want to use calculators.)

   a. Alexander's brother, Anthony, has 2 dollars, 3 quarters, 1 dime, 7 nickels, and 18 pennies. How much money does Anthony have altogether? What is the fewest number of bills and coins Anthony could have for this amount of money?

   b. Alexander's brother, Nicholas, has 1 dollar, 2 quarters, 5 dimes, 5 nickels, and 13 pennies. How much money does Nicholas have altogether? What is the fewest number of bills and coins Nicholas could have for this amount of money?

   c. How much more money would Nicholas have to save in order to have as much as Anthony? Write an equation showing this.

   d. If Anthony and Nicholas combined their money, how much would they have?

   e. When Alexander's grandparents came to visit, they gave him one dollar. Anthony has how much more money than Alexander? Nicholas has how much more money than Alexander?

2. Have students tell the story of how Alexander spent his one dollar in number sentences.

3. Have students list how they would have spent the money if their grandparents had given them a dollar.

4. Alexander wanted to buy a walkie-talkie. Have students research how much a walkie-talkie would cost in your community. If Alexander's grandparents came to visit every two weeks and brought him one dollar, how many months would it be before he could buy the walkie-talkie? (Standard 6)

5. After Alexander spent all his money, he tried to think of ways he could earn more. He thought about renting his toys, getting money for a loose tooth, looking for coins in a phone booth, and getting money for taking returnable bottles to the store.

   a. Have students find out how much money they could receive in your community for recycling glass bottles. How many bottles (or pounds of bottles) would they have to collect to save enough for a walkie-talkie?

   b. Ask students to each identify one item they would really like to own. Have them devise a plan for earning enough money to buy this item. Have them implement the plan and keep a record of their progress.

c. Have students plan a class "market day." Individually or in small groups, have students identify a product or service they want to barter. Each individual or group will set up shop, and everyone will have an opportunity to circulate among the shops and decide if and what they want to barter.

Example: One person may trade a drawing of a classmate for two brownies.

When finished, have students discuss how it worked. How does this compare to using money?

Anno's Mysterious Multiplying Jar
Masaichiro Anno and Mitsumasa Anno
(New York: Philomel Books, 1983)

We begin this story with 1 jar and discover there are 3,628,800 jars inside it. How this could be is clarified by an explanation of the concept of factorials.

Activities

1. In the book, the story is more difficult to follow because it is not contained in just one picture. Using a very large piece of butcher paper, have the students draw as much of the story as they can.

    Example: Draw one island with two countries, add three mountains in each country, and four walled kingdoms on each mountain.

2. Explain to the students that the term "factorial" is used by mathematicians to indicate that a number is multiplied by the next smaller number, then the next smaller number, and so on, all the way down to one. The symbol for this is an exclamation mark. Do one or two examples on the board and then have students practice writing out (not solving) 3!, 7!, 12!, and 25!.

3. Without a calculator, a factorial may look intimidating. At the board, show students how to solve 4! using a calculator.

    Example: $4 \times 3 = 12$
    $12 \times 2 = 24$
    $24 \times 1 = 24$

    Then, in pairs, have them use the calculators to solve the factorials they wrote above.

4. Factorials express the number of possibilities in which something can be arranged. For example, if there were four students and four desks, 4! would describe the number of different ways they could be combined. Have students brainstorm and research other situations in which factorials could be used.

5. Have students diagram the possibilities of four students and four desks. (This is shown in the back of Anno's book.)

How Much Is a Million?
David M. Schwartz
(New York: Lothrop, Lee & Shepard Books, 1985)

Marvelosissimo, the mathematical magician, takes the reader on a journey and explains the concept of million, billion, and trillion. With Stephen Kellogg's detailed illustrations, the reader can better understand large numbers.

Activities

1. Schwartz talks about very large numbers in the book. He also tries to help us understand them better by comparing them to things with which we are already familiar. Sometimes these things are not as familiar as we might think. Have students find out the following. (Standards 6 and 10)

   a. How high is the tallest building?

   b. How high is the highest mountain?

   c. How high do airplanes fly?

   d. What are the dimensions of a whale? How much does a whale weigh?

   e. How far away is the moon? In feet?

   f. How big is a stadium?

   g. How far away is Saturn?

   h. What is 10 miles away from your school?

   i. How far is it from New York to New Zealand?

   Students may also want to pace out some of these measurements with string.

2. Have students brainstorm times and places they might encounter large numbers. (One interesting fact is that scientists now estimate that the brain contains 100 trillion synapses.) (Standard 6)

   Have students consider why we need to be accurate about such large numbers. Why can't we just say there are lots and lots of synapses, or say that the stars are very far away?

3. Have students research the names for large numbers. Be sure they uncover the googol—a 1 with 100 zeros behind it.

4. Have students actually make one million. Have them draw 100 stars (or whatever shape they want) on each sheet of paper. As the papers are completed, hang them somewhere in the room so students can see what a large number this is. This will take a long time, so they may wish to enlist other classes or continue the project when they finish other work. Another option would be to draw the stars on adding machine rolls. (Standard 6)

5. Give students a page of math problems and allow them one minute to complete the calculations. Then have them do the same page in one minute using a calculator. Which way produces a greater number of correctly completed calculations per minute?

   Explain to the students that some computers can do almost one trillion calculations per second. The human brain can carry out 100 quadrillion operations per second.

6. To further help students understand the concept of large numbers, have them use calculators to determine how long it would take to buy one million pieces of candy, buying one piece every second of the day and night. A billion? A trillion? First have them explain how they would figure this out. After they have calculated how many seconds are in a year, they may also want to calculate how many seconds they have been alive. Some might even want to write a simple computer program to calculate it for themselves and others. (Standard 6)

7. Another way to help students understand large numbers is to have them imagine that their parents are going to give them $1 million. They will have $1,000 to spend each day. Have them estimate how many days, months, and years it will take to spend it all. Have them calculate the answer (3 years).

   Then tell them their parents will give them $1 billion to spend. If they spend $1,000 a day, have them estimate how long it will take to spend it all. Have them calculate the answer (3,000 years). (Standard 6)

8. In the book, children stand on each other's shoulders to make towers. Have students figure out the average height of their classmates. (Standards 10 and 11)

9. Explain to students that David Schwartz, author of *How Much Is a Million?*, found out that the average height of elementary school students is 4' 8". The shoulders of a 4' 8" child are about 4' high. Given that information, have students solve this problem: If four students stood on each other's shoulders, how high would the tower be?

   Therefore, using the information above, the height of a tower formed by children standing on each other's shoulders would equal four times the number of children included. Using the author's calculation, have the students find the height of the towers and complete the chart in figure 4.2.

   Fig. 4.2.

# of Children	x	Height	=	
10	x	4	=	
300	x	4	=	
2000	x	4	=	
450000	x	4	=	

10. In the aforementioned problem, children are standing on each other's shoulders. This could become heavy very quickly. Have students figure out the average weight of their classmates. Then have them use this information to calculate how much weight would be on the bottom child in the different towers mentioned in the book. (Standards 10 and 11)

11. In the book, Schwartz states that it would take about 23 days to count to one million. Based on this information, ask students to use their calculators to determine how long it takes to say each number. (If it takes so long to count, how can we use large numbers?)

    For something a little easier, ask students how Schwartz figured out that it would take about 23 days to count to one million once he calculated that it takes two seconds to say each number.

12. Schwartz also tells us that the amount of water required to keep one goldfish alive is one gallon. Based on this ratio, have students figure out the amount of water necessary to keep 10 goldfish alive. One hundred goldfish? One thousand goldfish? One million goldfish? (Standards 6 and 10)

13. Schwartz shows a whale in a large goldfish bowl. Have students find out the formula for water displacement and calculate how much of a splash the whale would make when placed into the water. Ask students how they would lift a whale into a large goldfish bowl.

14. Draw a large bull's-eye on a 2' x 2' square piece of cardboard. Label as follows: 1) inside circle, millions; 2) next circle, thousands; 3) next circle, hundreds; 4) next circle, tens; and 5) the last circle, ones. (See fig. 4.3.)

Fig. 4.3.

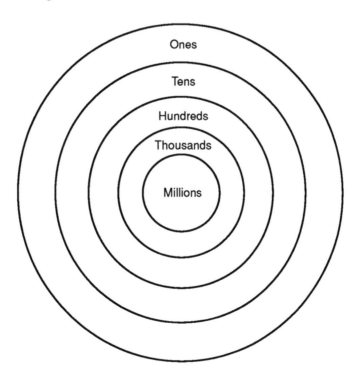

Let students pitch 25 paperclips at the bull's-eye, and then figure out their score. Have them use expanded notation first, and then write the number. (Standard 6)

Example: $2,000,000 + 6,000 + 500 + 40 + 8 = 2,006,548$. (Standards 6 and 8)

15. This is a great book to use for introducing scientific notation.

The Magic School Bus Lost in the Solar System
Joanna Cole
(New York: Scholastic, 1990)

Mrs. Frizzle is the weirdest teacher in the school. One day Mrs. Frizzle and her class depart on a field trip to the planetarium and end up traveling by bus through the solar system.

Activities

1. While waiting at a red light, the school bus suddenly tilts back and takes off into the sky. Divide students into groups and have them research the following questions related to this incident. (Standard 10)

    a. How far up would the bus have to go to escape Earth's gravity?

    b. What speed would the bus have to be traveling in order to escape the Earth's gravity?

    c. How much force would it take for the bus to escape the Earth's gravity?

    d. How much fuel would be needed to create that much force?

    e. How much time would it take for the bus to escape the Earth's gravity?

    f. How hot would the bus become due to friction?

    g. How much do the bus and passengers weigh?

2. Mrs. Frizzle's class takes a trip through the solar system and back in just one day. Have the students research how long it would really take for the class to make this trip. (Distances are listed in a chart towards the end of the book, and 200 miles per second can be used as a reasonable speed if no others are found.) (Standards 6 and 10)

3. In the book, the class reaches Pluto and sends back a radio message for help. Have students find out how long it would really take for anyone on Earth to receive that message. (Standards 6 and 10)

4. At various points in the book, weights on different planets are provided. Have students research how these were determined. Then, using this information, have them calculate their own weights on various planets. Some students may even want to write a computer program that will calculate these weights. (Standard 10)

5. When Mrs. Frizzle's students return from their trip, they set up a scale model of the solar system in the classroom. Using the size information provided in the book, have students scale down the size of the sun and planets in accurate proportions to make their own scaled-down planets. (Standard 10)

   Using the information provided in the book, have students also decrease the distances proportionally and use the information to place their planets in orbit. (Standard 10)

   By not scaling down the distances quite as far, students could pace out these distances outside to get a sense of the proportions. (Standards 6 and 10)

6. Using the revolution rate on the planet chart in the book, have the students calculate how many birthdays they would have celebrated on each planet. (Standard 10)

   Example: Since a year on Mercury is 88 days, you would have a birthday every 88 days. If you were now 10 years old on Earth, you would be over 41 years old on Mercury.

7. A light year is the distance light can travel in one year. If light travels at approximately 186,000 miles per second, have the students calculate how long it would take to get from Earth to the next closest star (not counting the sun). (Standards 6 and 10)

The Toothpaste Millionaire
Jean Merrill
(Boston: Houghton Mifflin, 1972)

One day sixth grader, Rufus Mayflower, becomes upset about the price of toothpaste in a local store. He goes home and begins making toothpaste in his kitchen. One thing leads to another, and soon he and his friend, Kate MacKinstrey, launch a very profitable business.

Activities

1. In the story, Rufus tells Kate he will make her a pair of saddlebags for her bike. In math class he passes her a note that says she will need 2¼ yards of 36-inch wide nylon. It costs $.97 per yard. Have students estimate the total cost of the material. Have them check their answers with calculators. This book was published in 1972. Have students find out how much this material would cost today, and recalculate Kate's cost. (Standards 10 and 12)

   Rufus draws a pattern for the saddlebags. One piece is 16" x 14½" and another is 16" x 8¼". Have students use paper to represent the nylon and then try to lay out a pattern for the saddlebags. (Standards 10 and 12)

2. Rufus is outraged about being asked to pay $.79 for a 6-inch tube of toothpaste. The 6-inch tube holds 3.5 ounces. Have students calculate the price per ounce. (Standard 12)

   Next have students find out the cost of toothpaste in a local store and calculate the cost per ounce. (Standard 12)

3. Kate is at the store when Rufus decides not to buy the toothpaste. She was going to buy some eye shadow for $.69, but calculates she can save $700 if she foregoes eye shadow until she is 80

years old. Have students figure out how much toothpaste they use per month or per year. Therefore, how much do they spend on toothpaste in a year? (Standard 12)

Have students calculate how much money they could save if they didn't buy toothpaste from their current age until age 70.

Toothpaste is not something they should do without, but have the students brainstorm some things they presently buy that they think could be done without, and calculate the lifetime savings.

4. When Rufus makes his first batch of toothpaste, he produces 40 tubes for $.79. Each tube contains 3.25 ounces. Have students calculate his cost per ounce. (Standard 12)

5. Have students experiment with making toothpaste using baking soda and flavorings. Have them keep track of amounts of ingredients and costs.

6. During math class, the teacher intercepted another note from Rufus to Kate. It read, "If there are 2½ billion tubes of toothpaste sold in the U.S. in one year, and 1 out of 10 people switched to a new brand, how many tubes of the new brand would they be buying?" Have the students figure out the answer. Then have them research current figures and recalculate.

7. The second part of the note read, "If the inventor of the new toothpaste made a profit of $.01 a tube on his toothpaste, what would his profit be at the end of the year?" Have students solve this. (Standard 12)

8. Later in the story, Rufus starts putting toothpaste in baby food jars. Have students find out how many ounces are in a baby food jar. If Rufus charges $.03 per jar, how much is he charging per ounce? Compare this to the store-bought brand. (Standard 12)

9. After Rufus appears on The Joe Smiley Show, he receives 689 orders for TOOTHPASTE. Have students estimate how much money he made and then check their answers.

10. Rufus pays his friends in company stock for helping. He uses stock certificates from the Stock Market game. Get a copy of the game and let the students participate.

Have a stockbroker visit the class to explain how the stock market works.

Have the students choose a stock in the newspaper, invest an imaginary amount of money, and keep track of losses and profits. (Standard 12)

11. Rufus pays his friends $100 worth of stock for every 100 hours they work. Have students calculate how much these friends are being paid. Why would they work for these wages?

Kate starts out with $200 worth of stock. Rufus says she should receive $5,000 if profits work out as he plans. Have students explain his reasoning.

12. Kate tries to find a birthday present for Rufus. She writes to the District Sales Manager of Tuxedo Tube and Container Corporation about purchasing a few toothpaste tubes. He responds by explaining that the company's minimum order is 10,000 tubes at $.05 per tube, but he can also quote prices for 50,000 and 100,000. Have the students calculate what the minimum order would cost Kate. Have them calculate what the larger amounts would cost if prices remained the same. (Standard 12)

13. At the auction, Kate bids on 50 gross of aluminum tubes. Ask students how much that is. (Standard 6)

    Kate pays $.10 per gross. Have students figure out her total cost. Have them figure out the cost per tube. (Standard 12)

14. After buying the tubes, Kate has to get them home. She calls Rufus and tells him there are five boxes. Ask students to calculate how many tubes are in each box if they are evenly divided.

    Rufus estimates that the tubes weigh about one ounce each. Again, if they are evenly distributed, how much does each box weigh? (Standard 10)

15. In the story, Hector says he needs $9,000 to support his wife and five kids. Have students find out what that amount is equivalent to in today's dollars, and then prepare a budget for Hector and his family. (Standard 12)

16. When Rufus and Kate go to the bank to get a loan, Kate tells Mr. Perkell that Rufus has sold more than 1000 jars of TOOTHPASTE in four weeks. Have the students figure out how much money Rufus made from these sales. What are his costs and what are his profits?

    If sales continue at this rate, how many jars would be sold in one year? What would be the costs and profits? (Standard 12)

17. Rufus offers Hector 15 percent of the business. If the company makes $2.5 million, have students calculate how much Hector will make. (Standards 11 and 12)

18. In *The Toothpaste Millionaire*, Rufus and Kate make up the final exam for their math class. Allow students to make up some questions for a math test.

19. Rufus figures a year's supply of TOOTHPASTE is 12 tubes. Have students calculate how much a year's supply would cost at $.15 per tube.

    If the cheapest store brand is $.79 per tube, how much is a year's supply of this brand? (Standard 12)

20. In an effort to keep costs down, Rufus decides against a cardboard package around each tube of TOOTHPASTE. In the book, Kate asks, "Do you know how many tons of cardboard it takes to make boxes for 250,000,000 tubes of toothpaste?" Have the students figure out the answer. Calculate the cost for the cardboard. (Standard 10)

    Today some toothpastes come in more rigid plastic containers that don't require a box. Does it cost the manufacturer more for the rigid plastic than for the soft tube and cardboard?

    Is the rigid tube that doesn't need cardboard better for the environment? If so, students might want to write to the manufacturer suggesting they discontinue the cardboard boxes.

21. Rufus and Company spend some of their money on commercials. Have students research the cost of making commercials and the cost of airing them.

Have them find out what percentage of the company's budget is for advertising. Have someone in advertising come in and speak with the class.

22. In the story, the magazine *Consumer Friend* does a very favorable report on TOOTHPASTE. Have students look at copies of consumer magazines such as *Consumer Reports* or *Zillions* (formerly *Penny Power*). Have them do their own research and report on toothpaste or some other product, and submit it to *Zillions*.

23. On p. 76 in the book, there are figures for sales of TOOTHPASTE. Have students figure sales, costs, and profits for each. (Standard 12)

24. Sparkle, Brite, and Dazzle, the other leading toothpaste companies, all make more profit per tube on their brand than Rufus does on TOOTHPASTE. Have students research what the markup is on consumer items. Contact a consumer advocate for more information about this.

25. At the end of the book Rufus writes a postcard to Kate. It reads, "Could you see if Vince's Army & Navy sells blow-up rafts at least 6' x 12'? And how much would two of them cost? And do they have army-surplus dried soup in 100-pound bags?" Have students guess what Rufus's next project might be.

RELATED BOOKS AND REFERENCES

ADDITION AND SUBTRACTION

Brenner, Barbara. *Annie's Pet.* New York: Byron Preiss Visual Publications, 1989. (K-3)

Burningham, John. *Mr. Gumpy's Outing.* New York: Holt, Rinehart & Winston, 1970. (K-3)

_____. *The Shopping Basket.* New York: Thomas Y. Crowell, 1980. (K-3)

Carle, Eric. *The Hungry Caterpillar.* New York: Philomel, 1969. (K-3)

Chalmers, Mary. *Six Dogs, Twenty-Three Cats, Forty-Five Mice and One Hundred Sixteen Spiders.* New York: Harper & Row, 1986. (K-3)

Christelow, Eileen. *Five Little Monkeys Jumping on the Bed.* New York: Clarion Books, 1989. (K-3)

dePaola, Tomie. *Too Many Hopkins.* New York: G. P. Putnam's Sons, 1989. (K-3)

Dunbar, Joyce. *A Cake for Barney.* New York: Orchard Books, 1987. (K-3)

Gisler, David. *Addition Annie.* Chicago: Children's Press, 1991. (K-3)

Gray, Catherine. *One, Two, Three, and Four. No More?* Boston: Houghton Mifflin, 1988. (K-3)

Krahn, Fernando. *The Family Minus.* New York: Parents Magazine Press, 1977. (K-3)

McLeod, Emilie Warren. *One Snail and Me.* Boston: Little, Brown, 1961. (K-3)

Samton, Sheila White. *On the River.* Honesdale, Pa.: Caroline House/Boyd Mills Press, 1991. (K-3)

Walsh, Ellen Stoll. *Mouse Count.* New York: Harcourt Brace Jovanovich, 1991. (K-3)

Whitney, David C. *Let's Find Out About Addition.* New York: Franklin Watts, 1966. (K-3)

_____. *Let's Find Out About Subtraction.* New York: Franklin Watts, 1968. (K-3)

CALCULATORS

Adler, David A. *Calculator Fun.* New York: Franklin Watts, 1981. (K-3)

Bitter, Gary G., and Thomas H. Metos. *Exploring with Pocket Calculators.* New York: Julian Messner, 1977. (4-6)

Donner, Michael. *Calculator Games.* Racine, Wis.: Western, 1977. (4-6)

MULTIPLICATION AND DIVISION

Birch, David. *The King's Chessboard.* New York: Dial Books for Young Readers, 1988. (4-6)

Conford, Ellen. *A Job for Jenny Archer.* Boston: Little, Brown, 1988. (4-6)

Friskey, Margaret. *Mystery of the Farmer's Three Fives.* Chicago: Children's Press, 1963. (K-3)

Froman, Robert. *The Greatest Guessing Game.* New York: Thomas Y. Crowell, 1978. (K-3)

Giganti, Paul, Jr. *Each Orange Had 8 Slices.* New York: Greenwillow Books, 1992. (K-3)

Peppe, Rodney. *Humphrey the Number Horse.* New York: Viking, 1978. (K-3)

Shapiro, Irwin. *Twice upon a Time.* New York: Charles Scribner's Sons, 1974. (4-6)

Trivett, John V. *Building Tables on Tables.* New York: Thomas Y. Crowell, 1975. (K-3)

MISCELLANEOUS

Belton, John, and Joella Cramblit. *Dice Games.* Milwaukee, Wis.: Raintree, 1976. (K-3)

_____. *Domino Games.* Milwaukee, Wis.: Raintree, 1976. (K-3)

Burns, Marilyn. *The I Hate Mathematics Book.* Boston: Little, Brown, 1975. (4-6)

Hall, Carolyn Vosburg. *I Love Popcorn.* Garden City, N.Y.: Doubleday, 1976. (4-6)

White, Laurence B., Jr., and Ray Broekel. *Math-a-Magic.* Niles, Ill.: Albert Whitman, 1990. (4-6)

Wyler, Rose, and Gerald Ames. *Funny Number Tricks.* New York: Parents Magazine Press, 1976. (4-6)

ADULT REFERENCES

Downie, Diane, et al. *Math for Girls and other Problem Solvers.* Berkeley, Calif.: the Regents, University of California, 1981.

Kerr, Jean, et al. *Family Math.* Berkeley, Calif.: the Regents, University of California, 1986.

Lieberthal, Edwin M. *Chisanbop Finger Calculation Method.* New York: Van Nostrand Reinhold, 1978.

5—Standard 9: Geometry and Spatial Sense

The mathematics curriculum should include two- and three-dimensional geometry so that students can

- describe, model, draw, and classify shapes;

- investigate and predict the results of combining, subdividing, and changing shapes;

- develop spatial sense;

- relate geometric ideas to number and measurement ideas; and

- recognize and appreciate geometry in their world.

Geometry gives children a different view of mathematics, and the practice with spatial skills (spatial sense is an intuitive feel for one's surroundings and the objects in them) can sharpen their intuitive skills. Geometry contributes to the development of number and measurement concepts.

BOOKS FOR GRADES K-3

MATHEMATICAL CONTENT VOCABULARY

angle	half circle	pyramid	symmetry
arc	heart	rectangle	tangrams
circle	heptagon	right angle	trapezoid
cone	hexagon	semicircle	triangle
crescent	octagon	silhouette	wavy line
cube	oval	sphere	zigzag
cylinder	parallelogram	square	
diamond	pentagon	star	
ellipse	petal	straight line	

The Shape of Me and Other Stuff
Dr. Seuss
(New York: Random House, 1988)

This book uses rhymes and silhouettes to spur children to think about the shape of many things, real and imaginary.

Activities

1. The first part of the title refers to "the shape of me." Have the children make life-size copies of themselves. With a partner, have one child lie down on a piece of butcher paper and have the other child trace around his partner. Do this twice and cut out the body image. Reverse roles. When the children are finished coloring on a face and clothing, have them staple the two pieces together. Leave a small opening to stuff the figure with newspaper and then finish stapling. Completed bodies can be hung from the ceiling or displayed elsewhere in the classroom.

2. Discuss with children why people, animals, and things have the shapes they do. For example, giraffes have long necks to reach their food supply.

3. Ask children if they can think of anything that doesn't have a shape. Demonstrate how liquids take the shape of their container. Explain that gases do the same thing.

4. Have children brainstorm things that change shape. Have them experiment with bubblegum, balloons, and clay to create and change shapes.

   If you have access to paint or draw computer software, have children draw an object on the screen, and then perform transformations such as rotating, stretching, distorting, scaling, etc.

5. Read *Hello Clouds!* or *It Looked Like Spilt Milk* and discuss how we decide what something looks like. Go outside and look at clouds and talk about what they look like.

6. In the book, the shapes of things are shown in silhouette. Have the children work in pairs to help each other make a silhouette picture of their profiles. Set up a bright light to shine on a piece of construction paper. Have one child stand between the light and the paper and have the other child trace the shadow. Cut this out and mount it on a black piece of paper.

7. Discuss shadows and reflections with children. Take them outside and have them experiment with their shadows. Talk about changes and distortions with shadows. Have students see how large a shadow they can create. Have them figure out how to make their shadows as small as they can.

   Have the children experiment with objects as well. If the weather isn't cooperative, set up a bright light in the classroom and have children draw or trace the shadows of smaller objects.

   Use a pond or a tub of water to find out more about reflections. Compare these to mirror reflections.

8. Discuss with children the difference between shapes and geometric shapes.

9. Ask children to identify geometric shapes on the human body. Have them choose one geometric shape, and then use only that shape to draw the body or another object. Repeat the exercise using a different geometric shape to draw the same object.

The Shapes Game
Paul Rogers
(New York: Henry Holt, 1989)

Colorful illustrations and a rhyming text ask children to identify nine geometric and other shapes. The book includes circles, triangles, squares, stars, ovals, crescents, rectangles, spirals, and diamonds.

Activities

1. Have children pick one of the geometric shapes mentioned in the book and identify objects in the classroom that have that shape. Have them think of as many objects as they can outside of the classroom that have that shape. Where would they find that shape in nature? Where would they find that shape in manmade objects?

2. Give children a piece of paper with a rectangle or some other geometric shape on it. Have them complete the picture on the paper. For example, a square could be a television screen, a book, a computer disk, etc. (You may also want to read *The Circle Sarah Drew*.)

3. Have children look through magazines for one or several geometric shapes and make a collage of what they find.

4. Have children take photographs that contain geometric shapes and make a book similar to those of Tana Hoban.

5. Find examples of Cubist paintings and share these with the children. Have them identify the various geometric shapes.

6. Have children help each other use their bodies to make geometric shapes and take "aerial" photographs.

7. Cut or have the children cut various sizes of these shapes out of construction paper. Have the children use just one shape to make pictures. (You may want to look at Rosalind Kightley's *Shapes*, and Graham Airey's *New Ideas in Card and Paper Crafts*, pp. 8-18, for examples.)

    Have them see how many different shapes they can use in one picture. You may want to use a different color paper for each shape. Using these shapes, have children experiment to find out what shapes cover other shapes.

8. Have children work with Ed Emberley's drawing books, particularly *Make a World*, to see how they can use geometric shapes to draw lots of different things.

9. Cut sponges into geometric shapes and have children dip them into paint to make pictures.

10. Have children glue toothpicks on paper in geometric shapes to make pictures.

11. Have children practice making geometric shapes using a geoboard.

12. Have children make geometric shapes out of clay, pipe cleaners, and wire.

13. Cut or have children cut construction paper into strips with different lengths. Then have them fold the strips into circles, squares, triangles, etc., and either glue or staple them. (Use a paperclip to hold the shape together while the glue dries if you choose this method.) Then have the children glue these different shapes together to make different designs. (Examples of this can be found in *New Ideas in Card and Paper Crafts*, pp. 43-53.)

14. Have children make mobiles out of geometric shapes. (You may want to refer to *Fast & Funny Paper Toys You Can Make*, pp. 103-105, for specific instructions.)

15. Have children make riddles using shape clues.

    Example: This is the third rectangle past the classroom door. What is it? (closet door) I am a circle on the wall. What am I? (clock)

16. Have children make a circle book using paper plates as pages. Have them list examples of circles or draw objects that are that shape, or cut out pictures with circles. Around the edge of the plate, have the children write a sentence about their picture.

17. Have the children make a book about other geometric shapes, including their own definitions.

    Example: In *If You Look Around You*, the author defines a circle this way. "A circle is what you see in the water after you drop a stone."

What Is Symmetry?
Mindel Sitomer and Harry Sitomer
(New York: Thomas Y. Crowell, 1970)

This book introduces the concepts of line symmetry, point symmetry, and plane symmetry in ways that are easy for children to understand.

SPECIAL NOTE: Activities can be done without the book. Symmetry is discussed on pages 96-97 in Burns, Marilyn. *The I Hate Mathematics! Book*. Boston: Little, Brown, 1975; pages 16-17 in Challoner, Jack. *The Science Book of Numbers*. NY: Harcourt Brace Jovanovich, 1992.

Activities

1. Give each child a piece of fingerpaint paper. Then have the child place a blob of either fingerpaint or pudding in the middle of the paper and fold it together. Open the paper back up, and there should be a symmetrical design.

2. Divide the children into pairs. Give each child some different colored blocks and a piece of paper. After each one draws a line down the middle of the paper (vertically or horizontally), have them create a design with the blocks on only one side of the paper. Then have them switch places with their partner and have the partner complete the other half of the design so that both halves are symmetrical. Children may also want to do this with colored rubber bands on a geoboard.

3. The book explains the folding test for line symmetry. Remind children that the way to do this is to "fold a picture along a line so that the parts on one side fit exactly over those on the other side." There can be a vertical line of symmetry, a horizontal line of symmetry, or both. Have students cut pictures out of magazines and fold them in half to test for vertical and horizontal symmetry. After they have some practice doing this, choose some pictures yourself and show them to the class. Have them try to identify a line symmetry just by sight.

    The children may want to collect pictures of symmetrical and asymmetrical items and make a chart or book of these. You may also want to discuss as a class if there is any pattern in which types of items fall into each category.

4. Divide the children into cooperative groups. Give each group 26 cards with a letter of the alphabet on each one. Have them try the folding test for each one, putting those with a vertical line of symmetry in one pile, those with a horizontal line of symmetry in another pile, those with both a vertical and horizontal line of symmetry in a third pile, and those with no line symmetry in a fourth pile.

5. Line symmetry can also be determined by using small mirrors cut to specifications at a hardware store. Have children place the mirror vertically along what they think is the line of symmetry. If the image in the mirror completes the object correctly, it has line symmetry.

6. In the book, there is a paper folding experiment to do. Give each child a piece of paper. Then have each one fold the paper in half once and then in half again. Finally, have each child carefully punch three holes in the folded paper near the second crease. Before opening it, have each one predict how many holes will be in the unfolded paper and where those holes will be. Then compare the predictions with the actual findings.

7. The book shows how to use the idea of line symmetry and a few cuts with the scissors to make symmetrical designs. Demonstrate and then let the children experiment with their own designs. (The book *Paper Cutting* contains many other examples of this, including a doily pattern on p. 49, and a monster pattern on pp. 56-57.)

8. The book also shows how to make paper dolls. Give each child a piece of lightweight paper. Instruct the class to fold about two inches of the paper up from the bottom. Then make the next fold the same size, but fold under. Continue this way until the whole page is folded in an accordion or fan pattern. Then help the children draw the outline of a person on the top layer. Next, have them cut it out and unfold. (Smaller folds can be used by students with better motor skills.)

Flat Stanley
Jeff Brown
(New York: Harper & Row, 1964)

An enormous bulletin board falls on Stanley Lambchop and squashes him flat as a pancake. Stanley is now 4' tall, about 1' wide, and ½" thick. The story tells how Stanley's life changes because of his new proportions, and his adventures while his brother, Arthur, figures out how to return Stanley to his former proportions.

Activities

1. A large bulletin board fell on Stanley and flattened him. When he went to the doctor, the nurse took his measurements and discovered he was 4' tall, 1' wide, and ½" thick. Construct Stanley according to his new proportions.

2. Have the children determine other things that are ½" thick. (Standard 10)

3. At least one of the illustrations shows Stanley standing up by himself. Have the children determine if he could really do this if he was ½" thick. (Standard 10)

4. Stanley's body is three-dimensional at the beginning of the story, but after the bulletin board falls on him, he becomes nearly two-dimensional. Discuss the differences between three-dimensional and two-dimensional. Have the children brainstorm lists of two- and three-dimensional objects.

5. Help children learn how to represent three-dimensional objects two-dimensionally. (You may want to ask an art teacher for assistance.)

6. A blueprint is a two-dimensional representation of a three-dimensional room or building. Divide students into groups and give each group a large piece of butcher paper and small cubes, or some other small three-dimensional objects. Direct them to place these objects on the paper to represent objects in the classroom. Then have them trace each small object on the paper to create a two-dimensional representation.

7. Have students make a list of two-dimensional geometric shapes and their three-dimensional counterparts. For example, a square is two-dimensional and a cube is its three-dimensional counterpart.

    Have students use toothpicks and small bits of clay, peas, or miniature marshmallows to create two- and three-dimensional geometric shapes.

8. At one point in the story, Mr. Lambchop rolls Stanley up to go walking. Have the children determine how much space Stanley would take rolled up. Into which size cylinder would he fit? (Standard 10)

9. Have the children make up more adventures for Stanley in his flattened proportions.

Anno's Math Games III
Mitsumasa Anno
(New York: Philomel Books, 1991)

This book explores many aspects of geometry and spatial relationships. It includes sections titled "Changing Shapes with Magic Liquid," "Exploring Triangles," "Mazes," "Topology," and "Left and Right."

Activities

1. In the first sections of the book, Kriss and Kross have a magic liquid that, when evenly mixed, makes whatever it is brushed on enlarge evenly. However, when it is not mixed evenly, it distorts the object unevenly. Silly Putty can be used to achieve a similar effect. Have the children choose partners and give each one a ball of Silly Putty and a black line image. Have each pair put the black line image face down on flattened Silly Putty. Then have them remove the image, pull the Silly Putty in only one direction, and observe how the image changes. Another way to achieve a similar effect is to draw on rubber or on balloons, and then stretch the material. If a computer paint program is available, have the children draw an object on the screen, then use the scaling, distort, or stretch options. Observe the results.

2. Kriss and Kross also make designs using triangles. Make copies of figure 5.1, and have the students color the triangles to make their own designs.

3. Find a kaleidoscope and have children take turns looking through it. Are the designs based on a triangle as shown in the book?

4. Kriss and Kross have some difficulty getting through various mazes. Make copies of figure 5.2, and have the children maneuver through the maze.

    Have them try to make their own mazes with paper and pencil.

    Have the children try to set up a 3-dimensional cardboard maze.

    (You may also want to discuss how behaviorists use rats and mazes in their research.)

5. Towards the end of the book, Kross wants to travel from the school to the barber shop, and Kriss wants to go to the train station. Have students draw a map from the classroom to the office or some other part of the school. Then have them draw a map from their house to the school.

(Text continues on page 72.)

Fig. 5.1. Triangle Design.

Fig. 5.2. Maze.

Grandfather Tang's Story
Ann Tompert
(New York: Crown, 1990)

Grandfather Tang and Little Soo spend the afternoon sitting under a peach tree in their backyard, making different shapes with their tangram pieces. Grandfather Tang uses his pieces to tell a story about the fox fairies, Wu Ling and Chou. The fox fairies are an important part of Chinese folklore and are believed to be capable of changing their shapes.

Activities

1. Have the children make their own tangram pieces out of construction paper. (See the instructions in fig. 5.3.)

    Have the children try to put the seven pieces back together to form a square.

2. As they follow along in the story, have the children make the shapes described with the tans they made.

3. Have the children make up their own designs. They may want to create their own story using the new designs.

    Have the children make the initial of their first name using all seven tans.

4. Give the students a variety of tangrams. Have them combine the tangrams to make geometric shapes, such as a square, triangle, rectangle, trapezoid, and so forth. Individually, in small groups, or as a class, ask the students to make a chart that shows how many shapes were made.

5. Make tans out of flannel for the children to use on a flannelboard.

6. Tangoes is a game that contains numerous designs using tans. Have children work with these.

7. Other shapes can also be divided to make a puzzle. Using the patterns in figures 5.4 and 5.5, cut the shapes into A, B, C, and D pieces. Paperclip all the A pieces together, the B pieces together, and so on. Divide the children into cooperative groups of four and give each person one clipped bundle of pieces. The objective is for each member of the group to try to create a hexagon. No one may take a shape from anyone else, and the person with the shape must offer it to the person who needs it. No talking is allowed.

(Text continues on page 76.)

Fig. 5.3. Making your own tangram.

Step One: Begin with any square piece of paper.(Show students how to make a square piece of paper from a rectangular one. Discard "extra piece.") Fold and cut into two congruent triangles.

Step Two: Fold and cut one of the two large congruent triangles into two smaller congruent triangles.

Step Three: Take the other large triangle and fold vertex A to the midpoint of segment BC. Then cut along the folded line. You will form a middle-sized triangle and a trapezoid.

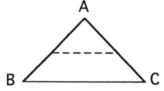

Step Four: Fold the trapezoid along the dotted line and cut into two congruent trapezoids.

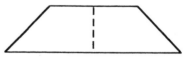

Step Five: Fold and cut each of the two trapezoids along the dotted lines.

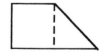

You should now have the seven pieces: 2 large congruent triangles
1 middle-sized triangle
2 small congruent triangles
1 square
1 parallelogram

Fig. 5.4. Cooperative geometry patterns.

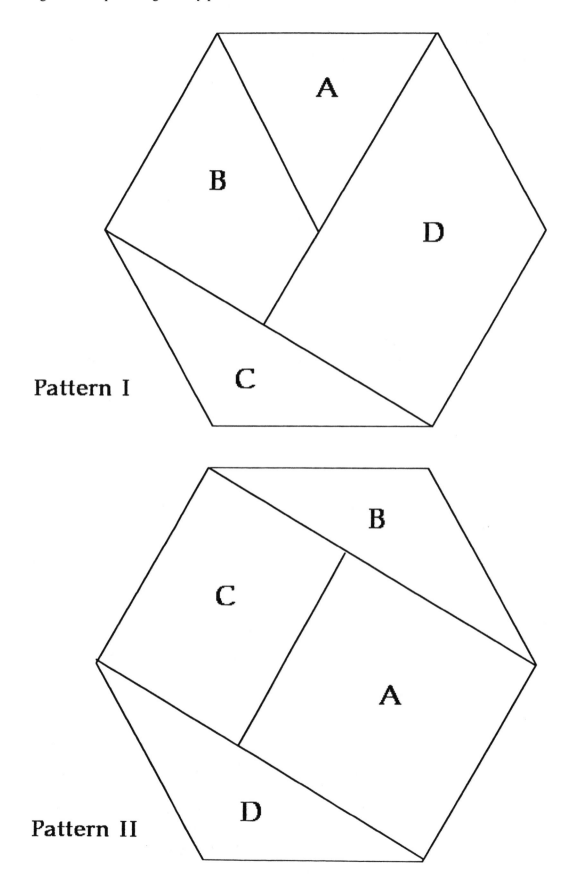

Pattern I

Pattern II

Fig. 5.5. Cooperative geometry patterns.

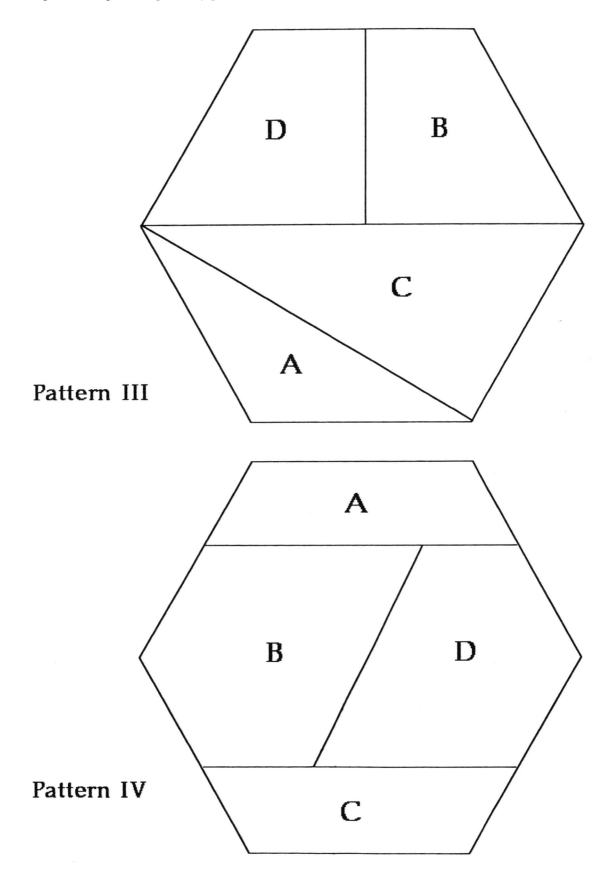

Pattern III

Pattern IV

BOOKS FOR GRADES 4-6

MATHEMATICAL CONTENT VOCABULARY

architect	genus	open figure	structural rigidity
axis	geometric solid	origami	tangram
blueprint	helix	pentagon	topology
closed figure	invariant	perspective	variant
compass	isosceles	pointillism	vertices
cubism	kirigami	quadrilateral	
curve	network	spiral	

Paper John
David Small
(New York: Farrar, Straus & Giroux, 1987)

Paper John is a stranger who comes to town. He builds himself a paper house and earns his living selling homemade paper items. While fishing one day, he rescues a demon. The demon's subsequent activities try Paper John's patience and ingenuity.

Activities

1. Paper John earns his living making various items out of paper. The Japanese art of paper folding is called origami. Have the students find books on origami with patterns for some of the items Paper John makes such as flowers, boats, a house, a kite, a table, a sheep, etc. (Check Related Books and References for suggested books. Patterns can be found for a sailboat, a flying bird, and a skiff in Elinor Massaglio's *Fun-Time Paper Folding*, pp. 7, 29-30, respectively. Patterns for a hut and a yacht can be found on pp. 19 and 53 of Claude Sarasas's *The ABCs of Origami*. In addition, *Easy Origami* by Dokuohtei Nakano contains patterns for building units, p. 12; talking masks, p. 13; a floating boat, p. 19; a box of triangles, p. 41; a rose, p. 57; a gentian, p. 58; and a yacht, p. 60.)

2. Have students make up their own origami patterns.

   Have them experiment with different kinds of paper.

   Ask them to estimate the maximum number of times they can fold one piece of paper in half, then try it.

3. In the book, Paper John makes a kite "round and golden like the sun." Later on, the demon uses this kite to try to escape. Have the students experiment to see if a round kite flies better than the usual quadrilateral kite.

   Students may also want to experiment with paper airplanes to determine which shapes work best.

4. Inside Paper John's house we see paper doll type designs. This involves paper cutting, which is sometimes called kirigami. Have students fold a piece of paper in half and make cuts along the fold. Unfold the paper to reveal a symmetrical design.

   Discuss the concept of symmetry and have them experiment some more. (You may want to refer to Robert Harbin's *Paper Folding Fun*, p. 83, and Florence Temko's *The Magic of Kirigami* which shows symmetrical cutting patterns on pp. 35-42. See Related Books and References at the end of this chapter.)

5. Since Paper John is so intrigued with paper, he may have also spent time figuring out paper puzzles. Examples of paper puzzles can be found in figure 5.6. (*Paper Folding Fun* includes additional paper puzzles on pp. 16-29.)

The Boy with Square Eyes
Juliet Snape and Charles Snape
(New York: Prentice-Hall Books for Young Readers, 1987)

Charlie watches so much television that his eyes become squared-shaped. His square-shaped eyes make everything look square until he finds a way to return them to normal.

Activities

1. Charlie develops square eyes from watching television. Have the students measure their television screens at home. What are the dimensions? Are they really square? Have students check computer screens as well. (Standard 10)

2. After Charlie's eyes change, everything looks very strange to him—everything is square-shaped. Have students pick an object in the classroom and draw it using only squares. Or cut out construction paper squares and use those to make a square picture.

3. Bit-mapped computer pictures use square pixels to create images. If you have access to a paint program, have students print out bit-mapped images and then create their own from scratch, pixel by pixel. If you do not have access to a computer, have students try this on graph paper.

4. Proportional drawing is done using squares. Make a copy of figure 5.7, and have students complete the drawing on the large grid. Students may want to make their own examples to share with others using graph paper.

5. Charlie supposedly is seeing everything as square-shaped. It might be more accurate to say that he is seeing straight lines and angles without any curves. Have students brainstorm how things would be different if there were no curves in the world, and then write a story about a world without curves.

   Have the students figure out how they could make a circle using only straight lines. If you have access to LOGO software, students could learn a lot about this and other geometric and spatial properties through experimenting with this computer language.

(Text continues on page 80.)

Fig. 5.6. Paper puzzles.

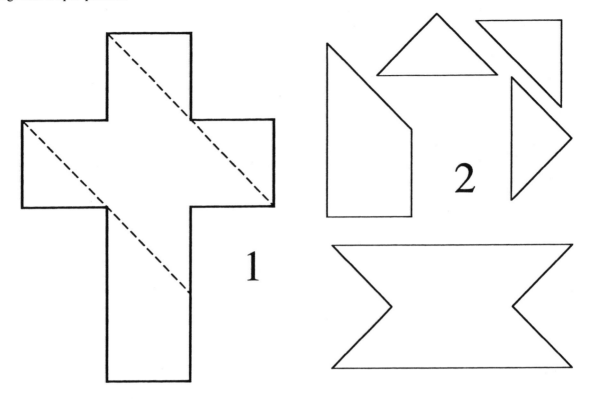

The Cross Puzzle: Cut out the cross in Figure 1 and cut on the dotted lines to make five pieces as shown in Figure 2. Mix the pieces and ask a friend to put it together again. You may find it difficult to reconstruct also.

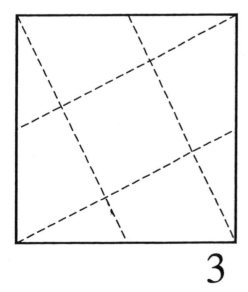

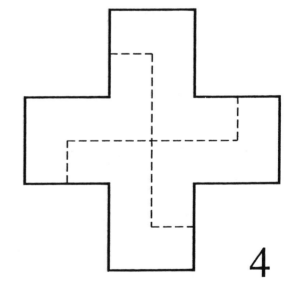

The Square Puzzle: Cut out Figure 3 and cut along the dotted lines to make nine pieces. Mix them up and try to reassemble.

Another Cross Puzzle: Cut out Figure 4 and cut along the inside dotted lines to make four pieces. The parts are exactly the same size and therefore, interchangeable. See if this makes it easier to reassemble.

Fig. 5.7. Proportional drawing.

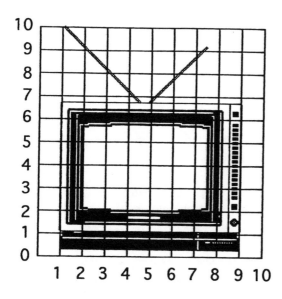

Make an enlargement of the drawing at the left on the grid below. Find the corresponding square on the large grid. Look carefully at the contents of that square on the small grid and draw the same thing in the corresponding square on the large grid.

The area of the two drawings are in the ratio of four to one.(If you double the dimension, you get four times the area.)

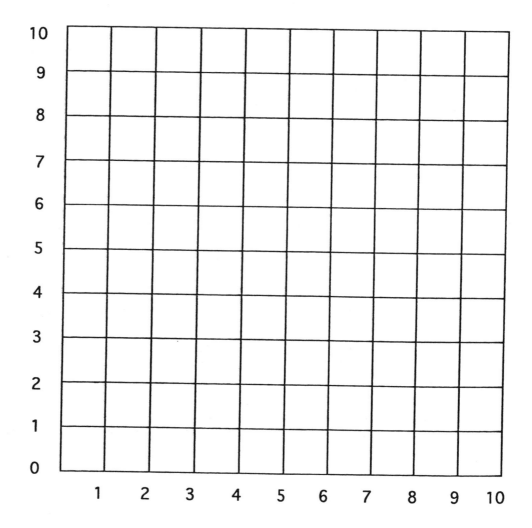

6. Introduce the students to cubism. Have them research artists who used this style and share examples of their work. (Pablo Picasso, Georges Braque, and Juan Gris are some artists who have used this style.) Have students try this style to create a painting.

7. Different cultures have used geometric forms in their art. Much Islamic art consists of geometric shapes, and Native Americans have used geometric shapes in weaving and pottery. Have the students research and share some of these designs. Then have them use geometric shapes to make their own designs or pictures.

8. Quilt patterns often contain geometric designs. Have the students research quilt designs, then choose one they like to reproduce, or create their own.

   After the students have made their own quilt squares (on paper or with cloth), have the class put them all together to make a whole quilt. Students might also want to assemble a book of quilting patterns.

9. Some groups have used geometric shapes for musical notation. These are called shape notes or Sacred Harp music. Have the students research shape notes and learn to sing a song using this notation. (There is a four-note and a seven-note system. The four-note system uses a triangle for fa, an oval for so, a square for la, and a diamond for mi. The Aiken seven-note system uses a pyramid-shaped triangle for do, a half-circle for re, a diamond for mi, a right triangle for fa, an oval for so, a square for la, and a cone for ti.)

   Your students may also want to create their own compositions using musical notation.

10. A square divided into seven pieces is a tangram puzzle. Your students may want to work with tangrams as well. (See *Grandfather Tang's Story* on pp. 141-42.)

11. If Charlie saw everything as square-shaped, he would see three-dimensional objects as well as two-dimensional. Have students create a sculpture using square objects such as gelatin cubes or sugar cubes.

12. The premise in the story is that Charlie sees square objects because he has square-shaped eyes. When his eyes return to normal, they are round. If he saw everything round, how would objects appear? Have students try to draw objects using only circles. (You may want to refer to *The I Hate Mathematics! Book* by Marilyn Burns, pp. 51-53, for printed examples.)

    The picture on your television screen consists of individual dots. Have the students use magnifying glasses to determine if they can see these dots when they look at the screen.

    In pointillist paintings, the artist dabs small bits of paint (almost little circles or dots) on a canvas that, from a distance, create a picture. Have the students research this type of art and experiment with this style.

13. Make copies of the activity Squaring Up in figure 5.8. Have the students cut these out. By making just one cut, they should be able to put the two pieces together to make a square.

Fig. 5.8. Squaring up.

Cut out these shapes. If you cut carefully, you should be able to make one cut somewhere on the shape, then put the two pieces together to make a square.

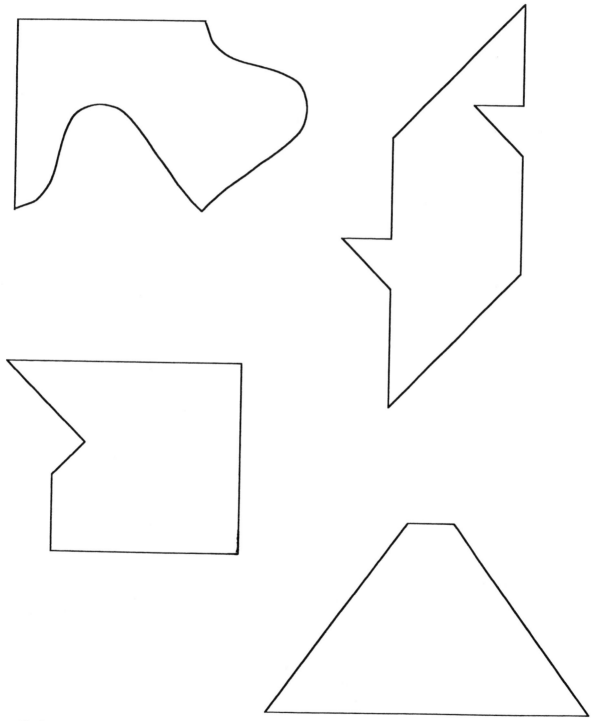

(From *The I Hate Mathematics! Book* by Marilyn Burns. Copyright © 1975 by the Yolla Bolly Press. By permission of Little, Brown and Company.)

Spirals
Mindel Sitomer and Harry Sitomer
(New York: Thomas Y. Crowell, 1974)

This book begins by clarifying the differences between spirals and circles, and goes on to discuss spirals in nature and in manmade items. It includes activities to aid readers in their understanding of this geometric form.

Activities

1. Using compasses, have the students draw the smallest circle they can. Then, opening the compasses about one-fourth inch wider, have them draw another circle surrounding the first. Have them draw a third and fourth circle the same way. Next, have the students roll clay into a long strip to make into small circles to fit on the paper. Each student should now have four small clay circles each inside the other. (Standard 12)

   Have the students use the compass to draw a three-inch circle on another piece of paper, then roll out another long strip of clay. Have them fasten one end near the center of the paper and wind the clay around this end. (Standard 10)

   Have students describe how these two figures are different.

2. Show the students an apple. Tell them you will pare the apple skin in just one piece. Ask them if they think this will make a spiral. Pare the apple, and have the students tell you why they do or why they do not think the skin forms a spiral.

3. The books states that it is not easy to draw a spiral. It explains one way to draw a spiral using graph paper. Have students follow the directions and draw a flat spiral.

   The authors describe how to draw a different shaped spiral and then suggest a third pattern. Have students try these, and then use their own counting patterns to create different spirals. (Standard 13)

   Your students may want to make a spiral sculpture as well. (A pattern for one can be found on p. 93 of *The Magic of Kirigami*.)

4. Using a compass, have students draw a six-inch circle on a piece of paper. Then have them try to cut a spiral by cutting into the circle at a slant, keeping an even width of about one inch. (Standard 10)

   Have them cut the spirals they drew in the previous activity and hang these in the classroom.

5. The book also discusses the helix, a spatial spiral that is three-dimensional. Have students brainstorm examples of both flat and spatial spirals.

6. Screw threads are one example of the use of a helical shape. To simulate this, have students form a cylinder out of clay. Next have them carefully wrap thread or string around the clay cylinder. Then remove the thread to see the pattern left on the cylinder.

7. A tornado is an example of wind whirling in a spiral. Have students make a tornado in a jar by following the directions below.

    1 quart jar filled ¾ with water
    1 drop blue food coloring
    1 drop green food coloring
    2 teaspoons clear vinegar
    2 teaspoons liquid dishwashing detergent (Joy, Palmolive, etc.)

    Put all ingredients in the jar. Tighten lid. Hold jar vertically and shake outward from your chest. Watch the white pet tornado. (Standard 10)

8. At the end of the book the authors describe a spiral game. Divide students into cooperative groups and have them experiment with the game. Then have them make up their own game using a spiral.

Shape: The Purpose of Forms
Eric Laithwaite
(New York: Franklin Watts, 1986)

This book helps students think more about the various kinds of shapes they encounter daily in the natural and manmade world. It addresses properties of shapes, purposes of shapes, how shapes are made and used, and symmetry.

SPECIAL NOTE: Activities can be done without the book. Substitutes include: Knapp, Brian. *Shapes and Structures and Their Influence on Our World*. Science in Our World Series. Danbury, CT: Grolier, 1991; Taylor, Barbara. *Structures and Materials*. NY: Franklin Watts, 1991.

Activities

1. Discuss with the students what similarities and differences they notice between natural and man-made objects.

2. The book states that "shape does not 'just happen'." Have the students brainstorm the factors that affect the shape of things, particularly manmade things.

3. Have the students pair up and select an object. Ask them to determine why their object has that particular shape. Would it be more effective, efficient, or both, if it were in another shape? Have the students explain their answers. For example, would there be any advantage in manufacturing a refrigerator in the shape of a cylinder?

4. Have students select a manmade object and list all the various shapes it contains.

5. The text states, "Sometimes the shape allows materials that are not very strong to resist large forces in a particular direction." For example, cylinders are strong when they are on end; an egg (arc) is strong when pushed from the top and bottom; triangles are a very stable shape. Have the students test this.

To test triangles, have the students cut out six 6" x ½" cardboard strips. Connect the ends with paper fasteners to create a hexagon. Twist the strips to make another hexagon. Then cut additional strips to make a pentagon, a quadrilateral, and a triangle. Try twisting them. (The triangle shouldn't twist much; this is called rigidity of form.) (Standard 10)

Later have the students find examples of how these structures are used in real life.

Students may want to do further research on bridge-building and make their own models to test what form will hold the most weight. (Standard 10)

6. The sphere, cube, pyramid, and cylinder are considered the most fundamental of three-dimensional shapes. Have the students find examples of each. Introduce other geometric solids and have them find examples of those as well. Students may want to make a book of what they find using photographs, drawings, or magazine pictures.

7. The book mentions soap bubbles as an example of spheres. Divide the students into cooperative groups. Have each group make a bubble solution in a tub. Then have them make two- and three-dimensional geometric shapes out of plastic straws and string. Have them experiment to see if they can create non-spherical three-dimensional bubbles. (They may want to look at *Tom Noddy's Bubble Magic*.)

8. On p. 15 of the book there is a two-dimensional diagram that, when folded correctly, makes a cube. This is called a nett. Using the diagrams in figures 5.9 and 5.10, have the students practice folding these netts into three-dimensional shapes. Then have them try to draw their own nett for a different three-dimensional object.

   The two netts provided are crystal shapes. There are more. Students may wish to explore this further. (Standard 13)

9. Have the students go to the grocery store, on their own time or as a school field trip. Have them keep track of the different shapes used for packaging items. Do certain types of foods only come in one shape? What is the most frequent shape? What is the least frequent shape? Why are these shapes used? (Standard 11)

10. The book mentions ideas that people have borrowed from nature. Have students find examples of shapes we have borrowed.

11. The book briefly discusses symmetry. Have students look for examples in nature of lateral symmetry and vertical symmetry. What are the advantages and disadvantages of a symmetrical arrangement?

(Text continues on page 87.)

Fig. 5.9.

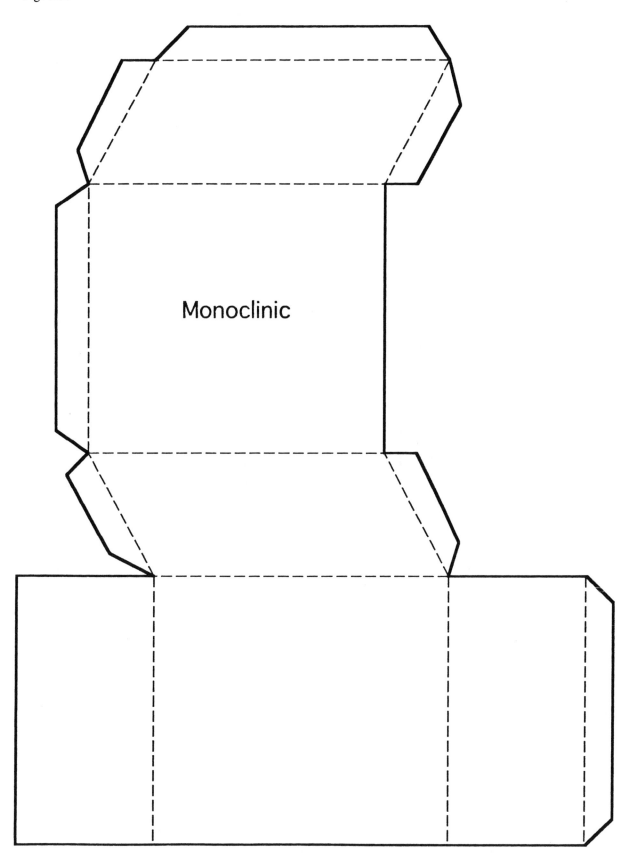

Fig. 5.10.

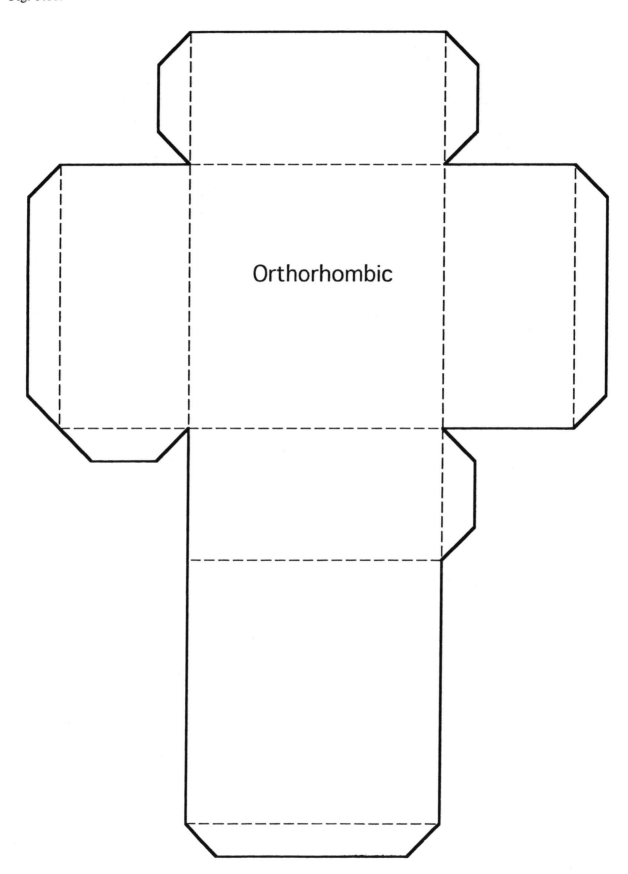

What Can She Be? An Architect
Gloria Goldreich and Esther Goldreich
(New York: Lothrop, Lee & Shepard, 1974)

Susan Brody is the architect spotlighted in this book. Readers discover what kinds of information and skills architects need to acquire while following Susan through several projects.

SPECIAL NOTE: Activities can be done without the book. Substitutes include: Clinton, Susan. *I Can Be an Architect*. Chicago: Childrens Press, 1986; Maddex, Diane. *Architects Make ZigZags*. Washington, D.C.: The National Trust for Historic Preservation, 1986; Wadsworth, Ginger. *Julia Morgan, Architect of Dreams*. Minneapolis: Lerner, 1990.

Activities

1. Invite an architect in your community to talk with the class. Have the architect bring some of the tools used in that profession, and explain their functions to the students.

2. Take a walking field trip with the students to observe different types of buildings. Discuss what types of geometric and non-geometric shapes are used and why these particular shapes are used. Do certain types of buildings, such as homes, businesses, churches, museums, libraries, and schools, have a common type of architecture?

3. Find out if the kindergarten has some geometric building blocks you can borrow and have your students build structures using these blocks. Ask them to notice what kinds of shapes work best as a base; what shapes are the most stable; what shapes work well in combination; etc.

4. Get a building drawing book and have the students practice some of the techniques used. (*Draw 50 Buildings and Other Structures* by Lee J. Ames is a good one.) By creating a structure step-by-step, they will become more observant of the shapes inherent in various buildings.

5. Architects must be able to see things from many perspectives. Divide students into cooperative groups and have them sit or stand in a circle. Give each group an irregular-shaped object, such as a coffee mug, and instruct them to put it in the center of the circle. Then have each student draw exactly what she sees from that position. When they have finished, collect the drawings from one group at a time and redistribute them to different students in the group. Have the students stand or sit in the position from which they think the object was drawn.

6. Architects use blueprints in their work. Have the students do the following activities to learn more about how to use blueprints.
    a. Divide students into cooperative groups. Give each group a large piece of butcher paper and several small cubes or other concrete objects. Have them place the objects on the paper to represent objects in the classroom. Have the students trace around the cubes and then remove the cubes one by one.
    b. Have the students try drawing another room without using the concrete objects first.
    c. Locate real blueprints for students to study. Have the students try to figure out the architectural symbols used for windows, doors, etc.
    d. Have the students design their ideal house, completing inside plans as well as outside plans.
    e. Obviously, blueprints are not as large as the buildings they represent. Discuss scaling with the students. Return to the "blueprint" of the classroom, and have the students draw it to scale. (Standards 10 and 12)

7. In the book, Bill, an apprentice architect, is shown building a scale model of a beach house. Have your students build a scale model of a building of their choice. (Standards 10 and 12)

Rubber Bands, Baseballs, and Doughnuts
Robert Froman
(New York: Thomas Y. Crowell, 1972)

This book uses experimentation with everyday objects to simplify the branch of mathematics known as topology. Topology is defined in the book as "the study of what does not change when line segments and different kinds of shapes are scrunched up, twisted around, or distorted in other ways." Cartographers, computer designers, and astronomers all use topology in their work.

SPECIAL NOTE: Activities can be done without the book. The concept of topology is discussed in Anno, Mitsumasa. *Math Games.* NY: Philomel, 1991; Burns, Marilyn. *The I Hate Mathematics! Book.* Boston: Little, Brown, 1975. A substitute is Wyler, Rose and Mary Elting. *Math Fun with Tricky Lines and Shapes.* NY: Julian Messner, 1992.

Activities

1. The book begins by asking readers to draw a line segment on a piece of paper. Readers are then instructed to mark four dots from left to right on the line segment. Have the students do this, and then crumple the paper and reopen it. Explain that although the line segment is now distorted in many ways, some things are still the same. Ask the students to identify what has not changed.

2. The next activity in the book involves cutting a rubber band and tying two knots in it. Have the students do this and then stretch the rubber band as far as they can without breaking it. Review with students what has changed and what has not. Explain that those things that do not change when distorted are called invariants; those things that do change when distorted are called variants.

3. Giving directions can involve topology. If a person tells you to go downstairs, turn left, walk past two doors, and turn right at the third corridor, the path of your travel will always look roughly the same regardless of the length of the stairway or the distance between the doors and corridors. Divide the students into cooperative groups and have one person create a set of directions like those above. Have the other students in the group draw different versions of the same directions. Switch roles.

4. Network theory involves lines connecting points or how places are linked. Have students choose a place to walk to and count how many streets they cross to reach their destination. Challenge the students to reach the same place by crossing fewer streets or crossing twice as many. Have them diagram those options. Could the same route be used if they were traveling by car? If not, how does it differ?

Challenge the students to walk through all the doors in their house once without passing through any more than once.

Students may also wish to investigate the bridges of Königsberg in conjunction with this. Michael Holt's *Maps, Tracks, and the Bridges of Königsberg* is a good reference for this. (See Related Books and References at the end of this chapter.)

Have students look at other networks such as highway systems, the circulatory system, rivers and streams, tree branches, electrical circuits, neural networks, and computer networks.

5. Divide students into cooperative groups. Have them draw as many shapes as they can without retracing any line, and without lifting the pencil from the paper. (You may want to do this outside using chalk on a sidewalk.)

   The shapes formed in a cat's cradle game can all be drawn with only one line. Have the students work in pairs with one person creating the different configurations with string, and the other person drawing these on paper.

   Simply by looking at a shape, students can learn to predict whether it can be drawn without lifting the pencil off the paper. Topologists do this by looking at the vertices (places where the lines intersect) to determine how many of them have an odd number of lines meeting there (odd vertices). Have the students look at different figures and chart the odd vertices. Have them record whether these can be drawn without lifting the pencil off the paper. What is the pattern that allows predictability? (Standard 13)

6. Sprouts is a topological game invented by two British mathematicians. Have each student choose a partner to play this game. The directions are in figure 5.11.

7. The author goes on to discuss simple closed curves. Have the students draw different shapes on a balloon and stretch them in a variety of ways. (This can also be done using a computer paint program.) Have them identify the variants and invariants.

8. A figure eight is not a simple closed curve because it divides the paper into one outside, but two insides. Have the students experiment with drawing different closed curves that separate the surface into one outside and several insides.

9. Topologists place solid objects into different categories based on how many cuts can be made in the objects before they become two separate pieces. The author uses balls and doughnuts to illustrate this more clearly. Have the students make a ball and a doughnut out of clay, and try the experiments in the book.

10. Any object that is classified as a specific genus can be changed into any other object belonging to the same genus without cutting or tearing. The book shows the doughnut stretching into a cup and a figure eight changing into a two-handled gravy bowl. Have the students try this with clay. Experiment with other objects as well.

Fig. 5.11. Sprouts.

Sprouts is a topological network game invented by two British mathematicians.

Directions:

Two players start with two points and take turns drawing according to the following rules:

A line must start and end at a point.

You can use curved lines, and you can start and end at the same point if you want.

After you draw a line, you must mark a new point somewhere on it.

No line can cross itself or another line, nor pass through any point.

No point can have more than three lines ending at it.

The winner is the last person able to play.

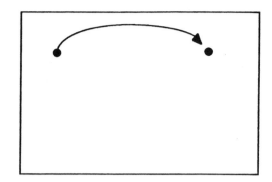

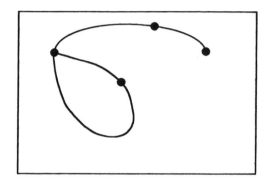

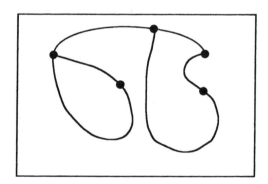

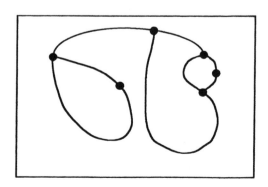

RELATED BOOKS AND REFERENCES

ARCHITECTURE

Clinton, Susan. *I Can Be an Architect.* Chicago: Children's Press, 1986. (K-3)

Devlin, Harry. *What Kind of a House Is That?* New York: Parents Magazine Press, 1969. (4-6)

Isaacson, Philip M. *Round Buildings, Square Buildings, & Buildings That Wiggle Like a Fish.* New York: Alfred A. Knopf, 1988. (4-6)

Lobel, Anita. *Sven's Bridge.* New York: Harper & Row, 1965. (4-6)

Macaulay, David. *Pyramid.* Boston: Houghton Mifflin, 1975. (4-6)

Maddex, Diane. *Architects Make Zigzags.* Washington, D.C.: Preservation Press, 1986. (4-6)

Robbins, Ken. *Building a House.* New York: Four Winds Press, 1984. (4-6)

Walker, Les. *Housebuilding for Children.* Woodstock, N.Y.: Overlook Press, 1977. (4-6)

Weiss, Harvey. *Model Buildings & How to Make Them.* New York: Thomas Y. Crowell, 1979. (4-6)

DIMENSIONALITY

Abbott, Edwin A. *Flatland: A Romance of Many Dimensions.* Boston: Little, Brown, 1899. (4-6)

Adler, David A. *3D, 2D, 1D.* New York: Thomas Y. Crowell, 1975. (K-3)

Dewdney, A. K. *The Planiverse: Computer Contact with a Two-Dimensional World.* New York: Poseidon Press, 1984. (4-6)

Impey, Rose. *The Flat Man.* New York: Barron's, 1988. (K-3)

DRAWING AND COMPUTER GRAPHICS

Ames, Lee J. *Draw 50 Buildings and Other Structures.* New York: Doubleday, 1980. (4-6)

Emberley, Ed. *Ed Emberley's Big Green Drawing Book.* Boston: Little, Brown, 1979. (K-3)

_____. *Ed Emberley's Drawing Book of Animals.* Boston: Little, Brown, 1970. (K-3)

_____. *Ed Emberley's Drawing Book of Faces.* Boston: Little, Brown, 1971. (K-3)

_____. *Ed Emberley's Drawing Book, Make a World.* Boston: Little, Brown, 1972. (K-3)

_____. *Ed Emberley's Great Thumbprint Drawing Book.* Boston: Little, Brown, 1977. (K-3)

_____. *Ed Emberley's Picture Pie.* Boston: Little, Brown, 1984. (K-3)

Holland, Penny. *Looking at Computer Graphics*. New York: Franklin Watts, 1985. (K-6)

Rauch, Hans-Georg. *The Lines Are Coming*. New York: Charles Scribner's Sons, 1978. (K-6)

GEOMETRIC SHAPES AND CONCEPTS

Allington, Richard L. *Beginning to Learn About Shapes*. Milwaukee, Wis.: Raintree Children's Books, 1979. (K-3)

Barrett, Peter, and Susan Barrett. *The Circle Sarah Drew*. New York: Scroll Press, 1972. (K-3)

Bendick, Jeanne. *Shapes*. New York: Franklin Watts, 1968. (4-6)

Budney, Blossom. *A Kiss Is Round*. New York: Lothrop, Lee & Shepard, 1954. (K-3)

Carle, Eric. *The Secret Birthday Message*. New York: Thomas Y. Crowell, 1983. (K-3)

Charosh, Mannis. *The Ellipse*. New York: Thomas Y. Crowell, 1971. (K-3)

_____. *Straight Lines, Parallel Lines, Perpendicular Lines*. New York: Thomas Y. Crowell, 1970. (K-3)

Charosh, Mannis, and Harry Sitomer. *Circles*. New York: Thomas Y. Crowell, 1971. (4-6)

Ehlert, Lois. *Color Farm*. New York: J. B. Lippincott, 1990. (K-3)

Emberley, Ed. *The Wing on a Flea*. Boston: Little, Brown, 1961. (K-3)

Fisher, Leonard Everett. *Look Around! A Book About Shapes*. New York: Puffin Books, 1987. (K-3)

Froman, Robert. *Angles Are Easy as Pie*. New York: Thomas Y. Crowell, 1975. (K-3)

Gundersheimer, Karen. *Shapes to Show*. New York: Harper & Row, 1986. (K-3)

Hoban, Tana. *Circles, Triangles, and Squares*. New York: Macmillan, 1974. (K-3)

Holland, Penny. *Looking at Logo*. New York: Franklin Watts, 1984. (K-3)

Kessler, Ethel, and Leonard Kessler. *Are You Square?* Garden City, N.Y.: Doubleday, 1966. (K-3)

Kightley, Rosalinda. *Shapes*. Boston: Little, Brown, 1986. (K-3)

Newth, Philip. *Roly Goes Exploring: A Book for Blind and Sighted Children, in Braille and Standard Type, with Pictures to Feel as Well as to See*. New York: Philomel Books, 1981. (K-3)

Pluckrose, Henry. *Think About Shape*. New York: Franklin Watts, 1986. (K-3)

Podendorf, Illa. *Shapes: Sides, Curves, and Corners*. Chicago: Children's Press, 1970. (K-3)

Razzell, Arthur G., and K. G. O. Watts. *Circles and Curves*. Garden City, N.Y.: Doubleday, 1968. (4-6)

_____. *Three and the Shape of Three*. Garden City, N.Y.: Doubleday, 1964. (4-6)

Reiss, John J. *Shapes*. New York: Bradbury Press, 1974. (K-3)

Russell, Solveig Paulson. *Lines and Shapes*. New York: Henry Z. Walck, 1965. (4-6)

Schlein, Miriam. *Shapes*. Reading, Mass.: Addison-Wesley, 1952. (K-3)

Testa, Fulvio. *If You Look Around You*. New York: Dial Books for Young Readers, 1983. (K-3)

Tester, Sylvia Root. *The Parade of Shapes*. Elgin, Ill.: Child's World, 1976. (K-3)

MISCELLANEOUS

Anno, Mitsumasa. *Anno's Math Games*. New York: Philomel Books, 1982. (K-3)

_____. *Anno's Math Games II*. New York: Philomel, 1982. (K-3)

Burns, Marilyn. *The I Hate Mathematics! Book*. Boston: Little, Brown, 1975. (4-6)

Fisher, Leonard Everett. *Symbol Art*. New York: Four Winds Press, 1985. (4-6)

Hewavisenti, Lakshmi. *Shapes and Solids*. New York: Gloucester Press, 1991. (K-6)

Lewis, David B. *Eureka!* New York: Perigee Books, 1983. (4-6)

Raboff, Ernest. *Pablo Picasso (Art for Children Series)*. New York: J. B. Lippincott, 1982. (4-6)

Zubrowski, Bernie. *Raceways: Have Fun with Balls and Tracks*. New York: William Morrow, 1985. (4-6)

NON-GEOMETRIC SHAPES

Bulloch, Ivan. *The Letter Book*. New York: Simon & Schuster Books for Young Readers, 1990. (K-3)

Grifalconi, Anne. *The Village of Round and Square Houses*. Boston: Little, Brown, 1986. (K-3)

Hoban, Tana. *Dots, Spots, Speckles and Stripes*. New York: Greenwillow Books, 1987. (K-3)

_____. *Round & Round & Round*. New York: Greenwillow Books, 1983. (K-3)

_____. *Shapes, Shapes, Shapes*. New York: Greenwillow Books, 1986. (K-3)

Renberg, Dalia Hardof. *Hello Clouds!* New York: Harper & Row, 1985. (K-3)

Shaw, Charles G. *It Looked Like Spilt Milk*. New York: Thomas Y. Crowell, 1974. (K-3)

Ungerer, Tomi. *Snail, Where Are You?* New York: Harper & Brothers, 1962. (K-3)

PAPER-FOLDING AND PAPER-CUTTING GEOMETRY/SYMMETRY

Airey, Graham, Ben Bates, and Ian Price. *New Ideas in Card and Paper Crafts.* New York: Van Nostrand Reinhold, 1973. (K-3)

Churchill, E. Richard. *Fast & Funny Paper Toys You Can Make.* New York: Sterling Publishing, 1989. (K-6)

Corwin, Judith Hoffman. *Papercrafts.* New York: Franklin Watts, 1988. (K-3)

Harbin, Robert. *Paper Folding Fun.* Newton Centre, Mass.: Charles T. Branford, 1960. (4-6)

Massaglio, Elinor. *Fun-Time Paper Folding.* Chicago: Children's Press, 1959. (K-3)

Nakano, Dokuohtei. *Easy Origami.* New York: Viking Penguin, 1985. (4-6)

Phillips, Jo. *Exploring Triangles: Paper-Folding Geometry.* New York: Thomas Y. Crowell, 1975. (4-6)

_____. *Right Angles. Paper-Folding Geometry.* New York: Thomas Y. Crowell, 1972. (K-3)

Sarasas, Claude. *The ABCs of Origami.* Rutland, Vt.: Charles E. Tuttle, 1964. (K-6)

Temko, Florence. *Paper Cutting.* Garden City, N.Y.: Doubleday, 1973. (K-3)

Temko, Florence, and Toshie Takahama. *The Magic of Kirigami.* Tokyo: Japan Publications, 1978. (4-6)

Tofts, Hannah. *The 3-D Paper Book.* New York: Simon & Schuster Books for Young Readers, 1989. (K-3)

PROPORTIONALITY

Anno, Mitsumasa. *The King's Flower.* New York: Philomel Books, 1976. (4-6)

Bridwell, Norman. *Clifford, the Big Red Dog.* New York: Scholastic, 1985. (K-3)

Mizumura, Kazue. *The Way of the Ant.* New York: Thomas Y. Crowell, 1970. (4-6)

Peterson, John. *The Littles.* New York: Scholastic, 1967. (4-6)

_____. *The Littles and the Big Storm.* New York: Scholastic, 1979. (4-6)

_____. *The Littles and the Trash Tinies.* New York: Scholastic, 1977. (4-6)

_____. *The Littles Go Exploring.* New York: Scholastic, 1978. (4-6)

_____. *The Littles' Great Halloween Scare.* New York: Scholastic, 1975. (4-6)

_____. *The Littles to the Rescue*. New York: Scholastic, 1968. (4-6)

Van Allsburg, Chris. *Two Bad Ants*. Boston: Houghton Mifflin, 1988. (4-6)

QUILTING

Ernst, Lisa Campbell. *Sam Johnson and the Blue Ribbon Quilt*. New York: Lothrop, Lee & Shepard, 1983. (4-6)

Sommer, Elyse, with Joellen Sommer. *A Patchwork, Applique, and Quilting Primer*. New York: Lothrop, Lee & Shepard, 1975. (4-6)

SHADOWS AND REFLECTIONS

Anno, Mitsumasa. *In Shadowland*. New York: Orchard Books, 1988. (K-3)

Brown, Marcia. *Shadow*. New York: Charles Scribner's Sons, 1982. (K-3)

Bursill, Henry. *Hand Shadows to Be Thrown upon the Wall*. New York: Dover Publications, 1967. (K-6)

Dorros, Arthur. *Me and My Shadow*. New York: Scholastic, 1990. (K-3)

Goor, Ron, and Nancy Goor. *Shadows*. New York: Thomas Y. Crowell, 1981. (K-3)

Hoban, Tana. *Shadows and Reflections*. New York: Greenwillow Books, 1990. (K-3)

Jonas, Ann. *Reflections*. New York: Greenwillow Books, 1987. (K-3)

_____. *Round Trip*. New York: Greenwillow Books, 1983. (K-3)

Kent, Jack. *The Biggest Shadow in the Zoo*. New York: Parents Magazine Press, 1981. (K-3)

Simon, Seymour. *Mirror Magic*. New York: Lothrop, Lee & Shepard, 1980. (K-3)

_____. *Shadow Magic*. New York: Lothrop, Lee & Shepard, 1985. (K-3)

Stevenson, Robert Louis. *My Shadow*. New York: G. P. Putnam's Sons, 1990. (K-3)

Taylor, Barbara. *Fun with Simple Science: Shadows and Reflections*. New York: Warwick Press, 1990. (4-6)

Trivett, Daphne Harwood. *Shadow Geometry*. New York: Thomas Y. Crowell, 1974. (K-3)

Webb, Angela. *Talkabout Reflections*. New York: Franklin Watts, 1988. (K-3)

TOPOLOGY

Helfman, Harry, and Elizabeth Helfman. *Strings on Your Fingers.* New York: William Morrow, 1965. (4-6)

Holt, Michael. *Maps, Tracks and the Bridges of Königsberg.* New York: Thomas Y. Crowell, 1975. (4-6)

Orii, Eiji, and Masako Orii. *Simple Science Experiments with Circles.* Milwaukee, Wis.: Gareth Stevens Children's Books, 1989. (K-3)

Snyder, Zilpha Keatley. *The Changing Maze.* New York: Macmillan, 1985. (4-6)

ADULT REFERENCES

Diggins, Julia. *String, Straightedge, and Shadow.* New York: Viking, 1965.

Holt, Michael. *More Math Puzzles and Games.* New York: Walker, 1978.

Hughes, Robert. *The Shock of the New.* New York: Alfred A. Knopf, 1981.

Pellman, Rachel, and Kenneth Pellman. *A Treasury of Amish Quilts.* Intercourse, Pa.: Good Books, 1990.

Reimer, Donald. *Ute Mountain Pottery Designs.* Towaoc, Colo.: Ute Mountain Indian Pottery, 1977.

Shared Horizons: Navajo Textiles. Santa Fe, N. Mex.: Wheelwright Museum of the American Indian, 1981.

Sutton, Keith. *Picasso.* New York: Marboro Books, 1962.

VanCleave, Janice. *Math for Every Kid.* New York: John Wiley, 1991.

Wadley, Nicolas. *Cubism.* New York: Hamlyn, 1970.

6—Standard 10: Measurement

The mathematics curriculum should include measurement so that readers can

- understand the attributes of length, capacity, weight, area, volume, time, temperature, and angle;
- develop the process of measuring and the concepts related to units of measurement;
- make and use estimates of measurement; and
- make and use measurement in problem and everyday situations.

Mathematics has value to students because of the power it gives them in everyday life, and the practice it provides in the development of mathematical skills and concepts. The beginning skills of measurement should include experience in comparing objects, covering the objects with units of measure, and counting the units of measure. Only after concept development should instruments and formulas be taught. As with other mathematics, measurement should involve estimation and real-world practice. Textbook activities and abstract learning by themselves are not effective.

U.S. standard units of measurement, metric units of measurement and nonstandard units of measurement should be learned. Elementary-age students need to understand the most basic estimation skills of conversion between the units, such as liter to quart, kilometer to mile, meter to yard, centimeter to inch, and grams in a pound. The primary goal is for the student to learn how to use each system.

BOOKS FOR GRADES K–3

MATHEMATICAL CONTENT VOCABULARY

April	half hour	metric	Sunday
area	heavy	minutes	surface area
August	hour	Monday	Thursday
balance	inch	month	time
calendar	January	nonstandard	ton
centimeter	July	November	Tuesday
clock	June	o'clock	volume
day	kilogram	October	Wednesday
December	light	ounce	week
estimate	linear measurement	pound	weigh
February	March	Saturday	weight
foot	May	scale	yard
Friday	measure	September	year
gram	meter	standard	

The Grouchy Ladybug
Eric Carle
(New York: Thomas Y. Crowell, 1977)

At five o'clock in the morning, a grouchy ladybug and a friendly ladybug both decide to have a breakfast of aphids on the same leaf. The grouchy ladybug doesn't want to share the aphids and tells the friendly ladybug to go away. He even threatens to fight the friendly ladybug, but finally the grouchy ladybug flies away. Every hour, he challenges another animal, backing down each time. When he gets to the whale, he challenges different parts of its body at each quarter hour. Finally at six o'clock he returns to the same leaf where he began, and decides to share the aphids with the friendly ladybug after all.

Activities

1. The grouchy ladybug had a very busy day. Write a one-sentence description on oaktag strips of his various encounters. Have the children put these in sequence.

2. Have the children make a picture clock, such as the one shown in figure 6.1, of their own daily schedules. They may want to make drawings or use pictures from magazines.

Fig. 6.1. Picture clock.

| Wake up | Go to school | Eat lunch | Watch TV |
| 7:30 a.m. | 9:00 a.m. | 12:15 p.m. | 4:00 p.m. |

3. Have the children make a paper plate clock and use it to illustrate the time of day while they tell the story of the grouchy ladybug.

4. The grouchy ladybug begins the day at five o'clock in the morning and ends it around six o'clock at night. How many hours was he flying around? (Standard 7 or 8)

5. It took a long time for the grouchy ladybug to travel from place to place. The children may want to research how fast a ladybug can travel. How long would it really take for him to fly the full length of a blue whale?

6. Have the children estimate how long it takes them to do certain things, such as making their beds and eating breakfast, and then have them time these activities.

    Have the children estimate how long it takes them to do certain activities at school and use a stopwatch to time them. Discuss how quickly or slowly time seems to pass depending on the activity.

7. The grouchy ladybug certainly didn't use a clock to tell time. Why do people use clocks to measure the passage of time? Have children brainstorm situations in which it is important to know the exact time.

8. The grouchy ladybug began the day at five o'clock in the morning when the sun came up. Ask the children where they are when the sun rises. When does the sun set? Does the sun always rise and set at the same time? Why not? (Standard 6)

9. The grouchy ladybug always backs out of a fight by saying, "Oh, you're not big enough." Have the children find out how big the different animals in the book really are. How big is a ladybug?

How Big Is a Foot?
Rolf Myller
(New York: Atheneum, 1962)

"Once upon a time there lived a King and his wife, the Queen." They had everything, so the King was stumped when he tried to think of a present for his wife's birthday. Finally, he decided to have a bed made for her, "which was an excellent idea since beds hadn't been invented yet." He ordered the bed to be built three feet wide and six feet long. Unfortunately, when the bed was presented to the Queen, it was too small. After being banished to the dungeon for this mistake, the apprentice carpenter figured out the problem, told the King of his solution, and went on to build a bed to fit the Queen.

Activities

1. The King used his feet to measure the Queen's length in order to pass on the dimensions to the apprentice carpenter. What else could the King have used to measure the Queen?

2. The King used his feet to measure the Queen for the bed. Have the children trace around their feet or shoes on a piece of paper. Have them cut out the foot and use it to measure various items in the classroom. Be sure to have them estimate the measurements first. You may want to use a sheet similar to the one shown in figure 6.2.

Fig. 6.2. Linear measurement data collection sheet.

Object	Estimate	Actual Measurement

3. The King ordered a bed for the Queen that was three feet wide and six feet long. That is exactly what the apprentice carpenter made. Why didn't it work?

    The King saw the completed bed before the Queen's birthday. Why didn't he know it was too small?

4. Lots of our measurements today were originally based on body parts. Ask the children why they think this was the case. Have the children research this and make a chart for the classroom.

    Have them measure their own thumbs, feet, etc., to see how close they are to an inch, a foot, etc., and to determine the variation.

5. Have the children experiment with the sizes of various body parts. With a partner, have them use string to measure the circumference of their heads. Cut the string and use this to measure their waist sizes. Are they the same? Measure wrists and ankles. Measure from head to toe. Have them stretch their arms out on either side and measure from fingertip to fingertip. Are they wider or taller? How much difference is there? Measure arm length and leg length. Measure waist to heel and waist to head. Which is longer? How much? (Standard 12)

6. The King needed to measure the Queen to get the right size bed. Why do people today need to use linear measurement?

7. The King used his feet to measure the Queen. The problem was that his feet and the apprentice carpenter's feet weren't the same size. Once the sculpture of the King's foot was made, a foot was always the same. Have the children discuss different measures and categorize them by those that are always the same size (standard) and those that aren't (nonstandard). (For example, peanuts are not all the same size; paperclips are.) Have the children measure the same items as above with an unofficial standard measure. Have them estimate first.

8. Have the children make a metric or nonmetric ruler and use it to measure various items. Have them estimate first. (Standard 8)

Pezzettino
Leo Lionni
(New York: Pantheon, 1975)

Pezzettino was a little piece. "All the others were big and did daring and wonderful things." Pezzettino thought he must be a missing part of somebody else. He asked the one-who-runs, the strong-one, the swimming-one, the one-on-the-mountain, the flying-one, and the wise-one, but he was not a piece of them. After voyaging to the Island of Wham, he realized he was himself.

Activities

1. Pezzettino looks like a little two-centimeter square. He doesn't take up very much space. Make little construction paper squares for the children or have them cut out their own. Tell them they will use Pezzettino to help them measure area. Give them the linear measurement data collection sheet in figure 6.2. Have them estimate how many Pezzettinos will cover each object. Then have them use the squares to measure.

2. Pezzettino thinks he is very small and must be part of someone else. He asks all the big ones if they have a missing piece. Divide the children into cooperative groups and have them use Pezzettino squares to make pictures of the big ones shown in the book. Which one has the largest area? For example, the one-who-runs has an area of approximately 37 Pezzettinos. (Standard 12)

3. Using the same number of Pezzettino squares as they used to make their particular big one, have each group make as many different big ones or designs as they can that still have the same area. Discuss how things that look different can have the same area.

4. Explain to the children that surface area is the total outside area of an object. Give each group a three-dimensional square, or rectangular object such as a box. Have the children estimate how many Pezzettino squares would cover all six sides. Then have them paste these construction paper squares onto the boxes and count the total. (Standard 9)

   Later, you may want them to do the same thing with a spherical object, such as a ball or a grapefruit.

5. For measuring the big areas such as floors, Pezzettino squares would take too long. Give the children giant Pezzettino squares (one foot square) to use for measuring these large objects. Prepare another measuring sheet for these and be sure to have the children estimate first.

6. Brainstorm with the children why people would want to know the area of something (carpeting, painting, sewing, etc.).

7. Do the students think that giant Pezzettino squares could be used to tell someone the area of the classroom floor? Why or why not? Use this discussion to move into standardized measurement when the children are ready.

Space, Shapes, and Sizes
Jane Jonas Srivastava
(New York: Thomas Y. Crowell, 1980)

In this book, bears, rabbits, dogs, pigs, and lions illustrate simple experiments children can do to learn more about volume.

SPECIAL NOTE: Activities can be done without the book. The concept of volume/capacity is discussed in: Anno, Mitsumasa. *Anno's Math Games II*. NY: Philomel, 1982; Lafferty, Peter. *Archimedes*. NY: Bookwright Press, 1991.

Activities

(Some of these activities will be harder if the children do not yet understand conservation of volume.)

1. The author begins by explaining that the shape of something can change without changing its volume. The first experiment involves sand. Divide the children into cooperative groups. Give each group a small box filled with sand. Have them pour the sand out of the box onto a piece of paper on a table or desk. Then have them spread the sand out on the paper into a flat shape. Using a funnel, have the children pour the sand back into the box. If none is spilled, it should still fill the box. Explain that the volume has not changed although the shape has. Ask the students to think of other situations in which this happens.

2. Divide children into cooperative groups. Give each group at least five containers of different sizes. Also give them an ample supply of beans, rice, sand, or water. Have them fill one container. Then have them estimate whether the others will hold more, less, or the same amount of beans, rice, sand, or water.

3. Show children the examples in the book of the "buildings" made with three, four, and six cubes. Explain that if a "building" was made with the same number of cubes, then it has the same volume. Divide the children into cooperative groups and give each group ten cubes. Have them make as many different "buildings" as they can. Have them share their results.

4. The author explains that different shaped boxes may have the same volume. One way to find out is to fill the boxes with pieces of popcorn. Make lots of popcorn. Show the class five or six different shaped boxes. Have them estimate and rank the boxes by volume. Then divide the children into cooperative groups and give each group one of the boxes and some popcorn. Have them fill their boxes with popcorn. (Before dumping the box to count the popcorn, have them cover it and shake it gently. Then open the box to see if more popcorn will fit inside.) Have each group count the number of kernels of corn inside their box and report. Which box has the greatest volume? (Standard 6)

5. The author also has a way to compare the volume of objects that you can't fill. Collect a golf ball; a lump of clay; a small metal car; a small potato; a black, brown, red, green, and blue crayon; and a jar with a wide mouth for each group. Before getting in cooperative groups, have the class estimate and rank the items according to volume. Have someone from each group fill the jar half full with water, and mark the water level on the outside of the jar with the black crayon. Have the children put what they think has the greatest volume in the jar. Mark the new water level with the brown crayon. Remove the object. Use the red crayon for the next object, the blue crayon for the next, and the green crayon for the last item. The object with the largest volume will take up the most space, and its mark will be the highest on the jar. Compare the results to the estimates.

Heavy Is a Hippopotamus
Miriam Schlein
(New York: William R. Scott, 1954)

This book begins with the concepts of heavy and light. It moves on to standardized measures for weight and provides examples of why we need these measures.

SPECIAL NOTE: Activities can be done without the book. A substitute is Taylor, Barbara. *Weight and Balance.* NY: Franklin Watts, 1990.

Activities

1. The book begins by asking, "What does heavy mean?" and gives a few examples. Have the children brainstorm examples of things that are heavy and things that are light. You may want to write a class book, "Heavy Is..."

2. Divide the class into cooperative groups. Give each group several objects of varying weights. Have the group list the objects from heaviest to lightest without touching them. Then use a balance scale to determine the order more accurately. Discuss why objects that appear different may weigh the same.

3. Divide the children into cooperative groups. For each group prepare two bags. In a small paper bag, place a jar of jelly and securely fasten the bag closed. In a large paper bag, place lots of crumpled newspaper and securely fasten the bag closed. Ask children to estimate which bag is heavier without lifting either one. Then ask the children to lift each bag and tell which is heavier. (Often, even after lifting, their perception is inaccurate.) Discuss that size and weight don't always correlate, and that it is important to know what is inside something before estimating weight.

4. As the book goes on, it shows that heavy and light are relative terms. For us a crumb is light; but to an ant, it is heavy. To use the terms heavy and light accurately, we must always compare them to something else. Ask the children to think of something that could be used as a comparison. Using that object as your basis for comparison, estimate whether other objects are heavier or lighter. Use a balance scale to categorize the objects more accurately.

5. Tell the children that a long time ago, stones were used as standards of measure. Divide the children into cooperative groups. Have each group go outside to collect several stones to use for measurement. Give each group the same five objects. Have them estimate how many stones each will weigh. Then, using their stones and the balance, have them record how many stones each one actually weighs. Have the groups compare their findings. Discuss why they aren't the same.

6. The results from the last activity aren't a problem unless you need to know exact or consistent weights. Have the children think of situations in which knowing exact or consistent weight is important.

7. Tell children that even if you used stones that were all exactly the same weight, weighing objects would still eventually become a problem. Why?

8. The book says a doughnut weighs about one ounce. Using a balance scale, have the children find out what else weighs about one ounce. (You may use the gram instead for this activity.) Have them get used to the feel of this weight in their hands.

9. The book goes on to state that 16 doughnuts weigh about one pound. Have the children use a marked scale to find other things that weigh about one pound. Bring in various grocery items that weigh one pound. Have them become accustomed to how heavy a pound feels in their hands. Discuss how different one pound can look. One pound of popped popcorn may look like a lot more than one pound of unpopped popcorn.

10. The book shows candy that is measured in ounces, potatoes that are measured in pounds, and coal that is measured in tons. Have the children make a chart that lists various items along with the standards that are used to measure these items. (Again, you may want to do this for metric instead.)

11. Children may also want to make a chart or book about heaviest and lightest records. (Standards 11 and 12)

    Example: The heaviest animal known is the blue whale weighing up to 200 tons. On the other hand, the Vervain hummingbird weighs only .08 ounce.

Or, perhaps they may want to make posters about how much different things weigh.

Example: A brachiosaurus was believed to have weighed 45,000 kilograms. A 4-x-5-foot bale of hay may weigh up to 850 pounds.

The Day That Monday Ran Away
Robert Heit
(New York: The Lion Press, 1969)

Monday feels unappreciated and thinks that people would be happier without him, so he decides to run away. Time tries to talk Monday out of it, but he can only think of one reason why Monday shouldn't run away. "People who have bought calendars expecting that there will be 365 days this year will not be getting their money's worth." That's not good enough for Monday, so he takes off. The story tells of all the problems this creates. All the other days help to search, but it is Saturday who discovers Monday's hiding place, and Monday is finally persuaded to return.

SPECIAL NOTE: Activities can be done without the book. Consult the bibliography and the following substitutes: Sulevitz, Uri. *One Monday Morning.* NY: Charles Scribner's Sons, 1967; Kachenmeister, Cherryl. *On Monday When It Rained.* Boston: Houghton Mifflin, 1989; Hooper, Meredith. *Seven Eggs.* NY: HarperCollins, 1986.

Activities

1. Monday is depressed at the beginning of the book. He thinks nobody likes him. Is this true in your classroom? Have the children vote on their favorite day of the week and graph the results. Have the children explain their choices. (Standard 11)

2. When Time has to think of a reason to keep Monday from running away, he can only think of one. "P.e.o.p.l.e. w.h.o. h.a.v.e. b.o.u.g.h.t. c.a.l.e.n.d.a.r.s. e.x.p.e.c.t.i.n.g. t.h.a.t. t.h.e.r.e. w.i.l.l. b.e. 365 d.a.y.s. t.h.i.s. y.e.a.r. w.i.l.l. n.o.t. b.e. g.e.t.t.i.n.g. t.h.e.i.r. m.o.n.e.y.'.s. w.o.r.t.h." If Mondays were removed from the calendar year, how many days would be left? (Standard 7 or 8)

3. When Monday ran away, people weren't able to do the things they normally do on Monday. Discuss with the children how their lives would change if there wasn't a Monday. What things, activities, and events occur on a weekly basis? On a monthly basis? On a yearly basis?

4. When Monday ran away, people whose birthdays were on Monday were not able to celebrate. How many children in the class were born on Monday? How many on other days? Graph this information. (Standard 11)

Share the following rhyme with the children.

Monday's child is fair of face,
Tuesday's child is full of grace,
Wednesday's child is full of woe,
Thursday's child has far to go;
Friday's child is loving and giving,
Saturday's child works hard for a living;
But the child that is born on the Sabbath day
Is blithe and bonny, good and gay.

There are also other sayings about different days of the week, such as:

If you sneeze on Monday, you sneeze for danger;
Sneeze on Tuesday, kiss a stranger;
Sneeze on Wednesday, sneeze for a letter;
Sneeze on Thursday, something better;
Sneeze on Friday, sneeze for sorrow;
Sneeze on Saturday, see your sweetheart tomorrow;
Sneeze on Sunday, the Devil will have you the rest of the week.

5. If there were no Mondays, there would only be six days per week. Have the children research why we have seven days in a week.

6. If Monday hadn't returned, a replacement day might have been found. What name do you think it should have had? Why do the days of the week have the names they do now? Have the children research this information.

7. Ask the children why we should keep track of the different days of the week anyway. Why can't they all be called today? Have the children use the calendar pattern in figure 6.3 to mark down important days they wish to remember.

Fig. 6.3.

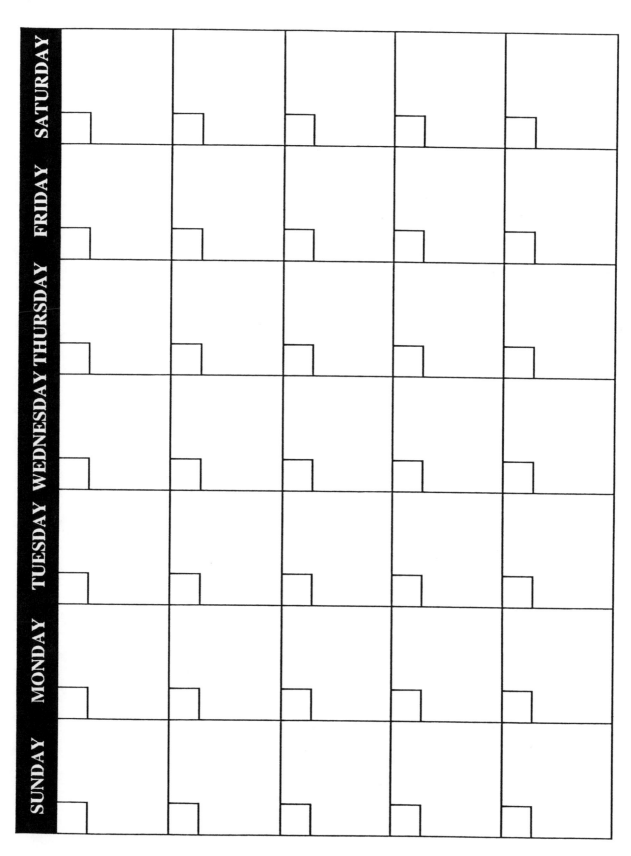

BOOKS FOR GRADES 4-6

MATHEMATICAL CONTENT VOCABULARY

A.D.
antipodes
B.C.
blood pressure
Celsius
centimeter
circumference
epoch
era
exponent
Fahrenheit
gram
Gregorian calendar
inch
kilogram

kilometer
latitude
longitude
magnification
mass
meridian
meter
miles
milligram
millimeter
newton
ounce
parallel
pound
pulse

quadrillon
Richter scale
shilling
sixpence
square foot
square inch
square mile
surface area
temperature
time zones
timeline
trillion
volume
weight

Diary of a Church Mouse
Graham Oakley
(New York: Atheneum, 1987)

Humphrey is a church mouse. His New Year's Resolution is to start on the Story of His Life right away. However, another mouse, Arthur, informs him that you have to wait until you are very old before you know how your life turned out. Humphrey protests that by then he will have forgotten, so Arthur suggests Humphrey keep a diary to help him remember what happens. This book contains one year in the life of Humphrey, the church mouse.

Activities

1. As per Arthur's suggestion, Humphrey, the church mouse, begins a diary. During the year, he makes note of vacations and holidays, including Valentine's Day, Halloween, and Christmas. Why doesn't he mention others such as Presidents' Day, Martin Luther King's birthday, St. Patrick's Day, and the Fourth of July?

2. Humphrey begins his diary on January 1. This is currently considered the beginning of our calendar year. In groups, have students research our calendar system to answer the following.

   a. Has this always been the beginning of the year? Why?

   b. What has changed about our calendar?

   c. Why do we have 12 months?

    d.   Why don't the months have the same number of days?

    e.   How did our months get their names?

    f.   Why do we have calendars anyway?

3.   Humphrey begins his diary on the first day of the new year. January 1 is not the first day of the new year for all calendars. Have the students research the Chinese calendar and others to find out how they are organized and why.

4.   At the end of the year, Humphrey was unimpressed with keeping a diary. He didn't think it had been very useful, partly because not enough exciting things had happened to him. Have students create a more exciting year's diary for Humphrey, or have them invent one for themselves.

5.   In 1792, the Gregorian calendar was changed in France. In 1929, the Soviet Union also abandoned the Gregorian calendar for a few years. Today, the World Calendar Association also wants to change the Gregorian calendar. Have the students devise what they think would be a better calendar than the one we have today. They may want to survey others to determine their preferences. They may also want to research what the World Calendar Association has proposed. (See *This Book Is About Time* by Marilyn Burns.)

6.   Sometimes groups make calendars to sell in order to raise money. Your class may want to think about doing this. You could include math facts and problems for each day or week; highlight a math standard every month; or highlight a specific number by making a collage for each month's picture. Students can calculate costs, set the price, and figure profits.

8,000 Stones
Diane Wolkstein
(Garden City, N.Y.: Doubleday, 1972)

    Ts'ao Ts'ao is the Most Supreme Governor of China. One year the Satrap, or prince, of India sends Ts'ao Ts'ao an elephant. No one in the kingdom has ever seen an elephant. When Ts'ao Ts'ao asks how tall the elephant is, he is told 10 feet. No one, however, knows how much the elephant weighs. Ts'ao Ts'ao is determined to know and orders his advisors to find out. No one can think of a way to weigh the elephant until Ts'ao Ts'ao's son, P'ei, comes up with the solution.

SPECIAL NOTE: Activities can be done without the book. Related substitutes include: Dahl, Roald. *Esio Trot.* NY: Viking, 1990; Taylor, Barbara. *Weight and Balance.* NY: Franklin Watts, 1990.

Activities

1.   The Satrap of India sends Ts'ao Ts'ao, the Most Supreme Governor of China, an elephant that is 10 feet tall. Have the students measure to find out how tall that is. What else is that tall? Is this the usual height of an elephant?

2.   Ts'ao Ts'ao orders his advisors to determine how much the elephant weighs, but they can't come up with a solution. Ask students how they would have figured it out in those days. How might they figure it out today? Students may want to call a zoo to find out if and how it is done there.

3.   Obviously, the way people determine weight has changed over the centuries. Have the students research the history of weights and measures.

4. Little Pe'i figures out how to weigh the elephant by using a boat. They determine that the elephant weighs 8,000 stones. If the elephant were weighed again in a different location, would he still weigh 8,000 stones? Why or why not? What else might be a problem with using stones to weigh things? (Hint: How much space do 8,000 stones take up?)

5. Have the students try the method Pe'i used to weigh his small ivory elephant. Use a toy boat in a large, deep basin of water and try weighing different objects. How many stones is each one equal to? You may want to use gram weights instead of stones.

6. Have the students research the weight of an average male Indian elephant. What else weighs this amount? Based on the initial information, and assuming each stone weighs the same amount, approximately how much does each stone weigh? (Standard 8)

7. Ts'ao Ts'ao is very interested in knowing how much the elephant weighs, although that information does not seem to prove very useful in the story. Ask students why knowing the weight of something is important today. Who uses this type of information and how?

8. There are many expressions that use the word weight such as pulling your own weight, throwing your weight around, weighing your words carefully, etc. Have the students find other weight-related sayings and make posters of these with illustrations.

9. Have students make a scale using the directions and illustrations in figure 6.4.

10. Explain to the students that weight is caused by the force of gravity pulling things toward the center of the Earth. Scientifically, it is measured in newtons. (A newton is a unit to measure force. One newton is the force needed to accelerate an object with a mass of 2.2046 pounds by 3.280 feet per second every second.) Inside a bathroom scale, your weight in newtons is converted into mass in pounds. Every pound of mass is pulled towards the center of the Earth by a force of about 4.5 newtons. Have the students calculate their weight in newtons. (Standards 8 and 12)

Time for Horatio
Penelope Colville Paine
(Santa Barbara, Calif.: Advocacy Press, 1990)

Oliver finds Horatio, a stray kitten, and takes him home. Home is a London pleasure steamer named Victorious. On Horatio's first trip, many of the tourists are mean to him. When he learns about Greenwich Mean Time, he misunderstands and thinks that is what is causing people to be mean. Oliver has a dream in which Horatio stops Big Ben in order to stop mean time.

Activities

1. Oliver takes Horatio to the boat, Victorious. Horatio just begins to relax when he is startled by the noise from Big Ben, probably the most famous clock in the world. Big Ben is the nickname given to the giant bell on which the great Westminster Clock strikes. Big Ben weighs 13½ tons. Each of the four clock faces is 23 feet in diameter and 180 feet from the ground. Have the students form ideas of how big this is. Have them research what else weighs this much—such as how many cars. Have them measure out a circle with a diameter of 23 feet. Have them find out what else is 180 feet tall. (Standard 6)

Fig. 6.4. How to build a balance scale.

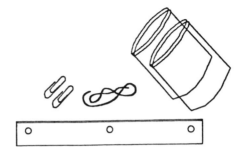

You will need:
A ruler with 3 holes
2 paperclips
2 Zip-lock bags
String

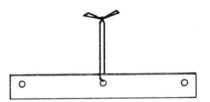

Step One:
Pull the string through the
middle hole of the ruler.
Tie the ends together.

Step Two:
Hook one end of the
paperclip just under
the Zip-lock strip and
attach the other end to
the hole at one end of
the ruler. Do the same
for the other end.

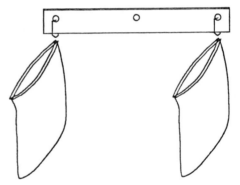

Step Three:
Hang the string on a
hook or a doorknob,
and it's ready to use.

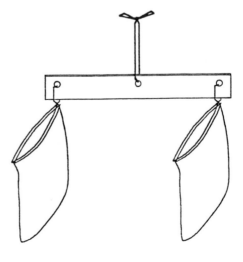

2. Oliver and Horatio visit the Royal Greenwich Observatory built in 1675. A royal warrant appointed John Flamsteed as the astronomical observator to research possible ways to measure time and distance accurately. It is filled with displays of all sorts of clocks and timepieces.

   Have students research the history of clocks and make posters or a book to illustrate what they have learned. They may want to share this with younger students at their school.

   Many books contain instructions for making models of these various timepieces, such as water clocks, hourglasses, and sundials. Have students make some of these.

3. Oliver and Horatio look at a map of the time zones of the world at the Observatory. Oliver explains that "scientists have divided the world up into strips ... a bit like an orange." Have the students make a large map of the world's time zones.

   Have the students write a story telling about what different people around the world are doing at the "same time."

   Example: When Linda is waking up in Los Angeles, what is Bruce doing in Tokyo? (Anno's *All in a Day* may be helpful.)

4. Oliver goes on to explain that the starting point is Greenwich, so they call that line the Greenwich meridian or prime meridian. It is zero degrees longitude. It divides the eastern half of the world from the western half. The meridian is used universally for timekeeping and navigation on land, at sea, and in the air. Have the students draw a map showing latitude and longitude lines. You may want them to lay this out on the classroom floor, or make a papier-mâché globe and mark the lines on that instead. Have them practice moving from place to place using the latitude and longitude directions. (Standard 9)

5. There is an official clock at the Observatory that people all over the world use to set their clocks. It's called Greenwich Mean Time. Have students research what people did before we had agreed-upon time zones. They may want to try to invent a better system.

The Magic School Bus Inside the Earth
Joanna Cole
(New York: Scholastic, 1987)

Each student in Mrs. Frizzle's class is supposed to bring a rock to school. However, most of the class doesn't do their homework, so Mrs. Frizzle decides to take them on a field trip to collect the rocks. They have quite an adventure traveling to the center of the Earth and back.

Activities

1. When the class reaches the field, Mrs. Frizzle tells them they will first dig through the Earth's crust. Have the students find out how thick the Earth's crust is. How many other layers are there, and how thick are they?

2. Some of the students find fossils. Have students find out how long it takes to make a fossil.

3. Mrs. Frizzle's students might have found a fossil of a trilobite. How long ago did trilobites live? You may want to have your students make a geologic timeline that includes different eras, epochs, and forms of life. (Standard 11)

4. The bus falls into a "huge limestone cave." Have the students do research to answer the following.

   a. How fast does the bus fall? If the bus falls two miles, how fast is it going? (Standard 8)

   b. What are the dimensions of the largest known natural underground cave or cavern?

   c. What is the volume of the largest "room"? How many students would fit in it? (Standard 8)

   d. Mrs. Frizzle's class sees stalagmites and stalactites. How long do they take to form? How much do they grow per year?

   e. Using the largest "room" dimensions and the rate of growth for stalagmites and stalactites, how long would it take for a stalactite and a stalagmite to grow together? (Standard 8)

5. As the class ventures deeper into the Earth, the temperature becomes higher and higher. The pressure also increases.

   a. Have the students find out the temperatures and amounts of pressure for each layer.

   b. What is the highest temperature a human can endure without dying?

   c. What is the greatest amount of pressure a human can survive?

6. During the trip, the students discuss the varying hardnesses of rocks. Have your students find out about the hardness scale used to classify rocks and what it is based on.

7. Rocks also vary in weight. Have students find out the lightest and heaviest types of rocks. They may want to make a chart listing different rocks and their weights. What is the amount of variation?

8. Mrs. Frizzle's class emerges from their trip to the center of the Earth on a volcanic island. Have students do some research on volcanoes.

   a. What is the biggest and smallest volcano?

   b. What volcano has had the most eruptions?

   c. What volcano has had the most violent eruptions?

   d. Earthquakes are measured on the Richter scale. How are volcanoes measured?

   e. How many active volcanoes do we know about in the world today?

   f. How hot is volcanic lava?

9. In the book, the class travels to the center of the Earth and back in one day. Ask the students to pretend that the heat and pressure wouldn't kill them, and ask them to calculate how long it would really take to make this trip. (Standard 8)

The Magic School Bus Inside the Human Body
Joanna Cole
(New York: Scholastic, 1990)

Once again, Mrs. Frizzle's class has an unusual field trip. On the way to the museum, they stop at a park for lunch. But as everyone else boards the bus to leave, Arnold is still sitting at the picnic table eating Cheesie-Weesies. Then instead of driving away, the bus becomes very small and slips into Arnold's bag of snacks. Arnold swallows the bus without noticing, and the class begins its trip through the human body.

Activities

1. In the beginning of the book, a student is looking through a microscope at her own cheek cells. What magnification is necessary to do this? Have your students draw various objects at different levels of magnification. Discuss how exponents are used for this. (Standard 6)

2. The bus shrinks enough to be mistaken for a Cheesie-Weesie. This allows it to travel through the esophagus and later, the bloodstream. Ask students to calculate how much the bus would have to shrink. You may want to specify using exponents, percentages, or fractions. (Standards 8 and/or 12)

3. The class begins its trip by traveling through the digestive system. Have students research the length of the human digestive system. If it were spread out in the human body, how tall would people have to be? They may want to compare the length of the human digestive system to that of other animals. (Standard 6)

4. The bus follows the food molecules into the blood.

   a. The book states that there are 250 million red blood cells in each drop of blood. Have students find out how we measure things that small.

   b. We normally discuss the amount of blood in the body in terms of pints. Have students find out how many pints of blood are in the human body. Have them pour an equivalent amount of liquid into a container to see how much that is. Have them calculate the total number of red blood cells in the body. (Standard 8)

   c. During the trip, the bus is attacked by a white blood cell. Have the students find out how many white blood cells are normally in the human body. What is the ratio of white blood cells to red blood cells? When the body has an infection, it produces more white blood cells. What is the rate of this production? Some diseases, such as leukemia, are marked by an overabundance of white blood cells. Have students find the ratio of white blood cells in a healthy person to those of a person with leukemia.

d. The Red Cross often holds blood drives. Have students find out how many pints of blood the Red Cross collects each year. There are several different blood types. Have the students find out the percentage for the occurrence of each in the general population. (Standard 12)

e. Michael's report claims that your blood makes a trip all around your body in less than a minute. Have the students research the length of the circulatory system and the speed at which blood travels. You may want to have a health professional talk with your class about blood and the circulatory system.

5. Meanwhile, Arnold is concerned because he thinks the bus has left without him, and he's not sure how to get back to school. His heart is pounding. Have the students find out how blood pressure and pulse rate are measured. How much does this vary in humans depending on their activity level? (Standard 11)

6. The class continues its trip through the body and reaches the brain. Have students find out how large a brain is. Does the size vary much? Do smarter people have bigger brains? (Standard 13)

Scientists now estimate that the brain contains 100 trillion synapses. Have students find out how this is measured or calculated. It is also estimated that the human brain can carry out 100 quadrillion operations per second. How is this measured? (You may want to mention that some computers can now perform almost 1 trillion calculations per second.)

7. Next the class climbs down the spine and notices the many nerve cells. Have students research the total length of the nervous system. If all the body's nerves were placed end to end, how far would they stretch? (Standard 8)

8. As the class slides down some muscle tissue, they notice that the leg muscles are working hard. Arnold is running to get back to school. As he runs, his body temperature is probably increasing. Have students find out what is considered normal temperature for human beings. What are the highest and lowest temperatures possible for human survival? (35° C and 42.8° C. Some marathon runners have gotten to 41° C, or 105.8° F.)

9. The bus escapes Arnold's body when he sneezes. Phoebe's report states that air rushes out of the nose at speeds of up to 100 miles per hour. How is this measured? How does the National Weather Service rate 100-mile-per-hour winds? (Standard 6)

10. At the end of the book a poster shows Arnold's favorite organ is a full stomach. Have the students research the size of the stomach. Have them find or make a container that has approximately the same volume. Have them experiment with what can be put into that size container.

11. On the trip through the body, the class goes through the heart and lungs, but misses the liver, kidney, bladder, etc. Have the students research the size of the different parts of the body, and make a chart, a book, or a life-size model to represent the numerical information they have learned about the body. What other measurement data could they include (vision, diameter of human hair, bone weight, etc.)? (Standard 11)

12. The book deals mainly with the inside of the human body, but you may want to have the students figure out the surface area (skin) of the body. (Standard 8)

Around the World in Eighty Days
Jules Verne
(New York: William Morrow, 1988)

In 1872, Phileas Fogg, an eccentric Englishman, wagers £20,000 that he can travel around the world in 80 days. This he does, despite numerous delays and adventures, returning just at the last moment.

Activities

1. In 1872, Phileas Fogg makes a wager with his friends that he can travel around the world in 80 days. In 1970, John Burningham, an author, also decided to go around the world in 80 days. They took quite different routes. Fogg traveled 26,000 miles and Burningham traveled 44,000 miles. Ask the students what they think it means to travel around the world. Do their criteria involve number of miles, number of countries visited, following a particular parallel, or something else? (The circumference of the earth at the equator is 24,901.46 miles, or 39,842.336 kilometers.)

2. The book states, "Could he have followed without deviation the fiftieth parallel, which is that of London, the whole distance would only have been about 12,000 miles." Have students find out if it would be possible today to follow the fiftieth parallel without deviation.

3. Phileas Fogg plans his journey based on the following estimates made by the *Daily Telegraph*.

From London to Suez, via Mont Cenis and Brindisi (Italy), by rail and steamboats	7 days
From Suez to Bombay, by steamer	13 days
From Bombay to Calcutta, by rail	3 days
From Calcutta to Hong Kong, by steamer	13 days
From Hong Kong to Yokohama (Japan), by steamer	6 days
From Yokohama to San Francisco, by steamer	22 days
From San Francisco to New York, by rail	7 days
From New York to London, by steamer and rail	9 days
Total	80 days

Have students trace this route on a map. Is it really 26,000 miles? Discuss the differences between distance as the crow flies and as transportation routes allow.

4. One of the whist players at the Reform Club states, "The world *has* grown smaller, since a man can now go round it ten times more quickly than a hundred years ago." That was said in 1872. Using the route followed by Phileas Fogg, have the students determine if we can travel around the world 10 times faster today (namely in eight days) than in 1872. (Standard 8)

5. Phileas Fogg uses a great deal of money on the trip for traveling expenses, bribes, fines, the purchase of an elephant, bail, the purchase of a boat, and so on. Have students make a list of how much he spent and on what. What would those things cost today? (Standard 8)

6. Passepartout, Fogg's manservant, left the gas burner on in his room. He tells the detective, Fix, that he is losing two shillings every four and twenty hours, exactly sixpence more than he earns. Have students calculate how much he will owe at the end of the trip. How much is that in dollars? (Standard 8)

7. On the 23d of November, Passepartout crossed over the 180th meridian, and was at the very antipodes of London. He thought that his watch was finally at the correct time again, but it was actually 12 hours off. Have the students determine where their watches would be exactly twelve hours off, starting out from your school. (You may want to explain that there are 360 degrees on the circumference of the earth; and these 360 degrees, multiplied by four minutes, equal precisely 24 hours.) (Standard 9)

8. In crossing the United States, we are told, "Thirteen hundred and eighty-two miles had been passed over from San Francisco, in three days and three nights; four days and nights more would probably bring them to New York." Have students find out how many miles are between San Francisco and New York. What is the quickest way to travel from one city to the other today, and how long would it take? How long would it take today by train? (Standard 8)

9. Using the criteria established above for what constitutes going around the world, have the students map out the route (starting from the school) they would follow, determine how long it would take, and how much it would cost. The class could be divided into cooperative groups with each group taking a different route. You may also want them to keep a notebook similar to the one Fogg used.

"Left London, Wednesday, October 2nd, at 8:45 P.M."
"Reached Paris, Thursday, October 3rd, at 7:20 A.M."
"Left Paris, Thursday, at 8:40 A.M."
"Reached Turin by Mont Cenis, Friday, October 4th, at 6:35 A.M."
"Left Turin, Friday, at 7:20 A.M."
"Arrived at Brindisi, Saturday, October 5th, at 4 P.M."
"Sailed on the *Mongolia*, Saturday, at 5 P.M."
"Reached Suez, Wednesday, October 5th, at 11 A.M."
"Total of hours spent 158½; or, in days, six days and a half."

10. "On the ninth day after leaving Yokohama, Phileas Fogg had traversed exactly one half of the terrestial globe. The *General Grant* passed, on the 23rd of November, the one hundred and eightieth meridian, and was at the very antipodes of London. Mr. Fogg had, it is true, exhausted fifty-two of the eighty days in which he was to complete the tour, and there were only twenty-eight left. But, though he was only half-way by the difference of meridians, he had really gone over two-thirds of the whole journey; for he had been obliged to make long circuits from London to Aden, from Aden to Bombay, from Calcutta to Singapore, and from Singapore to Yokohama. Could he have followed without deviation the fiftieth parallel, which is that of London, the whole distance would only have been about twelve thousand miles; whereas, he would be forced, by the irregular methods of locomotion, to traverse twenty-six thousand, of which he had, on the 23rd of November, accomplished seventeen thousand five hundred." Have the students calculate their halfway points, both by time and meridian. Are these as dissimilar as Fogg's? (Standard 8)

11. When the characters arrive in India, we are told that "India embraces fourteen hundred thousand square miles, upon which is spread unequally a population of one hundred and eighty million of souls." The Great Salt Lake is reported to be 72 miles long and 30 miles wide, and situated 4200 feet above sea level. The highest elevation of the journey was at Evans Pass, Colorado, 8,091 feet above sea level. You may want the students to include these types of statistics in their reports about the places they "visit." (Standard 11)

12. Have the students plot a trip that would allow them to visit every country in the world. How long would it take? (Standard 8)

RELATED BOOKS AND REFERENCES

AREA

Laurin, Anne. *Little Things*. New York: Atheneum, 1978. (4-6)

Srivastava, Jane Jonas. *Area*. New York: Thomas Y. Crowell, 1974. (K-3)

CALENDAR

Adler, Irving, and Ruth Adler. *The Calendar*. New York: John Day, 1967. (4-6)

Barrett, Judi. *Benjamin's 365 Birthdays*. New York: Atheneum, 1974. (K-3)

Blos, Joan W. *A Gathering of Days. A New England Girl's Journal, 1830-32*. New York: Charles Scribner's Sons, 1979. (4-6)

Brindze, Ruth. *The Story of Our Calendar*. New York: Vanguard Press, 1949. (4-6)

Fisher, Leonard Everett. *Calendar Art*. New York: Four Winds Press, 1987. (4-6)

Fleischman, Sid. *McBroom's Almanac*. Boston: Little, Brown, 1984. (4-6)

Goennel, Heidi. *Seasons*. Boston: Little, Brown, 1986. (K-3)

Ichikawa, Satomi. *Suzette and Nicholas and the Seasons Clock*. New York: Philomel Books, 1978. (K-3)

Lyon, George Ella. *Father Time and the Day Boxes*. New York: Bradbury Press, 1985. (K-3)

Sendak, Maurice. *Chicken Soup with Rice*. New York: Harper & Row, 1962. (K-3)

Yen, Clara. *Why Rat Comes First: A Story of the Chinese Zodiac*. San Francisco: Children's Book Press, 1991. (4-6)

DAYS OF THE WEEK

Carle, Eric. *The Very Hungry Caterpillar*. New York: Philomel Books, 1987. (K-3)

Domanska, Janina. *Busy Monday Morning*. New York: Greenwillow Books, 1985. (K-3)

Holabird, Katherine. *Angelina's Birthday Surprise.* New York: Clarkson N. Potter, 1989. (K-3)

Kraus, Robert. *Come Out and Play, Little Mouse.* New York: Greenwillow Books, 1987. (K-3)

Lasker, Joe. *Lentil Soup.* Chicago: Albert Whitman, 1977. (K-3)

Martin, Bill, Jr. *Monday, Monday, I Like Monday.* New York: Holt, Rinehart & Winston, 1970. (K-3)

Sharmat, Mitchell. *The Seven Sloppy Days of Phineas Pig.* San Diego, Calif.: Harcourt Brace Jovanovich, 1983. (K-3)

LINEAR MEASUREMENT

Allbright, Viv. *Ten Go Hopping.* London: Faber & Faber, 1985. (K-3)

Bate, Lucy. *How Georgina Drove the Car Very Carefully from Boston to New York.* New York: Crown, 1989. (K-3)

Beede, Gretchen. *Simple Sewing.* Minneapolis, Minn.: Lerner, 1975. (4-6)

Briggs, Raymond. *Jim and the Beanstalk.* New York: Coward-McCann, 1970. (4-6)

Burningham, John. *Around the World in Eighty Days.* London: Jonathan Cape, 1972. (4-6)

Corrigan, Barbara. *Of Course You Can Sew!* Garden City, N.Y.: Doubleday, 1971. (4-6)

Dolman, Sue. *The Brambly Hedge Pattern Book.* New York: Philomel Books, 1985. (4-6)

Fey, James T. *Long, Short, High, Low, Thin, Wide.* New York: Thomas Y. Crowell, 1971. (K-3)

Gilleo, Alma. *About Meters.* Elgin, Ill.: Child's World, 1977. (K-3)

Johnston, Tony. *Farmer Mack Measures His Pig.* New York: Harper & Row, 1986. (K-3)

Lionni, Leo. *Inch by Inch.* New York: Astor-Honor, 1960. (K-3)

Roth, Susan. *Marco Polo: His Notebook.* New York: Doubleday, 1990. (4-6)

Segan, Ann. *One Meter Max.* Englewood Cliffs, N.J.: Prentice-Hall, 1979. (K-3)

Walker, Les. *Housebuilding for Children.* Woodstock, N.Y.: Overlook Press, 1977. (4-6)

Yerian, Cameron, and Margaret Yerian, eds. *FunTime Easy Sewing Projects.* Chicago: Children's Press, 1975. (K-3)

_____. *FunTime Sew It! Wear It!* Chicago: Children's Press, 1975. (K-3)

MISCELLANEOUS MEASUREMENT

Adler, David A. *3-D, 2-D, 1-D.* New York: Thomas Y. Crowell, 1975. (K-3)

Adler, Peggy, and Irving Adler. *Metric Puzzles.* New York: Franklin Watts, 1977. (4-6)

Anno, Mitsumasa. *Anno's Math Games.* New York: Philomel Books, 1982. (K-3)

Arnold, Caroline. *Measurements.* New York: Franklin Watts, 1984. (K-3)

Baynton, Martin. *Fifty and the Great Race.* New York: Crown, 1987. (K-3)

Bendick, Jeanne. *Science Experiences: Measuring.* New York: Franklin Watts, 1971. (K-3)

Branley, Franklyn M. *How Little and How Much: A Book About Scales.* New York: Thomas Y. Crowell, 1976. (K-3)

Cobb, Vicki. *The Long and Short of Measurement.* New York: Parents Magazine Press, 1973. (K-3)

Conrad, Pam. *Pedro's Journal: A Voyage with Christopher Columbus.* Honesdale, Pa.: Boyds Mills Press, 1991. (4-6)

DuBois, William Pene. *The 21 Balloons.* New York: Viking, 1947. (4-6)

Froman, Robert. *Bigger and Smaller.* New York: Thomas Y. Crowell, 1971. (K-3)

Hennessy, B. G. *The Dinosaur Who Lived in My Backyard.* New York: Viking Kestrel, 1988. (K-3)

Hewavisenti, Lakshmi. *Measuring.* New York: Gloucester Press, 1991. (K-3)

Kennedy, Richard. *The Contests at Cowlick.* Boston: Little, Brown, 1975. (K-3)

Linn, Charles F. *Estimation.* New York: Thomas Y. Crowell, 1970. (K-3)

Lord, John Vernon. *The Giant Jam Sandwich.* Boston: Houghton Mifflin, 1972. (4-6)

Simon, Seymour. *The Largest Dinosaurs.* New York: Macmillan, 1986. (K-6)

_____. *The Smallest Dinosaurs.* New York: Crown Publishers, 1982. (K-6)

Webster, Harriet. *Going Places: The Young Traveler's Guide and Activity Book.* New York: Charles Scribner's Sons, 1991. (4-6)

TEMPERATURE

Branley, Franklyn M. *How Little and How Much: A Book About Scales.* New York: Thomas Y. Crowell, 1976. (K-3)

Gilleo, Alma. *About the Thermometer: A Metric Book.* Elgin, Ill.: Child's World, 1977. (K-3)

Maestro, Betsy, and Giulio Maestro. *Temperature and You.* New York: Lodestar Books, 1990. (K-3)

Munsch, Robert, and Michael Martchenko. *50 Below Zero.* Toronto: Annick Press, 1987. (K-3)

Simon, Seymour. *Hot & Cold.* New York: McGraw-Hill, 1972. (K-3)

TIME

Abisch, Roz. *Do You Know What Time It Is?* Englewood Cliffs, N.J.: Prentice-Hall, 1968. (K-3)

Allen, Jeffrey. *Mary Alice Operator Number 9.* Boston: Little, Brown, 1975. (K-3)

Anno, Mitsumasa. *All in a Day.* New York: Philomel Books, 1986. (4-6)

Burningham, John. *John Patrick Norman McHennessy — The Boy Who Was Always Late.* New York: Crown Publishers, 1987. (K-3)

Carlson, Natalie Savage. *Time for the White Egret.* New York: Charles Scribner's Sons, 1978. (4-6)

Delacre, Lulu. *Time for School, Nathan!* New York: Scholastic, 1989. (K-3)

Douglas, Barbara. *The Chocolate Chip Cookie Contest.* New York: Lothrop, Lee & Shepard, 1985. (K-3)

Francoise. *What Time Is It, Jeanne-Marie?* New York: Charles Scribner's Sons, 1963. (K-3)

Gerstein, Mordicai. *The Sun's Day.* New York: Harper & Row, 1989. (K-3)

Goennel, Heidi. *My Day.* Boston: Little, Brown, 1988. (K-3)

Gould, Deborah. *Brendan's Best-Timed Birthday.* New York: Bradbury Press, 1988. (K-3)

Grey, Judith. *What Time Is It?* Mahwah, N.J.: Troll Associates, 1981. (K-3)

Grossman, Bill. *The Guy Who Was Five Minutes Late.* New York: Harper & Row, 1990. (K-3)

Hutchins, Pat. *Clocks and More Clocks.* Macmillan, 1970. (K-3)

Jennings, Terry. *Time.* New York: Gloucester Press, 1988. (K-3)

Jupo, Frank. *A Day Around the World.* New York: Abelard-Schuman, 1968. (4-6)

Kantrowitz, Mildred. *Maxie.* New York: Four Winds Press, 1970. (4-6)

Krasilovsky, Phyllis. *The Man Who Tried to Save Time.* Garden City, N.Y.: Doubleday, 1979. (K-3)

McMillan, Bruce. *Time To...* New York: Lothrop, Lee & Shepard, 1989. (K-3)

Maestro, Betsy. *Around the Clock with Harriet.* New York: Crown, 1984. (K-3)

McMillan, Bruce. *Time To...* New York: Lothrop Lee & Shepard, 1989. (K-3)

Murphy, Jill. *Five Minutes Peace.* New York: G. P. Putnam's Sons, 1986. (K-3)

Ness, Evaline. *Do You Have the Time, Lydia?* New York: E. P. Dutton, 1971. (K-3)

Shapiro, Arnold. *Mr. Cuckoo's Clock Shop.* Los Angeles: Price Stern Sloan, 1981. (K-3)

Trivett, Daphne, and John Trivett. *Time for Clocks.* New York: Thomas Y. Crowell, 1979. (K-3)

Yolen, Jane. *The Bird of Time.* New York: Thomas Y. Crowell, 1971. (4-6)

Ziner, Feenie, and Elizabeth Thompson. *Time.* Chicago: Children's Press, 1982. (K-3)

Zubrowski, Bernie. *Clocks: Building and Experimenting with Model Timepieces.* New York: Morrow Junior Books, 1988. (4-6)

VOLUME AND CAPACITY

Anno, Mitsumasa. *Anno's Math Games II.* New York: Philomel Books, 1989. (K-3)

Douglas, Barbara. *The Chocolate Chip Cookie Contest.* New York: Lothrop, Lee & Shepard, 1985. (K-3)

Emerson, Anne. *Peter Rabbit's Cookery Book.* Middlesex, England: Frederick Warne, 1980. (K-3)

Gilleo, Alma. *About Liters.* Elgin, Ill.: Child's World, 1977. (K-3)

Howe, James. *Harold and Chester in Hot Fudge.* New York: Morrow Junior Books, 1990. (K-3)

MacGregor, Carol. *The Fairy Tale Cookbook.* New York: Macmillan, 1982. (K-3)

Modisett, Jeanne. *Vegetable Soup.* New York: Macmillan, 1988. (K-3)

Penner, Lucille Recht. *The Colonial Cookbook.* New York: Hastings House, 1976. (4-6)

Pluckrose, Henry. *Knowabout Capacity.* New York: Franklin Watts, 1988. (K-3)

Shapiro, Rebecca. *Wide World Cookbook*. Boston: Little, Brown, 1962. (4-6)

WEIGHT AND MASS

Branley, Franklyn M. *Gravity Is a Mystery*. New York: Thomas Y. Crowell, 1986. (K-3)

_____. *Weight and Weightlessness*. New York: Thomas Y. Crowell, 1971. (K-3)

Gilleo, Alma. *About Grams*. Elgin, Ill.: Child's World, 1977. (K-3)

Kellogg, Steven. *There Was an Old Woman*. New York: Parents Magazine Press, 1974. (4-6)

Pluckrose, Henry. *Knowabout Weight*. New York: Franklin Watts, 1988. (K-3)

Shapp, Martha, and Charles Shapp. *Let's Find Out What's Light and What's Heavy*. New York: Franklin Watts, 1975. (K-3)

Taylor, Barbara. *Weight and Balance*. New York: Franklin Watts, 1990. (4-6)

ADULT REFERENCES

Burns, Marilyn. *This Book Is About Time*. Boston: Little, Brown, 1978.

Hughes, Paul. *Days of the Week*. Ada, Okla.: Garrett Educational Corp., 1989.

Humphrey, Henry, and Deirdre O'Meara-Humphrey. *When Is Now?* Garden City, N.Y.: Doubleday, 1980.

Stenmark, Jean Kerr, Virginia Thompson, and Ruth Cossey. *Family Math*. Berkeley, Calif.: the Regents, University of California, 1986.

VanCleave, Janice. *Math for Every Kid*. New York: John Wiley, 1991.

Zaslavsky, Claudia. *Preparing Young Children for Math*. New York: Schocken Books, 1979.

7—Standard 11: Statistics and Probability

The mathematics curriculum should include experiences with data analysis and probability so that the students can

- collect, organize, and describe data;

- construct, read, and interpret displays of data;

- formulate and solve problems that involve collecting and analyzing data; and

- explore concepts of chance.

Children are able to use skills of collecting, organizing, describing, displaying, and interpreting data, as well as make decisions and predictions to help them better understand their world. The spirit of investigation and exploration should be the driving force in this instruction. Statistics and probability provide tools to connect other content areas, such as social studies, science, and language arts. Estimation and exactness are both skills required in statistics and probability.

BOOKS FOR GRADES K-3

MATHEMATICAL CONTENT VOCABULARY

arithmetic mean	data	mode	probability
average	divide	percentage	records
bar graph	estimate	pictograph	sample
census	graphs	pie graph	sampling
combinations	line graph	poll	statistics
cuboctahedron	median	prediction	tally

Statistics
Jane Jonas Srivastava
(New York: Thomas Y. Crowell, 1973)

This book starts by stating that "statistics are found by counting" and goes on to describe several examples. It also explains how statistics are gathered and how to communicate these statistics through graphs.

Activities

1. Have the children start a booklet about themselves titled "My Vital Statistics." They could include the number of people in their family, their ages, their number of teeth, their weights, their heights, the number of children in their class, the number of people that ride their bus, the number of pets they have, and so on. (Standard 6)

2. Once the children have collected their own statistics, they may wish to compare their information with others. Show them how to graph one of these items, such as shoe size. Draw the graph on the board or on a large piece of paper, and discuss size variations as well as which size is the most common.

3. The book states that many countries take a census every ten years. Ask the children why they think the census isn't taken every year. Have children find out what questions are asked on the U.S. census. Discuss why these are the questions asked. Have each child choose one statistic from the U.S. census that the child thinks is interesting, and then compile the statistics to make a bulletin board, a book, or a newsletter article.

4. The book discusses the idea of using a sample in taking polls. Explain that sample polls are also used for television ratings. Then, in cooperative groups, have the children conduct the experiment described in the book to show the difference the size of the sample makes.

5. The book also describes a sampling activity to determine which fruit the children in your school like best. Assign a group of children to each of the other classes in the school. Have each group ask five members of its assigned class to indicate the names of their favorite fruits. Help the children report their findings in a table on the chalkboard. Then have them make cutouts of the different fruits to use in making a pictograph of the information.

6. Have children find out how a fast food restaurant uses statistics to know how much food to buy, which items to keep on the menu, how much to charge, and so on.

7. The book lists some examples of statistics people may hear on television or read in a newspaper. Have each group look through a newspaper and cut out statistics they find.

Have the children bring to class examples of statistics they encounter outside of school. Have them consider how many were counted, who counted them, what was counted, where and when it was counted, if any of them indicate whether a sample was used, how the sample was chosen, and if it was a fair sample.

Fleet-Footed Florence
Marilyn Sachs
(Garden City, N.Y.: Doubleday, 1981)

Matt, the famous baseball hero, has three sons. He hopes they will grow up to be famous baseball players, too. However, it is Matt's daughter, Florence, who becomes the fastest runner in the East, West, North, and South. In fact, she joins her father's old team, the North Dakota Beavers, and "set so many records that there was no book big enough to hold them all."

SPECIAL NOTE: See *Matt's Mitt and Fleet-Footed Florence*. NY: Avon Books, 1991.

Activities

1. "Matt, the famous baseball hero, had three sons."

   a. Willie M. was named after the great hitter. Have the children find out who this refers to and what his record was. Has there been a hitter since then with a better record?

   b. Matt's second son, Lou B., was named after the great base-stealer. Have the children find out who this refers to and what his record was. Has there been a base stealer since then with a better record?

   c. Matt's third son, Johnny B., was named after the great catcher. Have the children find out who Johnny B. was and his record. Has there been a catcher since then with a better record?

2. Matt's daughter, Florence, became the fastest runner in the North, East, South, and West. Have children research the fastest speeds recorded for male and female runners. The children may want to have a race and record their own speeds. (Standard 10)

3. Baseball has many statistics. In the book the author refers to RBIs, ERAs, and BAs. Have the children find out what these acronyms mean and compare the statistics on various players. What other statistics are kept in baseball? Are statistics kept for Little League teams? How do they compare?

4. Ask how much money the children think the average baseball player earns. What is the highest salary? What is the lowest? (Standard 12)

5. Have the children research the average length of a baseball player's career. How does this compare to other professional sports?

6. Other sports keep statistics, too. What statistics are used in football, basketball, and soccer? Children may want to refer to the sports section of the newspaper. Ask the sports editor or a columnist to speak to the class about sports statistics. Why are these statistics important?

7. The children may want to research statistics on Olympic events. They may want to set up their own Olympic games and collect statistics on the events. You may want to work with the physical education teacher on this, particularly with regard to field days. (Standard 10)

8. At the end of the book, Florence and Frankie become a constellation. Research the twelve constellations of the zodiac. How many stars are in each one? Which constellation has the most stars? The fewest? What is the average number of stars in a constellation?

Moira's Birthday
Robert Munsch
(Toronto: Annick Press, 1989)

Moira invites "grade 1, grade 2, grade 3, grade 4, grade 5, grade 6, aaaaand kindergarten" to her birthday party. Her parents are expecting six of Moira's friends, but two hundred children show up. Moira orders two hundred pizzas and two hundred birthday cakes, but the pizza parlor and bakery can only deliver ten right away. Moira also receives two hundred birthday presents, which she offers to her guests to help her clean up. After everyone has gone home, the remainder of the pizzas and cakes are delivered. Her solution is to have another party the next day.

Activities

1. Moira is having a birthday. Help the children prepare a birthday graph, by month, for the class. (See fig. 7.1.)

Fig. 7.1. Class Birthdays.

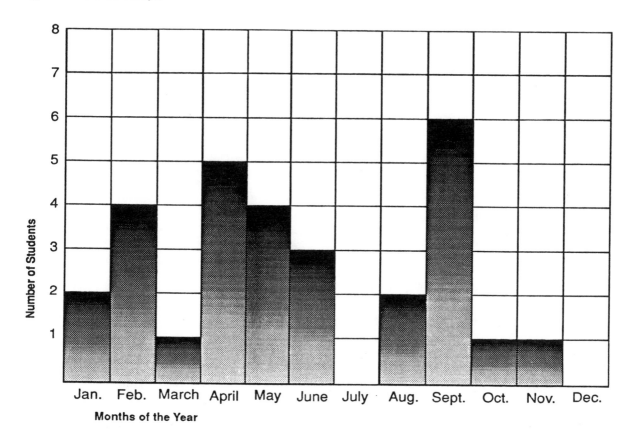

In any group of thirty people, chances are better than 2 to 1 that two people will have the same birthday. Are there two people in your class who have the same birthday? The children may want to poll other classes as well.

2. We don't know when Moira's birthday was, but the illustrations suggest it may be during the summer. Help the class show the number of children born in each season on the Seasons Birthday Bar Graph. (See fig. 7.2.)

Fig. 7.2. Seasons Birthday Bar Graph.

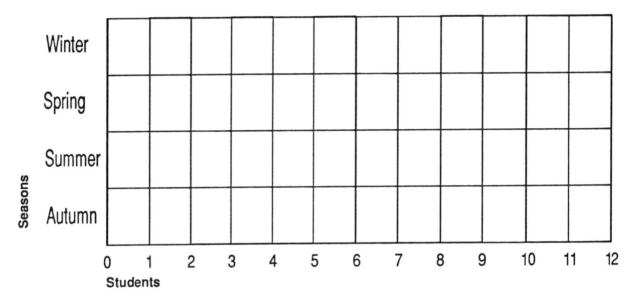

Using this bar graph, have the children answer the following questions.

a. In how many seasons do the children have birthdays?

b. Which season has the most birthdays?

c. How many birthdays are in that season?

d. Which season has the fewest birthdays?

e. How many birthdays are in this season?

3. Moira invited "grade 1, grade 2, grade 3, grade 4, grade 5, grade 6 aaaaand kindergarten." At Moira's school, this is 200 children. Have the children find out how many students this is at your school. (Standard 7 or 8)

4. When the kids come to Moira's party, they spread out all over the house—in the two bedrooms, the basement, the living room, the kitchen, the bathroom, and on the roof. Divide the class into cooperative groups. Have each group draw a picture of these rooms on a large piece of paper.

Give each group 200 counters to divide evenly in each room. Ask them if there were an equal number of children in each area, how many would be in each area? Is it likely that there would be an even number in each area? Why or why not? (Standard 7)

5. Moira orders 200 pizzas. The lady at the pizza parlor says she can only send ten. Tell the children to suppose there are only four varieties of pizza—pepperoni, cheese, sausage, and mushroom. Using decorated or labeled small paper plates to represent the pizzas, determine how many different combinations of varieties might arrive at Moira's house. To make this more challenging, increase the number of varieties and use all 200 pizzas. (Standard 7)

6. Have the children report on their favorite varieties of pizza and help them show this information in a pie graph. Which variety is most popular? Least popular? The children may want to check with a local pizza parlor to find out which varieties are ordered the most and which the least.

7. Moira ordered 200 pizzas and 200 birthday cakes for her 200 guests. This means each child is expected to eat one whole pizza and one whole cake. Do the children think Moira needed to order that much food? How would they figure out how much food to order? (Standard 7 or 8)

8. The word average is sometimes used to mean usual or common. Do the children think Moira had an average birthday party? How does it compare to their birthday parties? Did she have an average number of guests? Did she have an average amount of food? Do they think an average house could hold 200 people? Did Moira get an average number of gifts?

Averages
Jane Jonas Srivastava
(New York: Thomas Y. Crowell, 1975)

This book explains the concepts of median, mode, and arithmetic mean in easy-to-understand language. It provides examples and helps children understand that the type of average you use depends on the type of problem you want to solve.

Activities

1. Explain to the children that the word "average" is sometimes used to mean usual or common. If most children eat the same things for lunch, it could be said they had an average lunch. When parents ask what kind of a day their children had at school, and it was very much like any other day at school, the children could say they had an average day. Ask the children to list ways they think they are average. You may want to collect statistics to compare how accurate these perceptions are.

2. The "most of" kind of average is called the mode. Mode tells about the largest part of a group. Have the children take off one shoe and put it in one of three rows—laces, buckles, or other. Whichever row has the most shoes in it is the mode. Ask children why it wouldn't necessarily be the same as the longest row.

3. The median is the middle of a group when it is arranged in a specific order. Ask the children to identify which letter of the alphabet is the median. Then have them line up alphabetically to see if there is one child who is the median. The child who has the same number behind her as in front of her is standing in the middle of the line. (This will only work with odd numbers.)

4. Have the children line up in order of height. If one child is not the median, then the median height falls between the two children who are closest to the middle. Discuss how this type of average doesn't represent a real thing. If the children are ready to comprehend this concept, you may want to use the example that an average family used to have 2.5 children, but nobody really has half a child. (Standard 12)

5. The book describes an activity with pencils to illustrate how to find the arithmetic mean. Have the children do this.

6. Divide the children into cooperative groups. Have each child in the group take a handful of dry beans. Have each one write down the number of beans she has. Have each group combine its beans in the center. Divide the beans equally among each person so that everyone has the same number of beans. That number is the mean handful of beans. (You may want to show the children how to compute this with a calculator.) (Standard 7)

7. Using a scale or relying on self reports, list the weights of the children in the classroom. Then have the children use a calculator to add all the weights and divide by the number of children in the classroom to get the arithmetic mean. (Standards 7 and 10)

8. Give the children ten one-inch-square pieces of paper each. Have them write the letters of their first names on the squares, using one square for each letter. Then have them write the number of letters in their names on a separate square, putting their initials on the back of that square.

    a. Divide the class into three groups and have them lay out the letters in their names on a central table or desk, with the shortest name at the top and the longest at the bottom. To find the mean, have them move the letters from the longer names to the shorter ones until all the names have the same number of letters. This is the mean.

    b. Next have them lay down the squares with the numbers indicating the length of each person's name. Have the children put the squares in numerical order—lowest to highest. Find the center number in the row. This is the median. If there are two numbers in the middle, add them together and divide by two to obtain the median. (Standard 8)

    c. Finally, have the children glue the number squares onto a bar graph like the one shown below. The number that occurs most often is the mode. (See fig. 7.3)

    Fig. 7.3.

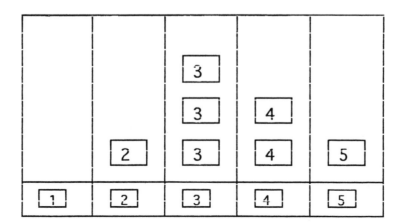

Probability
Charles F. Linn
(New York: Thomas Y. Crowell, 1972)

Two mice lead children through some simple experiments to help them understand the concept of probability. The book also suggests ways to organize the data from these experiments so they can be utilized for making predictions.

Activities

1. Tell the children that probability can be described as the chance that something will or won't happen. We use it all the time. There are things we are sure will not happen, things we are sure will happen, and things that may or may not happen.

   Example: I am sure I will not see a live dinosaur on my way home from school today. I am sure the sun will come up tomorrow. Maybe I will get a letter from a friend today.

   Make three lists—impossible, sure, and maybe—and have the children brainstorm statements for each one.

2. The book begins by discussing how probability is used in weather forecasts. One way we know what to expect is because of prior occurrences. Sometimes we use our memories, other times we keep records. The National Weather Service has kept records for years about weather in different areas of the country as well as which cloud patterns and other weather conditions go together. Have the children find out what kinds of records the National Weather Service keeps. How good are they at predicting the weather correctly?

   Have the students keep track of the forecasts and the actual weather conditions for 10 days. Each day the prediction is correct, write the number 1. For each day it is incorrect, write 0. Then help them calculate the percentage that the forecast was right. (Standards 8 and 12)

3. The book suggests tossing tacks to see how often they land point up. You may prefer to use coins and, in pairs, have the children record the number of times the coin lands heads up with a chart like this. (See fig. 7.4.)

   Fig. 7.4.

Tosses	Heads Up

Then have the children list the number of heads over the number of coins tossed to obtain the ratio expressing the probability. Compare the results from the different pairs.

4. The next experiment in the book involves rolling a cuboctahedron. The pattern for this is on page 8 of the book. Have the students trace the pattern and then cut it out. Fold and tape it together to make a three-dimensional object. (You may want to have these prepared ahead of time.) Predict how often it will land on a square face and how many times on a triangular face. Then, in pairs, have the children roll it 100 times. Compare their results to their predictions. Would the results help them to make future predictions? (Standard 13)

5. The experiment described has the children rolling 10 coins simultaneously to see how many heads turn up. In cooperative groups, have the children draw all the possible combinations for this on index cards. Then have half the groups tally the number of heads as described in the book. Have the other half of the groups put a counter (such as a bean) on the index card that shows the combination rolled each time. Discuss the results. Does a particular combination occur more often than others? Have the students graph their results.

6. The book suggests trying the coin-tossing experiment with different numbers of coins. Divide the class into cooperative groups and have each group toss a different number of coins recording the number of heads. Have each group graph the results and compare graphs.

7. Finally, the author discusses sampling as a way to improve predictions. He suggests two different colors of poker chips. (You may want to use M&Ms instead.) In any event, make up a bag of 100 objects for each of your cooperative groups. Make sure each group shakes up the bag. Without looking, have each group predict and record how many of each color, by number or percentage, are in the bag. Still without looking, have one person in each group remove 10 objects. Have the students revise their estimates. Remove 10 more objects and revise the estimates again. Remove 10 objects once more and revise the estimates. Finally, remove all the objects and count each color. Compare the estimates to the actual numbers or percentages. Did their predictions get better with more data? In what other situations does this apply? (Standards 12 and 13)

BOOKS FOR GRADES 4-6

MATHEMATICAL CONTENT VOCABULARY

arithmetic mean	frequency	odds	random sample
average	lottery	outcomes	raw data
census	margin of error	percentage	sampling
chances	market research	permutations	statistician
combinations	median	prediction	statistics
data	mode	probability	tally

What Do You Mean by "Average"?
Elizabeth James and Carol Barkin
(New York: Lothrop, Lee & Shepard, 1978)

Jill Slater is running for Student Council President in Normal City. Her strategy is to convince people that she'll be the best person to represent everyone by proving she's the most average person in the school. In the process of doing this, she and her campaign staff have to utilize different kinds of averages.

SPECIAL NOTE: Activities can be done without the book. Substitutes include: Mills, Claudia. *Dinah for President.* NY: Macmillan, 1992; Morris, Judy K. *The Kid Who Ran for President.* NY: J. B. Lippincott, 1989; Hewett, Joan. *Getting Elected: The Diary of a Campaign.* NY: E. P. Dutton, 1989.

<u>Activities</u>

1. Jill wants to prove she is the most average person in the school. Have students brainstorm ways she may be average.

2. Jill has her campaign staff calculate the mathematic mean for student height and weight in the school. Remind the students that mean averages are found by adding the numerical values of all the items and then dividing this total by the number of items. Then have them figure the average height and weight for your class. You may also want to divide the students into groups and have each group collect data on the height and weight of different classes in the school to calculate a school average. (The school nurse may be able to provide these data.) (Standards 8 and 10)

3. While attempting to calculate the average allowance, the campaign staff runs into a problem because the data are spread out very unevenly. They decide to locate the center point in the ordered list of raw data to find the median average. The book states that the U.S. Census uses a median to describe the average family income. What is the average family income according to the U.S. Census? Perhaps they can even find out what the raw data were.

   Students may also want to explore other statistics collected through the U.S. Census.

4. Jill and her staff calculate the median average for the number of children per family. Have your students do the same. Then calculate the mean average for children per family. Discuss any differences. (Standard 8)

5. Jill uses the modal average to prove that her gender makes her average. The mode is the item that occurs most often in a group. Modes are often used in television advertising. Have the students record examples of this to discuss in class.

6. Television advertising also relies on market research. Researchers use a sampling technique to identify the characteristics of people watching particular shows. Product advertisers want this information so they know when to reach their target audience. Have the class choose a specific television program and compile a list of characteristics they think would be true of the average person watching this show. Then have them watch the commercials aired during the show and make adjustments, if necessary, to their original list. You may prefer to divide the students into cooperative groups to analyze different shows. Finally, have students contact a person who sells advertising at a local television station to ask for his perception of the target audience.

7. Now that students know the three kinds of averages, have them make charts or a book listing or illustrating examples of each.

8. Jill wants to know what students think of her campaign issues, but there is not much time left before the election, so she and her staff decide to survey a random sample. However, obtaining a random sample is not as easy as it sounds. To illustrate this, have the students prepare 25 paper strips containing the numbers 1, 2, 3, 4. (See fig. 7.5.)

Fig. 7.5.

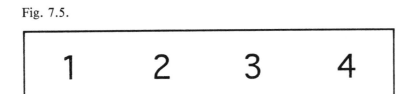

Have each student ask 25 people to cross out one number on the sheet. When they have collected the data, have them display their results using a line graph. (More people tend to cross out the number 3.)

Or, ask students to write any number from 1 to 9 on a piece of paper. (Seven is usually the favorite in this case.)

9. Jill's campaign staff surveys student opinions on what the Student Council should raise money for and what actions it should take to improve the school. Have your students choose one of these and compile a list of five survey questions. Conduct the survey and calculate percentages as explained in the book. Act on the results. (Standards 8 and 12)

10. This story takes place in Normal City. What do the students think a normal or average community would be like? Then research the following. (Standard 8)

   a. What is the population of this average community?

   b. What is the main occupation of the residents?

   c. What is the average age of the residents?

   d. Where is the geographic location of the city?

   e. What is the average income of the residents?

Miss Pickerell and the Weather Satellite
Ellen MacGregor and Dora Pantell
(New York: McGraw-Hill, 1971)

The weather satellites and weather station computers are forecasting sunshine and clear skies, but on Square Toe Mountain there are only heavy rains, thunder, lightning, and high winds. There is so much rain that the dam must be opened soon to prevent the flooding of Square Toe County. However, the dam can only be opened if the weather forecast predicts heavy rain. Miss Pickerell has to make a trip to the weather satellite itself to save the day.

SPECIAL NOTE: Activities can be done without the book. Substitutes include: Aardema, Verna. *Bringing the Rain to Kapiti Plain*. NY: Dial Books for Young Readers, 1981; Nelson, Theresa. *Devil Storm*. NY: Orchard Books, 1987.

Activities

1. In the beginning of the book, Miss Pickerell calls the weather report number to get the forecast. It states, "The next few days will be very sunny, warm, and clear." A few minutes later, it begins to pour.

   American Averages, published in 1980, reports, "In forecasting high and low temperatures a day ahead of time in the 48 contiguous states, the Weather Service was off by an average of 4.9 per cent in 1966. Ten years later, it had reduced its margin of error to 3.6 per cent."

   "But the Service's long-range forecasting was hardly better than guesswork. In predicting whether the next season would be warmer or cooler, wetter or drier than normal, the weatherman was right only 60 percent of the time."

   Have students find out how accurate weather forecasts are today. Is the National Weather Service more accurate than the *Farmer's Almanac*?

2. Weather forecasters often predict precipitation in terms of probability. For example, "forty percent chance of showers today." Have the students describe how they think forecasters arrive at those probabilities. Then have them consult with a professional. (Standard 12)

3. Euphus tries to explain to his aunt how weather satellites work. Have students research how weather satellites and other weather forecasting instruments work today. Students may want to contact the National Weather Service or a local television meteorologist.

4. Miss Pickerell is concerned about a flood in Square Toe County. Have students research statistics on floods. What is the largest amount of rain to fall in one day? One month?

5. According to *American Averages*, "In an average year, an average place in the continental United States gets 29 inches of precipitation." Have students find out what the average rainfall is for your part of the country. What is the highest annual rainfall in the world? What is the lowest?

   You may want to have the students set up rain gauges to measure rainfall in your area. You may also want to compare results with students in other areas. This can be done by mail or by modem.

6. Weather involves a lot of statistics. The National Climatic Center keeps detailed records on the number of hours of sunlight. What is the average percentage of sunshine in your part of the country? Which cities in the U.S. have the highest percentage? The lowest? (Standard 6)

7. In the book, Square Toe County is experiencing severe thunderstorms. Florida averages 80 to 100 thunderstorms per year. Have the students research thunderstorm frequency in your area. Is there a time of the year when the probability is greater for this type of weather? Have students find out the same information about hurricanes and tornados.

8. Chicago is known as the Windy City. The wind there blows at an average of 10.4 miles per hour. Have the students find out if there are windier cities in the United States.

9. According to *American Averages*, "At an average time on an average day or night at an average place in the continental United States, the temperature is 53.2 degrees Fahrenheit..." Have the students graph local temperatures for one month. Discuss the time of day the measurements are taken. Have them compare their results to the record highs and lows. They may also want to research high and low temperatures around the world or on other planets. (Standards 6 and 10)

Students may also research and record average monthly temperatures for your area on a graph such as the one found in figure 7.6.

Do You Wanna Bet?
Jean Cushman
(New York: Clarion Books, 1991)

Danny Johnson and Brian O'Shea find out that chance plays a big role in their lives. They learn about probability in coin tosses, weather forecasts, secret codes, birthday parties, baseball statistics, PTA carnivals, playing cards, and baby sisters.

Activities

1. Probability can be described as the branch of mathematics that deals with the likelihood of a given outcome. This book illustrates many everyday circumstances that involve probability. Before reading the book, have the students brainstorm situations that they think utilize a knowledge of probability. When you have completed the book and activities, have the students do this again.

2. Danny and Brian toss a coin to decide which television show to watch. Each time a coin is tossed, it has a 50 percent chance of landing heads up. However, this does not mean that if you toss a coin 100 times, it will land heads up exactly 50 times, but it will come close. With a partner, have the students try tossing a coin 100 times and keep track of how many times it comes up heads and how many tails.

3. Danny and Brian neglect their homework because the weather forecast says there is a 60% chance of six to eight inches of snow for the next day. The forecast was wrong. Have the students keep track of the weather for a month by recording the predicted and actual temperature and precipitation. (See fig. 7.6.) (Standard 10)

4. Brian and Danny's teacher give them a list of 12 sentences for homework. They have to decide if the statements are sure to happen, impossible to happen, or may happen. Give your students the list (see Probabilities from *Do You Wanna Bet?*) and have them mark each statement with an S, an I, or an M. Then, as a class, discuss the probabilities of each one. In cooperative groups, have the students make their own lists and exchange with other groups.

Fig. 7.6. Average Outside Temperature.

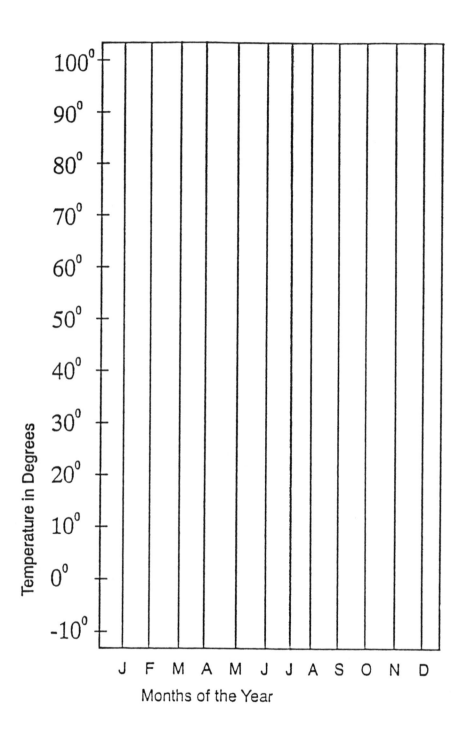

5. Mrs. Abrams intercepts a note being passed to Abigail from a girl in the back row. It is written in code. Mrs. Abrams suggests that knowing which letters are used most frequently in the English language would help students to decode the message. Have each student choose a separate paragraph from a reading book and tally the times each letter is found. (They should find that E, T, A, O, N, I, S, R, and H are the most frequently used letters, in that order. Q, Z, K, X, and J are the least used.)

   With partners, have the students use this information to write their own secret messages and then exchange them with a different pair to decode. (Standard 13)

   You may also want to play your own version of Wheel of Fortune.

6. Danny and Brian are both invited to Jamie's birthday party. Jamie takes his guests to a local bowling alley. Twelve boys go. Suppose each boy bowls three games, and their scores are as shown in figure 7.7. From this information have students determine the following. (Standard 8)

   a. What is each boy's average?

   b. Who has the highest average?

   c. Who bowls the highest game?

   d. What is the median score?

   e. What is the mode?

7. After bowling, the boys at Jamie's party play a game that involves guessing how many red, yellow, and brown candies are in a cannister. They use a sampling method to estimate actual amounts. A different sampling method often used by wildlife managers to estimate the number of fish in a lake is described on pp. 48-49 in the book. Have the students try this experiment by marking macaroni.

8. Sampling is used frequently when large numbers are involved. For example, you might read in an encyclopedia that the female codfish lays 9 million eggs per year, or that each year the Mississippi River carries 500 million tons of mud into the ocean. Have the students discuss how they think these numbers were determined. What other examples like this can they find?

   Have them use a sampling technique to determine how many words are in the school dictionary. In any library book. (Standard 6)

9. Brian and Danny are members of the Tomcats baseball team. Abigail is their statistician this year. Have students brainstorm, research, or both, the kinds of statistics Abigail might keep. Have them illustrate how those statistics are calculated, and explain why it is important to keep those statistics.

   The students may want to use record books or baseball cards to compile their own all-star team (decide if this team will be composed of current players), and then justify their selection based on statistical evidence.

Fig. 7.7.

Names	1st Game	2nd Game	3rd game
Brian	90	95	100
Danny	89	101	98
Jamie	79	82	90
Doug	110	125	111
Adam	102	97	105
Charles	96	103	104
Greg	75	77	81
Chris	76	82	78
John	91	93	98
Brandon	99	94	99
Cory	100	112	99
Matt	103	107	101

a. What is each boy's average?

b. Who has the highest average?

c. Who bowls the highest game?

d. What is the median score?

e. What is the mode?

10. At the PTA carnival, Brian plays a number on the Lucky Wheel. Have the students experiment with their own lucky wheels. Pass out or show students the three spinners in figure 7.8. The parts are unequal in spinner A, and equal in spinners B and C. Show the students spinner A and ask them which color has the best chance of having a spinner land on it. Then show them spinner B and ask the same question. Show them spinner C, where one number is used twice even though the spaces are divided equally, and ask the same question. The students should be able to see that there is a greater chance the spinner will land on four.

    Divide the class into three groups. Give each group a spinner. Have each group predict the number of times the spinner will land on each section if they spin 25 times. Compare the results with their predictions.

11. One rainy Saturday, Danny and Brian end up playing cards. When playing rummy, knowing something about the likelihood of drawing certain combinations can be helpful. Divide students into cooperative groups and give each group a regular deck of cards. Make sure they shuffle the deck seven times, and deal five hands of 10 cards each. Have them record the number of hands containing two of a kind, three of a kind, sequences, etc. Then have the groups compare results.

    Ask the students to calculate the probability of drawing a heart from a deck of cards. Two of a kind? A royal flush? (The chances of drawing a royal flush—ace, king, queen, jack, and ten from the same suit—are 1 in 2,598,960.) (Standard 8)

12. After playing cards the boys play Monopoly. Part of the game depends on rolling a pair of dice. To learn more about the probability of rolling certain combinations, have the students play Dice Toss. Divide the students into pairs and give each group a pair of dice. Follow the directions below. (Standard 8)

    a. Throw a pair of dice 50 times. Each time add the sum on the dice.

    b. Keep a tally of each time a sum is thrown. Record the tally marks as shown in figure 7.9.

    c. Add the tally marks and record the information on the bar graph labeled Dice Toss. (See fig. 7.10.)

    Ask students to predict and then compare actual results for the following questions.

    a. How many outcomes are possible when you roll a pair of dice?

    b. How often do doubles turn up?

    c. What is the most likely sum to turn up?

    d. What is the least likely sum?

13. Danny's mom is pregnant. What are the chances she will have a girl? Have students research how genetics influence this probability.

(Text continues on page 143.)

Fig. 7.8

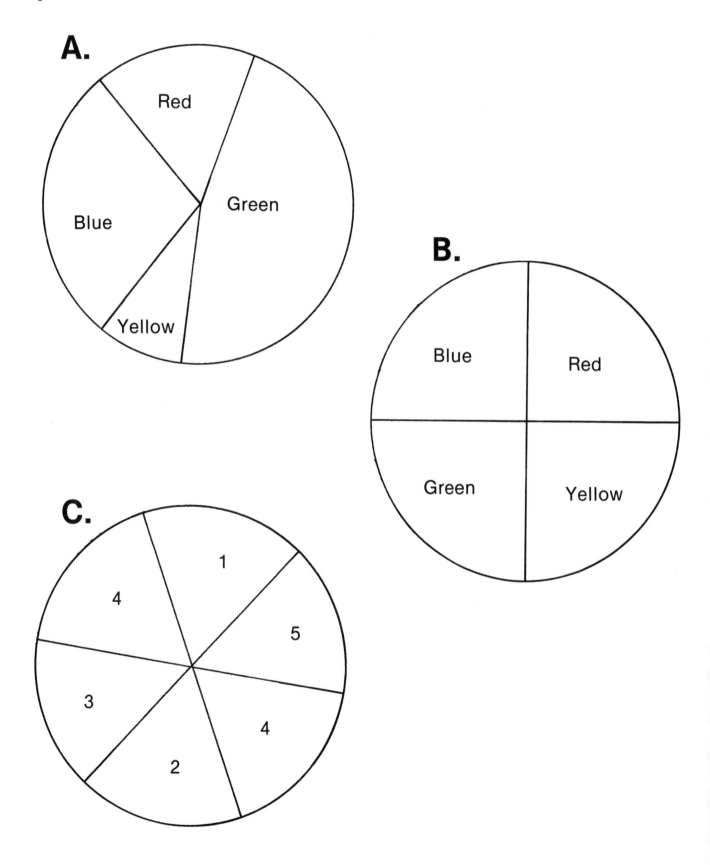

Fig. 7.9

Sum	Times Thrown	Sum	Times Thrown
2	_____	8	_____
3	_____	9	_____
4	_____	10	_____
5	_____	11	_____
6	_____	12	_____
7	_____		

Fig. 7.10. Dice Toss.

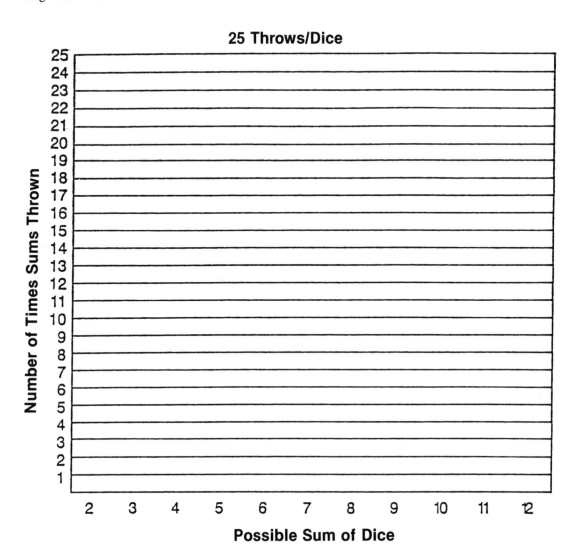

Probabilities
from
Do You Wanna Bet?
Jean Cushman
(New York: Clarion Books, 1991)

Directions

Some things are *sure* to happen. If today is Monday, tomorrow will be Tuesday. Some things are *impossible.* You can't roll a seven with only one pair of dice. Some things may or may not happen. *Maybe* it will snow, *maybe* it won't.

Mark each of the following statements with S for sure, I for impossible, or M for maybe.

1. There is a live dinosaur in the zoo.

2. You will get tails if you toss a coin.

3. It will rain on Saturday.

4. Superman will always beat the bad guys.

5. The next time you throw an ordinary ball, it will keep on going up into space.

6. Someone will win a state lottery twice in one year.

7. When you grow up, you will be 10 feet tall.

8. Outdoors at night you can see the stars in the sky.

9. Your little league team will win its next game.

10. The earth revolves around the sun.

11. You will be in school tomorrow.

12. In a new box of crayons at least one will be red.

Million Dollar Jeans
Ron Roy
(New York: E. P. Dutton, 1983)

Tommy Archer and Twig Collins are 10-year-olds who live relatively normal lives in Hartford, Connecticut. That is until a strange woman buys Tommy a lottery ticket as a reward for returning her wallet. The ticket turns out to be a million dollar winner, but it's in the pocket of a pair of jeans Mr. Archer dropped off at the church rummage sale. This is just the beginning of a circuitous search for the missing ticket. Their treasure hunts end successfully, but being millionaires is not quite what they imagined.

SPECIAL NOTE: Activities can be done without the book. A substitute is Sharmat, Marjorie Weinman. *Get Rich Mitch!* NY: William Morrow, 1985.

Activities

1. After Tommy returns her wallet, the woman at the drugstore buys him a lottery ticket. It has five numbers on it. The man at the counter explains that Tommy would win $50 for matching one number in the right position, $100 for two, $5,000 for three, $50,000 for four, and $1 million for five numbers in the right position. Assuming the numbers are only one-digit numbers 0-9, have students figure out the number of different arrangements possible for matching five numbers. Are these combinations or permutations? (Standard 8)

2. Have students research Lotto and lottery games in your area. What are the odds of winning at different levels? How is this calculated? How are the numbers chosen?

3. The winning numbers for Lotto games are supposedly picked randomly by a computer. Have the students research the winning numbers. Do some show up more frequently than others?

4. There are many legal games of chance. Have students investigate the chances of winning cereal box contests, soft drink contests, sweepstakes, etc. If the odds of winning are so low, why do so many people participate in these contests?

5. If someone says you have a better chance of being struck by lightning than winning the lottery, on what did they base their statement? Ask the students what they would like to know the odds on. Research the odds on these different occurrences.

6. Have the students research how a lottery game manages to make money. How many people must play just to support the prizes? How many people must play to make a profit? How much money does the average person spend on lottery tickets? You may want to have students investigate how a lottery is similar to various types of insurance. (Standard 8)

7. While the boys are waiting for the Salvation Army office to open on Monday morning, Tommy wonders what $1 million would look like dumped in his bedroom. Ask students to figure this out. (Standard 10)

8. Mr. Fallon at the Salvation Army office tells the boys that it is such a big operation that they'd be "neck-deep in people's discards" if things weren't moved quickly. Have the students gather some statistics on how much clothing is donated to the Salvation Army or Goodwill Industries in your area. (Standard 6)

9. When Rudy from Trash Flash, Inc. takes Tommy and Twig to the dump, he tells them how quickly the trash accumulates. Have the students research how much trash is dumped in your area. Have them collect statistics about the amount of trash an average family discards in a week, month, and year. How does this compare with their families?

Socrates and the Three Little Pigs
Tuyosi Mori
(New York: Philomel Books, 1986)

Socrates, the philosopher wolf, is watching three little pigs play in the meadow. His wife, Xanthippe, asks Socrates to catch one of the pigs for dinner. There are five houses in which the pigs live. To determine the best way to find one pig by itself, Socrates turns to his mathematician friend, Pythagoras, the frog. Pythagoras helps Socrates explore the various combinations and permutations involved in solving his problem. By the time they figure out a solution, it is daylight. They abandon their original plan, and decide instead to join the pigs playing in the meadow.

Activities

1. The notes at the back of the book state, "In a *combination*, the order of the objects in an arrangement does not matter." Students are used to manipulating different combinations of coins. Introduce them to this concept by having cooperative groups determine how many different combinations of quarters and half-dollars they can identify that will equal one dollar. Do the same with dimes, quarters, and half dollars. Repeat the activity using nickels, dimes, quarters, and half dollars. Finally, have them use all coins. Is there a way to predict the results? (Standard 13)

2. The author also states, "A *permutation* is any arrangement of the elements of a set in a definite order." Have the students determine all the possible permutations for the coin exercises in the activity above. Can they discern a pattern? (Standard 13)

3. The author asks the reader to suppose that the three pigs decided to find all the ways they could line up in groups of two. Since the order does make a difference, we are dealing with permutations. Have students determine the number of different arrangements. (Standard 8)

4. The author also suggests the reader suppose that the three pigs learn of Socrates's plan, and decide to form a committee of two pigs to deal with the dilemma while one pig stands guard. How many different committees can they form? Since the order does not matter in this situation, we are dealing with combinations. Have students determine the number of different arrangements. (Standard 8)

5. Ask the students to brainstorm other situations in which it would be important to determine combinations, permutations, or both. The author states, "Combinatorial analysis is a basis for computer programming, simplifying choices, and showing not just all, but also the **best** possibilities." Students may need to do some research to discover other real-life situations in which combinations and permutations are used.

6. Bring some doll clothes to class, and give one group two tops and two bottoms, the next group three and three, and so on. Have the students first predict how many outfit combinations can be created, and then put the outfits together (without regard to good taste). Look for a pattern in the results. The students may want to do this with their own wardrobes at home, comparing combinations and permutations. (See *Clementine's Winter Wardrobe* by Kate Spohn.)

7. Bring in wheat, rye, and white bread; Swiss, Monterey Jack, and cheddar cheese; and bologna, turkey, and ham. (The school cafeteria may be able to help, or you may want to use labeled cardboard instead of real food.) Have the students predict how many different combinations of sandwiches they could make using these ingredients. Then have them try it.

8. There are five houses in which the three pigs live. Pythagoras advises Socrates to catch one piggy alone. In cooperative groups, have the students come up with a way to solve the problem. Ask them to share their solutions.

9. As you continue through the book, have students draw diagrams or place pigs in houses on a flannelboard to help them understand the reasoning process of Socrates and Pythagoras.

RELATED BOOKS AND REFERENCES

PROBABILITY AND STATISTICS

Arthur, Lee, Elizabeth James, and Judith B. Taylor. *Sportsmath.* New York: Lothrop, Lee & Shepard, 1975. (4-6)

Buller, Laura, and Ron Taylor. *Calculation and Chance.* New York: Marshal Cavendish Corp., 1990. (4-6)

Frederique and Papy. *Graph Games.* New York: Thomas Y. Crowell, 1971. (K-3)

Hildick, E. W. *The Secret Winners.* New York: Crown, 1970. (4-6)

Nozaki, Akihiro, and Mitsumasa Anno. *Anno's Hat Tricks.* New York: Philomel Books, 1985. (K-3)

Razzell, Arthur G., and K. G. O. Watts. *Probability: The Science of Chance.* Garden City, N.Y.: Doubleday, 1967. (4-6)

Rockwell, Thomas. *How to Get Fabulously Rich.* New York: Franklin Watts, 1990. (4-6)

Shapiro, Irwin. *Twice upon a Time.* New York: Charles Scribner's Sons, 1973. (4-6)

Spohn, Kate. *Clementine's Winter Wardrobe.* New York: Orchard Books, 1989. (4-6)

WEATHER

Barrett, Judi. *Cloudy with a Chance of Meatballs.* New York: Atheneum, 1978. (K-3)

Branley, Franklyn M. *It's Raining Cats and Dogs.* Boston: Houghton Mifflin, 1987. (4-6)

Calhoun, Mary. *Jack and the Whoopee Wind*. New York: William Morrow, 1987. (K-3)

Gibbons, Gail. *Weather Forecasting*. New York: Four Winds Press, 1987. (K-3)

MacGregor, Ellen, and Dora Pantell. *Miss Pickerell and the Weather Satellite*. New York: McGraw-Hill, 1971. (4-6)

McVey, Vicki. *The Sierra Club Book of Weatherwisdom*. Boston: Little, Brown, 1991. (4-6)

Williams, Jay, and Raymond Abrashkin. *Danny Dunn and the Weather Machine*. New York: McGraw-Hill, 1959. (4-6)

Wyatt, Valerie. *Weatherwatch*. New York: Addison-Wesley, 1990. (K-3)

ADULT REFERENCES

Burns, Marilyn. *The I Hate Mathematics! Book*. Boston: Little, Brown, 1975.

_____. *Math for Smarty Pants*. Boston: Little, Brown, 1982.

Feinsilber, Mike, and William B. Mead. *American Averages*. Garden City, N.Y.: Doubleday, 1980. (This is an interesting book, but also details more adult topics, such as sexual habits.)

Stenmark, Jean Kerr, Virginia Thompson, and Ruth Cossey. *Family Math*. Berkeley Calif.: the Regents, University of California, 1986.

VanCleeve, Janice. *Math for Every Kid*. New York: John Wiley, 1991.

8—Standard 12: Fractions and Decimals

The mathematics curriculum should include fractions and decimals so that students can

- develop concepts of fractions, mixed numbers, and decimals;

- develop number sense for fractions and decimals;

- use models to relate fractions to decimals and to find equivalent fractions;

- apply fractions and decimals to problem situations.

Fractions and decimals are concepts necessary for children's understanding of the number system, and are necessary to help them understand the many real-world situations that they encounter. The students' understanding of the terms and interrelationships of fractions and decimals, and the different ways fractions and decimals express the same things are important concepts. As with measurement, the conceptual development of placing these partial units of measurement over the whole unit must precede more abstract thought and formula.

BOOKS FOR GRADES K-3

MATHEMATICAL CONTENT VOCABULARY

bar graph	divide	money	one-twelfth
business	dollars	more	parts
buy	doubling	nickels	pennies
cents	equally	one-eighth	pie
circle	equation	one-eleventh	piece
coins	equivalent	one-fifth	quarters
collects	expenses	one-half	sale
combine	fraction	one-hundredth	same
costs	greater	one-ninth	savings
count	group	one-quarter	size
cut	half-dollars	one-seventh	split
decimals	halving	one-sixth	unequal
denomination	less	one-tenth	value
dimes	line graph	one-third	whole

Gator Pie
Louise Mathews
(New York: Dodd, Mead, 1979)

Two alligators, Alice and Alvin, find a pie on a table near the edge of the swamp. Just as they are about to split it into halves to eat, another alligator stomps up and demands some of the pie. More and more alligators keep coming until Alice has to cut the pie into 100 pieces. When Alvin climbs onto the table and tells the waiting alligators to pick a piece warning them that the slices may not all be the same size, bedlam begins. While the other gators are fighting among themselves, Alice and Alvin whisk away the pie and hide. They divide the pie evenly, each eating 50 pieces of their favorite kind of pie—chocolate marshmallow.

SPECIAL NOTE: Activities are specific to the story. However, substitutes for fractions include: MacDonald, Elizabeth. *Mr. Badger's Birthday Pie*. NY: Dial Books for Young Readers, 1989; Watson, Clyde. *Tom Fox and the Apple Pie*. NY: Thomas Y. Crowell, 1972; Moncure, Jane Belk. *How Many Ways Can You Cut a Pie?* Chicago: Child's World, 1988.

Activities

1. Have the children solve the following problems based on the story.

   a. Alice and Alvin find a pie near the edge of the swamp and decide to divide it equally into two parts. What fraction of the pie will each one get?

   b. Before Alice and Alvin have a chance to cut the pie, another alligator comes along and demands a piece. If they divide the pie equally among themselves, what fraction of the pie will Alice and Alvin receive together? (Standard 7)

   c. A new gator slithers onto the beach and also wants some pie. If Alice cuts the pie into equal pieces for all of the alligators present, what fraction of the pie will Alice and Alvin receive apiece? How much smaller will Alice's and Alvin's pieces be now than they would have been before the other gators arrived? (Standard 7 or 8)

   d. Soon four more gators arrive, all demanding pie. What fraction of the pie will all of the intruders be eating? Can this be described by more than one fraction? (Standard 7 or 8)

2. Bring in some aluminum pie plates and have the children pair up to make pies out of clay to fit into the pie plates. Have them practice cutting the pie into the different number of slices described in *Gator Pie*.

   In the story, Alice has to cut the pie into 100 pieces. Have children discuss and share different strategies for doing this, and then experiment to see if one strategy works better than the others.

3. Before the pie is cut, the gators argue about what kind it is—lemon, banana, pumpkin, pineapple, or butterscotch. Including Alice and Alvin, there are 100 gators present. If the same number of gators guess each of the five different kinds of pie, what fraction of gators would that be? (Standard 7 or 8)

4. Make a real pie with the children, pointing out fractions used in the recipe. Discuss how to divide it evenly among everyone in the class. Some students may be ready to practice doubling or halving the recipe. (Standards 7 and 10)

5. Bring in eight aluminum pie tins and cut a cardboard circle to fit into the bottom of each one. Leave the first cardboard circle alone, divide the second circle into two equal pieces, divide the third circle into three equal pieces, and so on. Show the children that the pieces in a specific circle are all the same size, and that when they are put together they make a whole circle. Explain how to talk about and write fractions using these cardboard models. You may also wish to use these models to help the children understand equivalent fractions.

6. For additional practice understanding fractions, have the children figure out the fractional word riddles below. Using the clues, have them make a new word by combining the fractional parts of two words.

   Example: Combine the first two-thirds of PIE with the last one-fifth of ALVIN. Answer: PIN. Combine the first three-fifths of GATOR with the last one-fifth of TABLE. Answer: GATE.

   Have the children create their own riddles.

7. Make a deck of 40 to 52 cards illustrating the fractions and decimals you want your students to learn. Write fractions (½) on some of the cards, draw partially shaded figures on some, and write decimals (.75) on the others. Then, in pairs, have the children play a game similar to War. The dealer passes out all the cards face down, dividing them equally between players. Then both players reveal their top card. The player having the card with the greater value takes the trick. If the values are the same, each player must turn over another card. The player who wins this round takes the cards from both tricks. The game continues until one player has all the cards or the time limit expires. (Standard 6)

Dollars and Cents for Harriet
Betsy Maestro and Giulio Maestro
(New York: Crown, 1988)

Harriet the Elephant finds a toy she wants. It costs $5.00. She checks her piggybank and finds 100 pennies. The story shows how she earns the other $4.00 in different denominations of coins.

Activities

1. In the beginning of the story, Harriet finds something she wants to buy at the toy store. We know that it costs $5.00, but we don't know what it is. Have the children visit a toy store, or use a catalog to research toys that cost $5.00. (Standard 6)

2. When Harriet checks her piggybank, she finds 100 pennies. She knows this is equal to $1.00. Have the children work in groups to draw pictures showing what other combinations of coins Harriet might have found in her bank equal to $1.00. They can also write equations for these combinations.

3. Harriet tried to think of ways to earn the $4.00 she needed. She thought of washing windows, emptying trash, raking leaves, and painting fences. Have the children brainstorm other ways Harriet could earn money, or ways the children could earn money, and estimate how much could be earned for each task. Have them make a chart showing these data.

4. Harriet washes Monkey's car for $1.00 and he pays her with half-dollars. How many half-dollars does Harriet receive?

   Use play money or cut paper in the shape of $1.00 bills. Distribute the money to the children, then have them fold the paper in half and cut it to represent the half-dollars. Do this for the quarters, dimes, and nickels in the story as well.

5. Have the children represent the whole story using mathematical equations. Then have them create a different story using the same equations.

Fractions Are Parts of Things
J. Richard Dennis
(New York: Thomas Y. Crowell, 1971)

This book uses illustrations and activities to help children better understand the simple fractions—halves, thirds, and fourths.

Activities

1. The name of the book is *Fractions Are Parts of Things*. This is true, but the parts must be equal. Divide the children into cooperative groups of five. Give each group an apple that has been divided into five unequal pieces. Have the group decide how to distribute these so that each person receives one piece. Is everyone happy with what they have received? Did each child receive the same amount—one piece out of five or one-fifth? Discuss the difference between parts and equal parts. Then you may want to give each group a Hershey bar and have them divide it equally.

2. The book begins, "You can find one half in lots of places." Have the children brainstorm places they can see one-half in the classroom. Discuss situations when one-half or other fractions are used. (Standard 6)

3. There is an illustration in the book of six children. One-half have brown hair and one-half have black hair. One-half of the six children are girls. Group your students according to these categories. Is it one-half for your class? If not, what fractions are these divisions? Ask the children to figure out at least one way to divide themselves into two halves. You may also want them to practice categorizing with attribute blocks, and identify the fractional part of each category.

4. The book shows many ways to find and cut shapes in halves, thirds, and fourths. Cut different shapes out of construction paper beforehand. Have the children practice folding or cutting these shapes into these fractions. Is there more than one way to fold a shape in half?

5. Sometimes fractional parts are not obvious. Re-create the illustration on p. 8 of *Fractions Are Parts of Things* and have the children cut out the black and white pieces. Try to fit the white pieces on top of the black piece to see if the black piece and the white pieces are each one-half of the shape. (Standard 9)

6. Using the dot paper in figure 8.1, have the children outline different shapes, divide the shapes into specified fractional parts, and then shade in a portion of each shape.

    Example: Have a child draw a rectangle five dots long and two dots wide. Then draw lines to divide this rectangle into fourths, and shade three-fourths.

    This activity can also be used with equivalent fractions. You may want to use geoboards instead of dot paper to do this activity.

7. Cuisenaire rods also are used for teaching fractions. The orange rod can represent one whole and the other pieces fractional parts. Ten white pieces equal one orange, so each one is one-tenth. Each yellow is one-half, and so on.

8. As students progress in their understanding of fractions, give each pair a copy of the worksheet Search for Fractional Wholes. (See fig. 8.2.) Tell them to search for fractions that when added together will make a whole. The fractions may align horizontally, vertically, diagonally, or all three ways. Explain that their circles may overlap. Students may wish to use manipulatives to help them arrive at the correct answers. (Standard 8)

Henry's Pennies
Louise McNamara
(New York: Franklin Watts, 1972)

Henry is a little boy who collects pennies. Henry sometimes finds pennies under the sofa or chair cushions, in his mother's pin dish, or on sidewalks and driveways. On Sundays, Henry's father gives him all of the pennies he has in his pockets. Henry likes the feel of pennies in his pocket, and the noise they make when he walks. He especially likes to count them.

One day he hears about a white elephant sale to be held at the school fair, and decides to use his pennies to buy himself a new pet. Obviously, there are no real white elephants at the sale, but he does manage to buy a special pet with his money.

SPECIAL NOTE: Activities can be done without the book. Substitutes include: Brenner, Barbara. *Annie's Pet*. NY: Bryon Preiss Books, 1989; Caple, Kathy. *The Purse*. Boston: Houghton Mifflin, 1986; Berenstain, Stan and Jan Berenstain. *Berenstain Bears' Trouble with Money*. NY: Random House, 1983.

Activities

1. Henry's dad gives him all of the pennies he has in his pockets. When Henry counts all of his pennies, he finds he has 252 pennies. Henry imagines spending his pennies on candy. Have the children list their favorite kinds of candy, and how much each kind costs. Have them show how they would spend Henry's $2.52 on candy. (Standard 8)

2. Henry isn't sure how to spend his money until he discovers there will be a white elephant sale at the school fair. Then he decides to buy a white elephant for a pet. Have the children come up with suggestions for other types of pets. Then have them research how much these pets would cost to buy.

(Text continues on page 155.)

Fig. 8.1.

Fig. 8.2. Search for Fractional Wholes.

1/8	1/4	1/4	3/8	1/2	1/3	1/3	1/3	1/6
2/5	1/5	2/5	3/8	1/3	1/4	3/4	1/2	5/6
1/4	1/2	3/4	1/4	2/3	1/6	2/3	2/4	2/5
3/6	3/8	2/12	3/6	2/6	1/4	1/4	2/8	1/4
6/12	1/4	1/6	1/5	2/10	1/4	1/6	2/10	3/6
1/4	2/3	2/6	1/4	2/4	4/8	1/4	2/8	1/6
1/4	4/8	1/2	5/12	1/3	1/6	3/6	2/4	2/6

(Answer key on page 171.)

Have children make a chart of the information they find. They may want to publish it in a school or local newspaper. (Standard 11)

3. Henry ended up with a white rabbit for a pet. Have the children survey their classmates, or a larger group, to discover the most popular type of pet. Have them display their findings using a bar graph, a line graph, or a pictogram. (See figs. 8.3 and 8.4.) They may wish to publish these findings as well. Have them express the results in fractions also. (Standard 11)

Example: One-third of the people polled said that a dog is their favorite pet.

4. Henry doesn't find a real white elephant at the fair, but he does buy a white rabbit with a collar and a leash for 200 pennies. Have the children write an equation to show how much money he has left. (Standard 7)

Henry also buys a big balloon and a dozen sugar cookies with the money he has left. Have the children write an equation to show how they think the rest of his money was split. (Standard 7)

5. At the end of the book Henry has a rabbit, but no money. Have the children research the kinds of expenses Henry will incur taking care of his pet. Calculate how much it will cost Henry to take care of his rabbit during the first year. Be sure to include shots, food, cage, and so on. Students may wish to do this for their favorite type of pet as well.

Arthur's Funny Money
Lillian Hoban
(New York: Harper & Row, 1981)

Arthur wants to buy a "Far Out Frisbees" T-shirt and matching cap. His total cost will be $5.00. He does not have enough money, so with the help of his little sister, Violet, he sets up a bike-washing business. Norman and his little brother are their first customers. Bubbles, Norman's dog, is with them. When no one is looking, Bubbles eats the soap out of the box. Subsequently, Arthur and Violet must walk to the store to buy more. As they are walking home, they pass the general store. In the window are the T-shirt and matching cap that Arthur wants. Displayed next to the clothes is a sign that reads Window Samples Reduced. Now Arthur has enough money for the T-shirt and the cap, plus $.18 left to buy licorice twists.

Activities

1. In the beginning of the book, Arthur's sister, Violet, is trying to solve a math problem. She asks Arthur, "If I have five peas and you take three and give me back two, how many peas will I have?" Have the children write an equation to express her question, and then solve it. (Standards 7 and 8)

2. Arthur wants to buy a "Far-Out Frisbees" T-shirt and matching cap, and the total cost is $5.00. When he counts the money in his piggy bank, he finds he only has $3.78. Have the children write two different equations that could help them determine how much more money Arthur needs. Solve the equations. (Standards 7 and 8)

Fig. 8.3.

Favorite Pets		
Name of Pet	Tally	Total
Birds	|||	3
Cats	卌 ||||	9
Dogs	卌 ||	7
Goldfish	||	2
Guinea Pigs	||||	4
Hamsters			1
Rabbits	卌	5
Snakes			1
Others	||	2

Fig. 8.4.

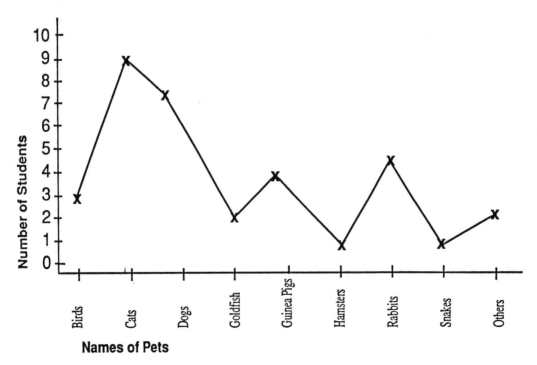

Favorite Pets

3. When Arthur and Violet decide to have a bike wash to raise money, Arthur has to buy supplies. He buys a box of soap for $.53 and a box of Brillo for $.27. How much money has he spent so far? How much of his savings does he have left? (Standard 8)

4. Arthur decides to charge $.25 to wash a bicycle. Ask children how many bicycles he will have to wash before he has $5.25. (Standard 8)

5. The bike washing doesn't go quite as Arthur had planned. Have children answer the following questions about the day. (Standard 8)

   a. Norman pays Arthur $.42 to wash a bicycle and a tricycle. How much money does Arthur have now?

   b. Wilma gives Arthur $.34 for washing a buggy, a stroller, and a rocking horse. How much money does he have now?

   c. Arthur washes a fire engine, a sled, and a wagon for Peter for $.36. How much does he have now?

   d. Arthur washes a scooter and a skateboard for John and charges him $.33. How much money does Arthur have now?

   e. How much money does Arthur earn from the bike wash?

   f. When Arthur goes to the store to buy more soap, he is surprised to find the price has increased. In the morning it had been $.53, and in the afternoon it was $.64. How much cheaper is the soap in the morning than in the afternoon?

6. Arthur is upset about the price change on the soap and decides not to buy it. On the way home, he and Violet walk by the general store and notice the price of the T-shirt and cap has been reduced to $4.25. How much less than $5.00 do the items cost? How much money does Arthur have left? (Standard 8)

7. Have the children research other items Arthur could have purchased with his $4.43 if the T-shirts and caps had all been sold. (Standard 6)

Harold & Chester in Hot Fudge
James Howe
(New York: Morrow Junior Books, 1990)

The Monroe family lives with four pets—Chester the cat, Harold and Howie the dogs, and Bunnicula the rabbit—who often have adventures. This time there is a mix-up concerning the fudge Mr. Monroe makes for the Library Bake Sale. It seems the fudge has been stolen, or at least the chocolate coloring. The animals do their best to clear up the mystery and ensure the fudge gets to the bake sale.

SPECIAL NOTE: Same as *Hot Fudge*.

1. Mr. Monroe makes his famous fudge for the Library Bake Sale. Mrs. Monroe needs to take the car, but Mr. Monroe wants to wait 10 more minutes for the fudge to cool. Ask the children to figure out what fraction of an hour 10 minutes is. In small groups, have them create problems for each other involving time and fractions. (Standard 7)

2. After the Monroes leave, Chester, the cat, starts reading the newspaper. Give the students copies of a newspaper and have them circle fractions and decimals found in the paper. Discuss these instances and applications. (Standard 6)

3. Chester tells Harold and Howie that the three of them are just a cheap burglar alarm system. Have the students research the initial cost and maintenance of a burglar alarm system, and the initial cost and maintenance for two dogs and a cat. Is Chester's statement accurate? (Standard 6)

4. When the animals think the fudge may have been stolen, Harold pulls himself up to his full height and peers over the top of the pan. Howie, the dachshund, would never be able to reach the windowsill. Perhaps Howie is only one-fourth as tall as Harold. Have students practice drawing dogs or other objects that are fractionally smaller or larger. (Standard 9)

   Example: Draw a dog. Draw a dog half that size. Draw another dog one-quarter the size of the first.

   If possible, have students experiment with the scaling tools found in computer paint programs.

5. There is a recipe for Mr. Monroe's famous fudge in the back of the book. Make this with the students and emphasize the fractions used in measurement. (Standard 10)

6. Mr. Monroe takes his fudge to the Library Bake Sale. Students may wish to organize their own bake sale to raise money for a special project, or to donate to their library or another worthy cause. (Standard 6)

BOOKS FOR GRADES 4-6

MATHEMATICAL CONTENT VOCABULARY

account	counterfeit	gallons	price range
advertising	coupons	income	prices
allowance	credit	income tax	profit
average	credit cards	inventory	proportion
banks	decimals	investment	sales
bulk pricing	discount	loan	sales tax
calories	earnings	market share	savings account
checking account	equivalent	markup	square foot
commission	expenses	minimum wage	survey
consumer	fares	money	undercut
consumer advocate	flat rate	percent	
cost	fractions	percentage	

Alice and the Boa Constrictor
Laurie Adams and Allison Coudert
(Boston: Houghton Mifflin, 1983)

When Alice Whipple begins studying reptiles in the fourth grade at Miss Barton's School for Girls, she decides she wants to buy her very own boa constrictor. Her father reluctantly agrees, thinking Alice will never be able to raise all the money herself. However, he doesn't bargain on Alice's creative ideas for earning money.

Activities

1. Alice tells her father that Virginia Robinson's boa constrictor costs $85. She plans to save her allowance to buy the boa constrictor herself. Her father agrees because he thinks Alice will change her mind before she can save enough money. Her allowance is $.75 each week.

   a. How many weeks will Alice have to save her allowance to pay for the boa constrictor? How many months is this? What fraction of a year is this? (Standards 8 and 10)

   b. Alice knows where she can buy a boa constrictor for only $25. How many weeks will she have to save her allowance for this snake? She also needs to buy a cage for $10. How many weeks will she have to save her allowance for both the snake and the cage? How many months is this? What fraction of a year is this? (Standards 8 and 10)

   c. If the students in your class receive an allowance, have them calculate the number of weeks they would have to save it to buy Alice's boa constrictor and cage. How much would a boa constrictor and cage cost in your area? How long would Alice have to save for this? How long would the students have to save? (Standards 8 and 10)

   d. Have the students survey the class to find out how many receive allowances, if they have to do chores to earn their money, and how much they earn. Survey the parents to find out the same things.

   e. Have the students calculate the average allowance of classmates or of students at their grade level. (Standards 8 and 11)

   f. Have the students discuss how they spend their allowances or the money they earn.

2. Alice decides she will have to wait too long to buy her boa constrictor if she only saves her allowance, so she tries to think of other ways to earn money.

   a. Have students brainstorm other ways that kids could earn money. (See Money-Making Ideas for Kids in Related Books and References.)

   b. Have the students list jobs they do at home or elsewhere, and how much money they earn. Or, conduct a survey of how much they earn. Graph the results. (Standard 11)

3. The first way that Alice decides to make money is to become an inventor. She decides to invent a "new, super-duper no-wax floor polish," but later changes to furniture polish. To make it, she mixes water, Comet, olive oil, hand lotion, and chocolate syrup. The specific amounts are not mentioned, but have students estimate how much she uses of each one. Then have them research

the costs of these ingredients and calculate her cost to produce this "super-duper" furniture polish. How does this compare to the price of other furniture polishes already on the market? What would her markup be? What is the usual markup on consumer items? You may wish to contact a consumer advocacy group to talk with students about markups. (Standard 8)

4. Next, Alice becomes a street musician and has her sister, Beatrice, dress up in old clothes to gain sympathy. Students may want to research how much street musicians make. What is the range? What is the average? (Standard 11)

5. Finally, Alice, Beatrice, and a friend go to the movies and are shocked at the price of popcorn—$1 for a small bag and $2 for a large. Alice decides she can sell popcorn at lower prices. She goes to the store and spends $7.76 on popcorn. They pop 47 bags of popcorn and charge $.75 per bag. (Standard 8)

   a. Assuming Alice's bags of popcorn are equal to the theater's small bag, by what percentage did Alice undercut the theater prices?

   b. What were Alice's costs per bag to make the popcorn?

   c. What percent profit did Alice make on each bag?

   d. If it costs the theater the same amount of money to make popcorn, what is the theater's profit expressed in a percentage?

   e. What does your local theater charge for popcorn? How much is this per ounce? How much does unpopped popcorn cost per ounce at the store? Without taking into account bulk pricing, how much profit is the theater making?

   f. What other factors need to be taken into account in calculating profit (advertising, butter, salt, bulk pricing, equipment, etc.)?

6. When Alice finally is ready to buy her boa constrictor and cage, she is expecting to pay $35. Instead the bill comes to $37.80 with tax.

   a. What percent sales tax is being charged?

   b. What is your local sales tax? What would the snake and cage cost with tax in your community?

   c. Have the students list several things they would like to buy and have them figure the cost with tax included.

   d. Research how much of the sales tax is local and how much is state, and how those taxes are spent. You may want to contact local or state officials to discuss these issues with the class.

7. Once Alice brings Sir Lancelot home, she has to feed him a dead mouse once per week. Will her allowance cover the cost of feeding Sir Lancelot? (Standard 8)

What's Cooking, Jenny Archer?
Ellen Conford
(Boston: Little, Brown, 1989)

Jenny Archer decides to make her own lunches because she doesn't like school lunches. At first her friends are impressed and offer her their lunch money to make their lunches, too. Jenny quickly calculates her anticipated profit and agrees. However, she didn't count on expenses, "finicky" eaters, and hungry dogs.

Activities

1. Once Jenny decides to make her own lunches, she and her mom go shopping. Using a chart like the one in figure 8.5, have students research the costs for these items. (Standard 6)

Fig. 8.5.

Jenny Archer's Shopping List

Grocery Items	Store 1 Price	Store 2 Price
Deviled Ham		
Cheese		
Shrimp Salad		
Sweet Pickles		
Clam Dip		
Pita Bread		
Mushrooms		

2. Jenny watches a show called "Kids in the Kitchen." Danny and Denise suggest making different sandwiches including:

   • peanut butter, bacon, and banana;

   • walnuts, olives, and cream cheese;

   • chutney and cream cheese; and

   • carrots, raisins, and cream cheese.

   Have students figure out what the cheapest sandwich is. Which one contains the most calories? (Standard 8)

3. The next day, Jenny includes in her lunch a deviled ham and sweet pickle sandwich on wheat bread, three cherry tomatoes with a green olive on top, a wedge of honeydew melon, and four oatmeal cookies. Have the students calculate the cost of this lunch. Is this more or less than the cost of a school lunch? (Standard 8)

4. School lunches cost $1.50 per day. The first day Jenny brings her lunch, they serve chicken noodle soup, pizza, canned peas, and a slice of peach pie. Have the students research the costs of these same items at a grocery store and at a restaurant. Why are the prices different? (Standard 6)

   You may want to have someone from the school cafeteria, a grocery store, and a restaurant come in to discuss their expenses and profits with the class.

5. On the first day, four people offer Jenny $1.50 to make their lunches. Jenny quickly calculates that she will make $30 each week. If this continues, how much will she earn in one year? Later, Sarah and Howard also offer Jenny their lunch money. Now how much would she earn in one year? (Standard 8)

6. Jenny goes to Mr. Marvel's Deli to buy roast beef for seven sandwiches. He tells her she needs three slices of beef for each sandwich—about one and one-half pounds and it will cost $9.

   a. How many slices are in one pound of roast beef? What is the cost per slice? (Standards 8 and/or 10)

   b. He also tells her she can buy sliced chicken for seven sandwiches for $6.50. Assuming the number of slices is the same for chicken as for roast beef, how much is this per slice? What is the percentage difference in cost between the chicken and the roast beef? (Standard 8)

   c. Jenny decides to spend $5.50 on 15 slices of chicken to make five sandwiches. How much does each sandwich cost? (Standard 8)

7. Because one cookie costs $.50 at the deli Jenny decides to bake her own. Using a recipe for chocolate chip cookies, have the students research the total cost of the ingredients, and calculate the cost per cookie. (Standard 8)

8. Jenny's lunches don't go over very well. She has to give back three dollars and six quarters. She has already spent $5.50 to buy chicken. What is her profit or loss? (Standard 8)

If You Made a Million
David M. Schwartz
(New York: Lothrop, Lee & Shepard, 1989)

Marvelosissimo, the mathematical magician, begins with simple concepts of equivalence, such as "one dime has the same value as two nickels or ten pennies," until he reaches $1 million. He explains about interest, writing checks, and the buying power of various amounts of money. The illustrations are clever and help provide a good introduction to money matters and large numbers.

Activities

1. On the first page, Marvelosissimo congratulates a girl for earning a penny. Have the students research and list all of the things, if any, they can find that cost one cent. Do the same for 5 or 10 cents.

    Have the students ask their parents, grandparents, or look in old newspapers, to find out what kinds of things could be bought for one cent 20 or 30 years ago. Research the prices for things such as a candy bar, a loaf of bread, a pair of shoes, a movie ticket, a car, and a house.

2. The book shows four different combinations of coins that are equivalent to a one dollar bill. Have the students list as many combinations as they can of coins and bills that are equivalent to a five dollar bill.

3. The author states that $10 is equivalent to a five-foot stack of pennies. Divide the students into cooperative groups to complete the following activities.

    a. Have the students research and list other things that are five feet high. Have the groups share their lists with the whole class. (Standard 6)

    b. Have students think of three ways to determine how high the stack of pennies equivalent to $100 would be. Research other things that are 50 feet high. (Standards 7 and 10)

    c. Have students determine which combination of coins equaling $100 would make the shortest stack. Which would make the tallest stack? Ask the same questions for $1000. Could this be the reason people write checks? (Standard 8 or 10)

4. In the book *If You Made a Million*, author David Schwartz states that if you save a one-dollar bill in a bank for a year, it will be worth $1.05.

    a. Have the students figure how much money the dollar earned in interest. What fraction of the dollar is this? What percentage of the dollar is this? (Standard 8)

    b. Have the students study the information in figure 8.6. Then have them estimate the amount of interest their dollar would earn if they left it in the bank for five years. For 25 years.

Fig. 8.6.

Investment	Length of Time in Bank	Amount of Interest
$1.00	1 year	$.05
	10 years	.64
	20 years	1.70

c. Have students explain why $1.00 earns $.64 interest in 10 years instead of $.50.

d. Ask students to find out why banks pay interest. Then have the students research interest rates at local banks. They may want to discuss why interest rates vary from bank to bank and from account to account. (Standard 6)

e. Using the highest interest rate they can find, have the students use calculators to calculate how much interest they would earn in one year if they saved $1 per week. How much would they earn if they saved $5 per week? (Standards 7 and 8)

5. Give the students the following scenario: Your parents give you $.01 on your birthday. The next day they give you double that amount. The following day, they double what they gave you on day 2, and so on. How long would it take before you had $1 million? (Standard 8) (You may also want to refer to *The King's Chessboard* by David Birch and listed in Related Books and References on p. 61).

6. David Schwartz states that $1 million is equivalent to a stack of pennies 95 miles high, a whale's weight in quarters, a 360-foot pile of one-dollar bills, or the number of nickels necessary to fill a school bus.

a. Have the students find out how high 95 miles is. Do we know of anything that high? (Standard 6)

b. How much does a whale weigh? Can the students find anything else that weighs the same amount? (Standard 6)

c. Ask students to make a list of things that are 360 feet high. They may have to convert feet to yards first. (Standards 6, 8, and 10)

d. How big is the interior of a school bus? (Standards 6 and 10)

7. The author states that $1 million is equivalent to a whale's weight in quarters. Have the students think of three ways to determine the weight of $100 worth of quarters.

8. One illustration in the book indicates that it takes 20 million nickels to fill a school bus. Have students think of at least three ways to determine how many nickels it would take to fill their classroom. (Standards 7 and 10)

9. Ask students to make a list of how they would spend $1 million. Have them include prices for items. Schwartz states that the interest on $1 million is about $1,000 per week. Ask students to make a list of how they might spend just the interest.

10. Tell the students that even if they had $1000 per week, there might be other things they would like to buy.

    a. They might choose to purchase things using a credit card. Have the students research how credit cards work. (Standard 6)

    b. Have students find out what kinds of interest rates are charged by different companies. Ask them to explain when and why companies charge interest on credit card balances. (Standard 6)

    c. Using the interest rates they discovered, have the students calculate the amount of interest they would pay if they charged $100 this month and didn't pay it off. How much money would they have to pay the next month if they didn't make any more purchases? (Standard 8)

11. In the book, you buy a $100,000 castle. You must borrow $50,000 from the bank to do this. If you paid $100 per month, and if you didn't have to pay interest on the loan, how long would it be before the loan was paid off? (Standards 8 and 10)

Jason and the Money Tree
Sonia Levitin
(New York: Harcourt Brace Jovanovich, 1974)

Jason Galloway is 11 years old when his grandfather dies and leaves him a box of treasures, including a ten-dollar bill. "As a result of a strange dream he had, the message he found in his fortune cookie and Grandpa's admonition that 'Nothing is impossible'," Jason plants the bill in the backyard. Nonetheless, he is astounded when he discovers the bill has sprouted, and he has his own money tree. This is not quite the good fortune it seems, and Jason encounters many unanticipated complications before the story ends.

SPECIAL NOTE: Activities can be done without the book. Substitutes include: Aiello, Barbara. *Business Is Looking Up*. Frederick, MD: Twenty-First Century Books, 1988; Van Leeuwen, Jean. *Benjy in Business*. NY: Dial Books for Young Readers, 1983; Conford, Ellen. *A Job for Jenny Archer*. Boston: Little, Brown, 1988.

Activities

1. After six weeks of working at the store, Mr. Matroni tells Jason he will give him one dollar for every day he works at the store. Jason will be working three days per week during summer vacation. How much money will he earn by the time school starts in the fall? (Standard 8)

2. At one point, Jason thinks never again would he have to clip coupons out of magazines for free samples or enter contests for free prizes." Have the students look through different magazines to find coupons. Calculate how much money would be spent using these coupons, and how much money would be saved. Which coupon has the largest percent discount and which has the smallest? What is the average? (Standards 8 and 11)

   Have the students ask their parents if they use grocery coupons and how much they save.

3. Jason's family has several unexpected expenses—the washer breaks down, the car breaks down, the roof needs fixing and a broken leg—that negatively impact the family budget. Have students assume a minimum wage income and devise their own monthly budget using newspapers to estimate expenses. (Standard 8)

4. After Jason harvests the first ten-dollar bill from his money tree, he notices two more sprouts. He wonders if he doubles the amount from his tree every day, how long it will take him to become a millionaire. Have students calculate the answer and share their strategies for solving the problem. (Standard 6 or 8)

5. The IRS man comes to audit Mr. Matroni. What percentage of a person's income is consumed by income tax? Give students some annual income figures and have them figure the amount of tax owed to the government. (Standard 8)

   You may want to have a tax accountant or an IRS agent talk to the class about taxes. You may also want to contact a government official to explain how state and federal income tax is spent.

6. Jason has $73. He plans to buy the Super-Duper fishing pole at Matroni's for $38.95. How much money will he have left? Mr. Matroni says he will give Jason a 10 percent discount. How much money will that be? How much will Jason have left if he takes advantage of the discount? (Standard 8)

7. Jason plans to give his dad a laundry basket filled to the brim with ten-dollar bills. Divide students into cooperative groups and ask them how they would determine how much money this would be. Then have them do the actual calculations. (Standards 7 and/or 10)

8. Jason makes a deal with Mr. Quinley, his next door neighbor, to weed his pumpkin patch for $.50 per hour. Jason must weed two hours per day, two days per week for five weeks to earn $10 to pay for an engraving for his mother. Have students write an equation illustrating this arrangement. (Standard 7)

9. Jason harvests 44 ten-dollar bills. One is deformed, he cuts up two with the lawnmower, three blow into other yards, and a bird pecks holes in another. What percentage of the bills produced by his money tree are not usable? When gardeners plant seeds, what percentage do they expect will not germinate? How do these percentages compare? (Standards 6 and 8)

10. Jason's parents make an offer on a house. Real estate agents receive a commission on their sales. Have students research other kinds of jobs that involve commissions and the percentages they pay. (Standard 6)

    Have the students look at real estate ads and calculate the commissions on these houses. If they wanted to make $50,000 per year, approximately how many houses would they have to sell? You may want to do this activity with cars instead. (Standard 8)

The Turtle Street Trading Co.
Jill Ross Klevin
(New York: Delacorte Press, 1982)

Four 12-year-olds, Morgan Pierpont III, P. J. Alberoy, Mikey McGrath, and Fergy Weinstein, make up a secret society known as the Turtles. They make little progress in raising money for a trip to Disneyland and are on the verge of disbanding when they decide to form The Turtle Street Trading Co. With the assistance of Morgan's younger brother, Sanford, they recycle old junk and collect an inventory that includes used toys, tapes, records, posters, models, and T-shirts for which other kids can trade their old stuff. For this service, they charge a commission. After a discouraging start, the business becomes a huge success.

Activities

1. Morgan orders the secret society T-shirts from a catalog his mom receives in the mail. "On the front was a bright green turtle outlined in orange on a purple background. On the back was their official club motto: TURTLES TOGETHER FOREVER!" Have the students research the cost of printing the shirts in your community. (Standard 6)

2. The Turtles want to go to Disneyland. They live in Calabasas, California. Have students calculate the cost for each person to travel to Disneyland and back. Include transportation costs, motel costs, meals, and admission charges. Is it cheaper to travel by car or by bus? (Standard 8)

   Calculate the costs to travel to Disneyland and back from your location. Students may want to investigate train and plane fares, too. (Standard 8)

3. "You know," [Morgan] said as casually as he could under the circumstances, "I was reading just the other day. Kids make up fifty percent of the population in this area." What percentage of the population are kids in your area? How many kids is this? (Standards 6 and 8)

4. At dinner one night, Mrs. Pierpont serves broiled fish. Sandy wants hamburgers. Morgan tells him that hamburgers aren't good for him because they have too much cholesterol. Research cholesterol percentages in various foods.

5. Morgan's mom is a journalist at the *Valley Herald*, "the biggest local newspaper, and the one with the highest circulation." Have the students research newspapers in your area to find out what percentage of market share they have. You may want to contact a marketing representative to explain to the class more about the concept of market share and how it is determined. (Standard 6)

6. To start their business, the Turtles borrow $25 at six percent interest from Fergie's sister, Felicia. How much money will they have to pay back to Felicia? Of this money, they spend $21.85 on supplies. What percentage of their initial investment is this? (Standard 8)

7. The Turtles place the following ad in the *Pennysaver.*

    > Kids! Bring all your old junk and trade it at the grand opening of the
    > TURTLE STREET TRADING COMPANY, the Turtles' answer to
    > being rich, in the parking lot outside of Ralph's in the Mulview
    > Shopping Center at Mulwood & San Luis roads, Calabasas, on July 21
    > from 10 a.m. to 6 p.m. and on Sunday, July 22, same hours. Free
    > prizes, free refreshments and a famous secret celebrity to sign
    > autographs.

    a. The ad costs $3.70. What is the cost per word? (Standard 8)

    b. How much does Morgan have to contribute from his leftover allowance to pay for the ad? (Standard 8)

    c. With Morgan's contribution, their initial investment was $25.55. What percentage did they spend on advertising? Is this percentage consistent with what other businesses spend on advertising? (Standard 8)

    d. Have students research how much this ad would cost to run in your community. (Standard 6)

    e. Have the students compare the costs of advertising in a newspaper, on radio, and on television. (Standard 6)

8. By 3:00 P.M. on the second day, the Turtles have $30.42 in the cash box. (Standard 8)

    a. Five kids have been working since 10:00 A.M. How much has each one earned?

    b. The Turtles are charging 25 percent commission. What is the cash value of the items brought in to trade?

9. By the end of the first week, the Turtles have cleared $300 above their overhead.

    a. Knowing that they are open Tuesdays through Sundays from 10:00 A.M. to 6:00 P.M., how much money do they average each day? (Standards 8 and 11)

    b. How much is each Turtle earning per hour? (Standard 8)

10. By the end of the second week, the Turtles have earned over $700. (Standard 8)

    a. By what percentage has their profit increased?

    b. If business keeps up at this rate, and school starts September 7, how much profit will they have made by then?

    c. Once school starts, they will only be open on Saturdays, Sundays, and Wednesdays from 1:00 P.M. to 8:00 P.M. If they continue to make the same profit, how much will they make each week? How much will they make by June 1? Is this enough for them to go to Disneyland?

11. Morgan's dad reminds him about income taxes. He says they could run from 15 or 20 percent up to 50 percent.

    a. Have students calculate how much the Turtle Street Trading Company will owe in taxes in either case. (Standard 8)

    b. Mr. Pierpont also suggests they hire an accountant. How much do accountants typically charge? (Standard 6)

    c. Furthermore, Mr. Pierpont points out that they may want to rent a small store in case of bad weather and so their parents don't have to constantly haul the merchandise to the parking lot. Have the students research rental costs for commercial properties in your area.

    d. Based on their research, have the students deduct these various expenses from the company's profit. Is this still a profitable business? (Standard 8)

12. Start your own version of the Turtle Street Trading Company. (Standard 6)

The Magic School Bus at the Waterworks
Joanna Cole
(New York: Scholastic, 1986)

Mrs. Frizzle and her class have an unusual trip to the waterworks, beginning with the bus evaporating into the sky in the same way water does, and ending with the children encased in the water droplets coming out of the faucet in the girls' bathroom.

Activities

1. The book states that approximately two-thirds of your body is made up of water. How much water is that? (Standards 6 and 8)

2. At the beginning of the field trip, the bus seems to evaporate into the clouds. Have students find out how long it takes water to evaporate.

3. Humidity is often expressed in percentages. Have the students find out what humidity reports mean, and how to measure humidity. (Standard 6)

4. At one point in the story the students shrink to the size of a raindrop. Have your students research the size of a raindrop. Assuming Mrs. Frizzle's students are the same size as your students, ask your students to determine what fraction of their former size they would have to become to be the size of a raindrop. (Standard 8)

5. Mrs. Frizzle and her class return to Earth as rain. What is the average rainfall in your area? How do water officials determine how much to restrict water usage when an area experiences a drought? (Standard 6)

6. Tell the students that water covers three-fourths of the Earth's surface. Ask them to calculate how much water this is. How much is fresh water? How much of the world's fresh water is in the United States? (Standards 6 and 8)

7. In the book, the class swims through a reservoir of water. Have students find out if there is a reservoir that stores water for your community and answer the following questions. (Standards 6 and 8)

   a. How much water does the reservoir hold?

   b. How much water is this per person?

   c. How many gallons of water does your community use in one year?

   d. By what percentage or fraction does water use increase during high volume times?

   e. Are there other sources for your local water supply, and what percent of the water comes from each source?

8. At the waterworks, the students find that chlorine and fluorine are added to the water. Have your students find out if this is done in your community, and in what proportions.

   Using that information, have them calculate how many gallons of chlorine, fluorine, or both, would be added to 100,000 gallons of water. Are these the same proportions used for swimming pools? (Standards 6 and 8)

9. Tell students that water pressure is 64 pounds per square foot. Then give them this problem: If you swam to the bottom of the reservoir, and it was 50 feet deep, how many pounds of pressure per square foot would be on your body? (Standard 8)

10. Mrs. Frizzle and the class swim through water pipes. Ask students how they would calculate the size of pipe needed to carry 1,000 cubic feet of water per minute. (Standards 7 and 10)

11. The book states that the average city loses one-fifth of all its water through leaks. Have students find out how many gallons of water this is for your community. (Standards 6 and 8)

12. Most communities charge for water. Some have a flat rate and others charge based on usage. (Standards 6 and 8)

    a. Have students find out what your community does.

    b. How do they decide how much to charge? Do water rates differ depending on area rainfall?

    c. Have the students find out how much water the average household uses per month.

d. Have the students find out how much water is used for activities such as watering the lawn, doing the dishes, flushing the toilet, etc. Have the students use this information to estimate their family's daily water use in gallons.

e. Have students research water conservation measures and calculate the percentage of water saved when these are implemented.

Search for Fractional Wholes

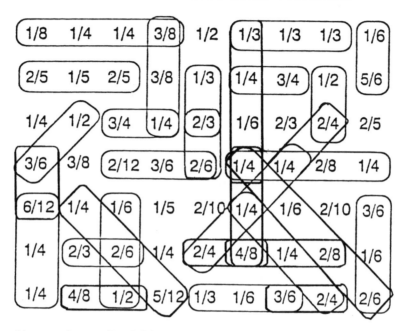

(Answer key to fig. 8.2.)

RELATED BOOKS AND REFERENCES

FRACTIONS—COOKING

Blain, Diane. *The Boxcar Children Cookbook*. Morton Grove, Ill.: Albert Whitman, 1991. (4-6)

Douglass, Barbara. *The Chocolate Chip Cookie Contest*. New York: Lothrop, Lee & Shepard, 1985. (K-3)

MacDonald, Kate. *The Anne of Green Gables Cookbook*. Toronto: Oxford University Press, 1985. (4-6)

MacGregor, Carol. *The Storybook Cookbook*. Garden City, N.Y.: Doubleday, 1967. (4-6)

Watson, N. Cameron. *The Little Pigs' First Cookbook*. Boston: Little, Brown, 1987. (K-3)

Willard, Nancy. *The High Rise Glorious Skittle Skat Roarious Sky Pie Angel Food Cake*. New York: Harcourt Brace Jovanovich, 1990. (4-6)

FRACTIONS—MUSIC

Landeck, Beatrice. *Songs to Grow On.* New York: Edward B. Marks Music Corp., 1950. (K-3)

Langstaff, John. *Sweetly Sings the Donkey.* New York: Atheneum, 1976. (K-3)

Miller, Carl S., ed. *Sing, Children, Sing.* New York: Chappell, 1972. (4-6)

Seeger, Ruth Crawford. *American Folk Songs for Children.* Garden City, N.Y.: Doubleday, 1948. (4-6)

FRACTIONS—PIES AND PIZZAS/FOOD

Cresswell, Helen. *The Piemakers.* New York: J. B. Lippincott, 1968. (4-6)

Khalsa, Dayal Kaur. *How Pizza Came to Queens.* New York: Clarkson N. Potter, 1989. (K-3)

Levitin, Sonia. *Nobody Stole the Pie.* New York: Harcourt Brace Jovanovich, 1980. (4-6)

MacDonald, Elizabeth. *Mr. Badger's Birthday Pie.* New York: Dial Books for Young Readers, 1989. (K-3)

McMillan, Bruce. *Eating Fractions.* New York: Scholastic, 1991. (K-3)

Moncure, Jane Belk. *How Many Ways Can You Cut a Pie?* Mankato, Minn.: Child's World, 1988. (K-3)

Wellington, Anne. *Apple Pie.* Englewood Cliffs, N.J.: Prentice-Hall, 1978. (K-3)

FRACTIONS—MISCELLANEOUS

Emberley, Ed. *Picture Pie.* Boston: Little, Brown, 1984. (K-3)

Holl, Adelaide. *The Runaway Giant.* New York: Lothrop, Lee & Shepard, 1967. (K-3)

Macaulay, David. *Black and White.* New York: Houghton Mifflin, 1990. (4-6)

Ungerer, Tomi. *Moon Man.* New York: Harper & Row, 1967. (K-3)

VanCleave, Janice. *Math for Every Kid.* New York: John Wiley, 1991. (Adult Reference)

Whitney, David C. *The Easy Book of Fractions.* New York: Franklin Watts, 1970. (4-6)

DECIMALS

Anno, Mitsumasa. *Anno's Flea Market.* New York: Philomel Books, 1984. (4-6)

Berenstain, Stan, and Jan Berenstain. *The Berenstain Bears' Trouble with Money.* New York: Random House, 1983. (K-3)

Brenner, Barbara. *Annie's Pet.* New York: Bantam Books, 1989. (K-3)

Butterworth, Nick, and Mick Inkpen. *Just Like Jasper!* Boston: Little, Brown, 1989. (K-3)

Caple, Kathy. *The Purse.* Boston: Houghton Mifflin, 1986. (K-3)

Conford, Ellen. *A Job for Jenny Archer.* Boston: Little, Brown, 1988. (4-6)

Day, Alexandra. *Paddy's Pay-Day.* New York: Viking Kestrel, 1989. (K-3)

Dumbleton, Mike. *Dial-a-Croc.* New York: Orchard Books, 1991. (K-3)

Heide, Florence Parry. *Treehorn's Treasures.* New York: Holiday House, 1981. (4-6)

Kotzwinkle, William. *The Day the Gang Got Rich.* New York: Viking Press, 1970. (K-3)

Marshall, James. *Yummers Too.* Boston: Houghton Mifflin, 1986. (K-3)

Martin, Charles E. *Summer Business.* New York: Greenwillow Books, 1984. (4-6)

Shaw, Nancy. *Sheep in a Shop.* Boston: Houghton Mifflin, 1991. (K-3)

Van Leeuwen, Jean. *Benjy in Business.* New York: E. P. Dutton, 1983. (K-3)

MONEY—MISCELLANEOUS

Adler, David A. *Inflation.* New York: Franklin Watts, 1985. (4-6)

_____. *Prices Go Up, Prices Go Down.* New York: Franklin Watts, 1984. (4-6)

Houser, Peggy, and Hassell Bradley. *How to Teach Children About Money.* Denver, Colo.: Western Freelance Writing Services, 1989. (4-6)

Scott, Elaine. *Stocks and Bonds, Profits and Losses: A Quick Look at Financial Markets.* New York: Franklin Watts, 1985. (4-6)

MONEY-MAKING IDEAS FOR KIDS

The Amazing Life Games Co. *Good Cents.* Boston: Houghton Mifflin, 1974. (4-6)

Barkin, Carol, and Elizabeth James. *Jobs for Kids.* New York: Lothrop, Lee & Shepard, 1990. (4-6)

Wilkinson, Elizabeth. *Making Cents: Every Kid's Guide to Money.* Boston: Little, Brown, 1989. (4-6)

Yerian, Cameron, and Margaret Yerian, eds. *Fun Time Money-Making Ideas.* Chicago: Children's Press, 1975. (K-6)

Young, Jim, and Jean Young. *The Kids' Money-Making Book.* Garden City, N.Y.: Doubleday, 1976. (4-6)

9—Standard 13: Patterns and Relationships

The mathematics curriculum should include the study of patterns and relationships so that students can

- recognize, describe, extend, and create a wide variety of patterns;

- represent and describe mathematical relationships; and

- explore the use of variables and open sentences to express relationships.

Children should learn that their world is made up of many predictable patterns and that much within their world is related. Physical materials should be used to help children explore, recognize, and create patterns and relationships. The curriculum should allow children to focus on regularities in events, shapes, designs, and sets of numbers. Children should explore the connections among numbers, geometry, and measurement.

BOOKS FOR GRADES K-3

MATHEMATICAL CONTENT VOCABULARY

alliteration	function machine	patterns
cipher	hundreds chart	square numbers
code	number patterns	triangular numbers
consecutive	odd numbers	visual patterns
even numbers	parquetry	

Some Things Go Together
Charlotte Zolotow
(New York: Thomas Y. Crowell, 1969)

The author uses rhyming couplets to describe various ideas, objects, descriptors, and actions that we often think of as connected in some way.

Activities

1. Have children identify the patterns in the text (rhyming, two groups of three words each, etc.).

2. Write a class story based on the same pattern or patterns.

3. Explain to the children that just as words sometimes go together in patterns, numbers can go together in patterns too. As a whole group or in pairs, have them work on the patterns in figure 9.1. The children may want to place beans on the Hundred Chart to help them figure out the patterns. (See fig. 3.1. on page 18.) (Standard 7 or 8)

4. In pairs, have the children make up other patterns to exchange with other groups and solve the patterns.

5. Draw a large box on the board and tell the children this is a function machine. When a number goes into the box, something happens to it and it comes out the other side as a different number. They should be able to figure out what happened inside the box by comparing the number before it went into the box with the number that comes out. For example, if a 1 goes into the box and a 3 comes out, the function machine added 2 to the number. Play this game with the children. (Standards 7 and 8)

A, My Name Is Alice
Jane Bayer
(New York: Dial Books for Young Readers, 1984)

"A, My Name Is Alice and my husband's name is Alex. We come from Alaska and we sell ants." This book is based on an old game that takes children through the alphabet from A to Z. In the original game, a child had to think of the name of a woman, the name of her husband, where they came from, and a business venture, all beginning with the same letter of the alphabet. The author shares her creative combinations using this alliterative pattern.

Activities

1. Read the book to the children and discuss the concept of alliteration. Have the children follow the pattern in the book, but use new names for each letter.

    In cooperative groups, have the children brainstorm as many words as they can for an assigned letter. Have them use those words to make a story or to create tongue twisters.

2. Have the children make up a few sentences or a short story using as many numbers as they can.

    Example: 4 fun I'll just dash off a line and send it off 2 U.

3. The author remembers reciting this type of rhyme while bouncing a ball. The player bounces the ball one time for each word. Each time a word beginning with the correct letter of the alphabet comes up, the player must lift one leg over the ball as it bounces. You may want to collaborate with a physical education teacher on this activity.

4. Repeat the bouncing ball game, but this time use math patterns. For example: $1 + 9 = 10, 2 + 8 = 10$. Bounce the ball for each element in the number sentence. Lift one leg over the ball when ten is repeated. (Standard 8)

5. Have the children clap out the syllables for the couplets and list the number of syllables in each one. Do they all have the same number of syllables? (Standard 6)

Fig. 9.1. Number patterns.

1. 0, 1, 2, 3, 4, ___, ___, ___, ___, ___, ___,

2. 0 ___, ___, ___, 4, 5, ___, ___, ___, ___

3. 1 ___ 3 ___5 ___ 7 ___ 9 ___ 11 ___ 13 ___

4. ___, ___, ___, 5, ___, ___, ___

5. ___, ___, ___, ___, ___, ___, ___, ___, 9

6. 10, 20, 30, ___, ___, ___, ___, ___, ___, ___

7. 6, ___, 8, ___, 10, ___, 12, ___, 14, ___, 16

8. 1, 4, 9, 16, ___, ___, ___, ___, ___, ___, ___

9. 7, 14, 21, 28, ___, ___, ___, ___, ___, ___

10. 24, 21, 18, ___, ___, ___, ___, ___, ___

11. 3, 13, 23, ___, ___, ___, ___, ___, ___, ___

12. 1, 12, 23, 34, ___, ___, ___, ___, ___, ___

Number Ideas Through Pictures
Mannis Charosh
(New York: Thomas Y. Crowell, 1974)

This book uses clear illustrations and simple explanations to clarify the concepts of odd and even numbers, triangular numbers, and square numbers. It suggests ways for children to use manipulatives to concretely understand what are often considered abstract concepts.

SPECIAL NOTE: Activities can be done without the book. Substitutes include: O'Brien, Thomas C. *Odds and Evens*. NY: Thomas Y. Crowell, 1971; Hulme, Joy N. *Sea Squares*. NY: Hyperion Books, 1991.

Activities

1. The beginning of the book shows children a simple way to tell if a number is odd or even. They count the specified number of objects, put them on a desk or table, and pair them up. If there are none left, it is an even number. If there is an object left, it is an odd number. Let the children try this. (Standard 6)

2. Ask the children to predict whether adding two even numbers will produce an odd or an even number. Have them try several examples. Then ask the same question using two odd numbers.

    What do they predict for adding an even and an odd number? (Standard 8)

3. Give the students a handful of wooden cubes. Have them count out four cubes and form them into the shape of a square. Have them find another number of cubes that will form a square. What is the number? Explain that these are called square numbers. Have them discover the first five square numbers and list these on the board. (Standard 9)

4. The book states that you can also discover square numbers by adding consecutive odd numbers. Have the children verify this with their blocks. (Standards 8 and 9)

5. Explain the concept of triangular numbers to the children. Have them count out six cubes. By placing three cubes in one row, two above it, and one above that, they should have something that looks like a triangle.

    The book claims that triangular numbers can be found by adding consecutive numbers. Have the children verify this with their blocks. (Standards 8 and 9)

6. The author goes on to illustrate how adding two consecutive triangular numbers produces a square number. You may want to have the children use different colored blocks to illustrate this more clearly. The children may also want to use different colors on graph paper to represent the blocks or to draw different symbols as shown in the book. (Standards 8 and 9)

7. Using the Hundreds Chart in fig. 3.1 on p. 18, use one color for marking square numbers and another for marking triangular numbers. (If you want to reuse the charts, beans may be placed on the numbers instead of coloring.) Discuss any patterns.

8. If the children are ready for a challenge, have them predict whether adding two square numbers will form another square number. Have them test their predictions. (Standards 8 and 9)

Sam Johnson and the Blue Ribbon Quilt
Lisa Campbell Ernst
(New York: Lothrop, Lee & Shepard, 1983)

Sam Johnson is a farmer who learns to quilt while his wife is away. When she returns, he decides to join her quilting club, but the women laugh at him. So Sam starts the Rosedale Men's Quilting Club. Both groups are competing to win the prize at the county fair. Problems arise before the two clubs get their quilts to the fair, but they are able to create a winning design by working together.

Activities

1. In addition to the two patterns selected by the Rosedale Men's Quilting Club and the Rosedale Women's Quilting Club, there are several quilt patterns shown as borders for the pages of the book. Have the children select one or create their own, then draw it repeatedly on graph paper and color it in. (Standard 9)

2. Quilt patterns are often based on geometric designs or patterns. If you have parquetry blocks, have the children experiment with making and copying patterns with these manipulatives. (Standard 9)

3. Tangrams also involve geometric patterns. Have the children make designs or objects using the tangram pieces or tans. (Standard 9)

4. Divide the children into pairs. Have one child make a pattern on a geoboard. Have her partner copy it. Reverse roles. (Standard 9)

5. Remaining in pairs, have the children make a design with five or six blocks on a piece of graph paper. Remove one block at a time and color the design on the graph paper. Next have the children surround the base design by placing a block in each space that touches only one side of the base design. (You may want to check their progress before they remove the blocks and color the spaces.) (See fig. 9.2.) (Standard 9)

6. Visual patterns don't always involve geometric shapes; they are sometimes more dependent on color. Have the children string beads according to a specified pattern. Or, you may want to divide children into pairs and have one child create a pattern for the partner to copy, and then switch roles.

7. Explain that numbers can make visual patterns, too. Copy the Hundreds Chart in figure 3.1. Have the children use beans or other markers to cover all the numbers containing a 4. Then cover or color all the numbers with two digits the same (22, 33, etc.). Have them color all numbers with digits that add to nine. Think of some more to try. Discuss the patterns. (Standard 8)

Fig. 9.2.

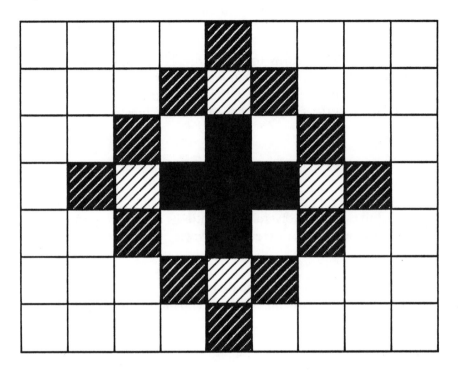

From *Mathematics Their Way* by Mary Baratta-Lorton (Addison-Wesley Publishing Company, 1976).

◼ This is the base design. ▨ This is the second step.

▨ This shows step three.

8. Have the children use graph paper to make addition, subtraction, multiplication, and division patterns as shown in the chart below. (Standard 8)

Fig. 9.3.

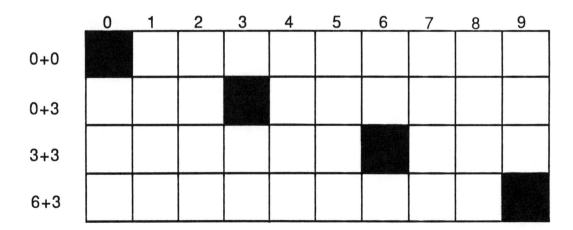

9. Explain that the brain uses patterns to recognize familiar objects. This activity will give children a chance to see how this works. Divide the children into pairs. Give each pair a piece of cardboard with a one-inch square cut out of it. Have one child find a picture in a book or magazine and place the cardboard over it. Then have the partner guess what the whole picture is from the small part that is visible.

10. Patterns can also be used to hide things. Show the children figure 9.4. Have them use graph paper to create their own words.

Fig. 9.4.

The Case of the Stolen Code Book
Barbara Rinkoff
(New York: Crown, 1971)

Winnie, Alex, John, and Holly have a Secret Agents club. One day they forget their code book in the yard. Bob, a new boy in the neighborhood, finds it. He wants to meet the others so he leaves clues, including codes, for them to follow to recover their missing book. Winnie, Alex, John, and Holly are impressed with Bob's abilities and ask him to join the club.

SPECIAL NOTE: Activities can be done without the book. Consult the bibliography and the following substitutes: Burton, Albert, Jr. *Code Busters!* Niles, IL: Albert Whitman, 1985; Jonas, Ann. *The 13th Clue.* NY: Greenwillow Books, 1992; Stanley, George Edward. *The Codebreaker Kids.* NY: Avon Books, 1987.

Activities

1. In the book, Bob uses a simple substitution code in which A = 1, B = 2, C = 3, and so on. Divide the children into pairs. Using this code, have the children make up their own messages. Then have them exchange codes with their partners and decode.

2. There are many types of secret codes. One that might have been in the Secret Agents Code Book is a backward number code in which A = 26, B = 25, C = 24, and so on. Have the children try this code.

3. Using the skip number code (A = 2, B = 4, C = 6, and so on), write a message on the board. Have the students try to decipher the code by analyzing the patterns. After they understand the code, have them write their own messages using this method. Exchange and decode.

4. A more complicated code known as the grid number cipher, or the square box code, was first devised by Polybius, a writer in ancient Greece.

Fig. 9.5.

	1	2	3	4	5
1	A	B	C	D	E
2	F	G	H	I	J
3	K	L	M	N	O
4	P	Q	R	S	T
5	U	V	W/X	Y	Z

Look at the row and then the column to determine which numbers represent which letters. For example: A = 11, B = 12, R = 43.

5. Have the children work in pairs or small groups to use patterns to make their own secret codes. Have them exchange their coded messages with other groups and then try to decode the messages.

BOOKS FOR GRADES 4-6

MATHEMATICAL CONTENT VOCABULARY

alliteration	frequency	optical illusion
arithmetic sequence	geometric sequence	palindromes
cipher	haiku	Pascal
code	infinite system	pixel
constant	limerick	plane
decipher	M. C. Escher	power sequence
encipher	multiple	prediction
extrapolate	Nim games	strategies
Fibonacci	number pattern	substitution
finite system	number sequence	tessellations

Too Hot to Hoot
Marvin Terban
(New York: Clarion Books, 1985)

Palindromes are words, phrases, sentences, or numbers that are written the same forwards and backwards. This book primarily deals with language palindromes, starting with simple three-letter palindrome riddles and working toward whole sentences. However, numerical palindromes are mentioned and the patterns can be extrapolated.

Activities

1. Tell the students that a palindrome is a word, a phrase, or a sentence that is spelled the same way backwards and forwards. There are several three-letter palindrome riddles in the beginning of the book. Provide a few examples and have the students guess the rest. Then have them make up their own riddles.

   Have the students do the same for four- and five-letter palindromes. Do the same for phrases and sentences too.

2. Explain to the students that numbers with two or more digits can be palindromes too. Have the students give you several examples of palindromic numbers.

3. Give the students a 0-99 chart such as the one in figure 9.6, and have them color all the palindromic numbers. Discuss any patterns.

4. Tell the students that one year in each century is a palindrome. The book tells us that 1001 was an early one. Have students figure out which years these were for the last 500 years. What will be the palindrome for the next century? How many years separate these numbers? Is there a pattern? (Standard 7 or 8)

5. The author explains that writing out full dates in numbers can also produce palindromes. The example he provides is January 4, 1941, 1/4/41.

   Have the students think of others. How frequently does this occur? A perfect palindrome is the same number repeated. An example is June 6, 1966, or 6/6/66. Have the students name other perfect palindromes. How often do they occur? When will the next one occur?

6. Tell students that every integer can be made into a palindromic number. The process begins by adding the reverse to the first number. If the sum is not a palindrome, add the sum and its reverse. Continue to do this until a palindrome is produced. (Standard 8)

   One step palindrome:
   $$\begin{array}{r} 423 \\ + 324 \\ \hline 747 \end{array}$$

   Two-step palindrome:
   $$\begin{array}{r} 49 \\ + 94 \\ \hline 143 \\ + 341 \\ \hline 484 \end{array}$$

Have the students test the numbers from 10 to 99. Divide the students into cooperative groups and give each group a set of these numbers to make into palindromic numbers. How many steps does each one take? Is there a pattern? Refer back to the 0-99 chart (see fig. 9.6) and have the students color the one-step palindromes in one color, the two-step palindromes in another color, and so on. Is there a visual pattern? Can they predict how many steps it will take to make a given integer into a palindrome?

Fig. 9.6. 0-99 Chart.

0	1	2	3	4	5	6	7	8	9
10	11	12	13	14	15	16	17	18	19
20	21	22	23	24	25	26	27	28	29
30	31	32	33	34	35	36	37	38	39
40	41	42	43	44	45	46	47	48	49
50	51	52	53	54	55	56	57	58	59
60	61	62	63	64	65	66	67	68	69
70	71	72	73	74	75	76	77	78	79
80	81	82	83	84	85	86	87	88	89
90	91	92	93	94	95	96	97	98	99

Sea Witches
Joanne Robertson and Laszlo Gal
(New York: Dial Books for Young Readers, 1991)

A Scottish grandmother warns her grandson to never leave his eggshells whole. According to the superstition she recounts, sea witches turn uncrushed eggshells into boats and search the seas for sailors. Then these ghost witches cause terrible storms to sink the ships and drown the crews. The whole story is told in 26 stanzas of haiku verse.

Activities

1. The story is told in 26 stanzas of haiku verse. Have the students examine the text to identify the pattern or patterns used for writing this type of verse. Haiku is defined by very strict patterns. It always consists of three lines with five, seven, and five syllables respectively. (Standard 6)

2. After reading this and other examples of haiku, have the students follow the pattern and write their own haiku verse.

3. Haiku is not the only type of poetry that follows a pattern. Limericks have a very distinctive pattern as well. Have the students read several limericks and identify the pattern or patterns used. (There are three main patterns for limericks. Each one is five lines long; lines one, two, and five have three beats; lines three and four have two beats.)

4. Just as in many types of poetry, numbers have patterns, too. Have students calculate the following. (Calculators may be used.) (Standard 7 or 8)

    $0 \times 9 + 1 =$ $37 \times 3 =$
    $1 \times 9 + 2 =$ $37 \times 6 =$
    $12 \times 9 + 3 =$ $37 \times 9 =$
    $123 \times 9 + 4 =$ $37 \times 12 =$
    $1234 \times 9 + 5 =$ $37 \times 27 =$
    $12345 \times 9 + 6 =$
    $123456 \times 9 + 7 =$

    What are the patterns? Why do they happen? Can the students find others?

5. Patterns make it possible to predict what will come next. Divide students into pairs. Have them work on the pattern sequences worksheet in figure 9.7. While one partner listens, have the other child tell what she is thinking as she identifies the pattern. Have them write down the pattern description. Switch roles. Afterwards, discuss the various strategies as well as the different types of patterns. (Standard 6 or 8)

    Arithmetic Sequence

    Add or subtract the same constant to each term.
    3, 8, 13, 18, ...

    Geometric Sequence

    Multiply or divide each term by a constant.
    12, 48, 192, 768, ...

Fig. 9.7. Pattern sequences.

1. O, T, T, F, F, S, ___,___, ___, ___, ___, ___...

2. S, M, T, W, ___, ___, ___.

3. 3, 4, 6, 7, 9, 10, ___, ___, ___, ___, ___, ...

4. 9, 14, 11, 16, 13, 18, 15, ___, ___, ___, ___...

5. JKLMNO, JKLOMN, JKOLMN, _____, _____...

6. J, F, M, A, M, J, ___, ___, ___, ___, ___, ___.

7. 4, 8, 16, 32, ___, ___, ___, ___, ___, ___...

8. 2187, 729, 243, ___, ___, ___, ___, ___,___...

9. 4, 9, 16, 25, ___, ___, ___, ___, ___, ___...

10. 5, 3, 8, 5, 13, 7, 20, ___, ___, ___, ___...

11. 1z, 2w, 4t, 6q, ___, ___, ___, ___, ___...

12. 1, 5, 7, 11, 13, ___, ___, ___, ___, ___...

Power Sequence

Raise or lower each term to the same power or exponent.

9, 16, 25, 36, ...

Remaining in pairs, have the students invent their own pattern sequences and have their partners identify the pattern.

6. Introduce your students to the following special number patterns. Put the sequences on the board and ask students to determine the pattern. (Standard 8)

1, 1, 2, 3, 5, 8, 13, 21, ...
2, 4, 6, 10, 16, 26, 42, 68, ...
1, 3, 4, 7, 11, 18, 29, 47, ...
1, 4, 5, 9, 14, 23, 37, 60, ...

The first example is the only true Fibonacci sequence. Discuss how the Fibonacci sequence can be designated as F_1, F_2, F_3, and so on. You may also want to explain how the sum of the first n Fibonacci numbers is one less than the (n+2)nd Fibonacci number. ($F_1 + F_2 + ... + F_n = F_{n+2} - 1$)

7. Pascal's Triangle is another special number pattern. It is shown in figure 9.8. (Standard 8)

Fig. 9.8. Pascal's Triangle.

a. Have the students fill in the blanks for the partially completed triangular array of numbers.

b. Ask the students to complete the numbers for each row and its related sum as shown in figure 9.9. Have them discover the relationship between the number of each row and its related sum.

Fig. 9.9. Pascal's Triangle.

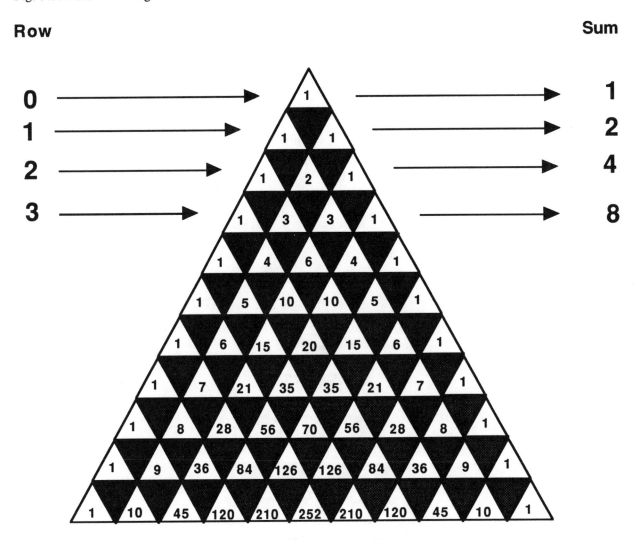

c. Make multiple copies of the triangle and have the students circle various patterns they find such as even numbers, multiples of 3, multiples of 5, and so forth.

8. Patterns sometimes make it possible to predict future occurrences. Have students brainstorm ways that patterns can be used in the real world for prediction purposes (weather, sales, insurance statistics, etc.). Students may want to interview people in these fields about how they use patterns to make predictions. (Standard 6)

Or, you may want to have these people visit the class to talk about how they use patterns to make predictions.

9. Have the students research the rainfall and temperatures for your area during the past three years. Make predictions for the next year and keep track, if possible. (See fig. 9.10.) (Standards 6 and 11)

Fig. 9.10.

Year	1990				1991				1992			
Month	Jan.	Apr.	July	Oct.	Jan.	Apr.	July	Oct.	Jan.	Apr.	July	Oct.
Temp.												

Solomon Grundy, Born on Oneday
Malcolm E. Weiss
(New York: Thomas Y. Crowell, 1977)

"Solomon Grundy, born on Monday, christened on Tuesday, married on Wednesday, took sick on Thursday, buried on Sunday." Did this really all happen in one week, or is there another way to explain this nursery rhyme?

SPECIAL NOTE: Most activities can be done without the book. A substitute is Hogett, Susan Samsay. *Solomon Grundy.* NY: E. P. Dutton, 1986.

Activities

1. Read the nursery rhyme to the students and ask how they could explain it. Discuss the repeating pattern in all our time measurements. (Standard 10)

2. Have the students make a calendar for a month. Look for number patterns. (Standard 10)

3. Have the students make a week-clock as explained in the book on pp. 11-13. Have them use this finite system to do arithmetic as shown in the book. (Standards 7 and 8)

    Ask students if they can think of other finite systems and how they work. Can they think of some infinite systems too?

4. Have the students make addition charts from 1 to 9 using regular arithmetic and week-clock arithmetic. Have them look for patterns. (Standards 7 and 8)

5. Nim games are also based on a finite system. Nim is an old Chinese game. In these games, the players choose the number of objects to take away from a set. The player who takes the last object wins the game. Show students that this is very easy when there are only two objects; the second player will always win. Ask the students what their strategy would be if there were four objects in a set. Six objects? (They may want to mentally divide the set into two parts. If the two piles have the same number of objects, the second player can win by doing just what the first player does.)

6. A more complicated Nim game is called Poison. Give each pair of students 12 items that are the same and one that is different. Each player may take away one or two items during each turn. The player left with the different object (Poison) loses. Have students determine if it is better to go first or second. Does their strategy change if one, two, or three objects are taken at a time?

Visual Magic
Dr. David Thomson
(New York: Dial Books, 1991)

Our visual system tries to make sense of the world around us by interpreting what we think we see. The brain often relies on past experiences or tries to make stimuli fit a pattern, or both. This book explores how effective these strategies can be and how we can sometimes be fooled.

Activities

1. The picture on p. 8 of the book was produced by putting a photograph into a computer. The computer translated the image into little squares called pixels. Have the students make a face using small construction paper squares, by coloring graph paper squares, or by using a computer drawing program. Discuss what types of patterns are involved. (Standard 9)

2. Sometimes lines or shapes can be placed in such a way to make our visual system see other patterns. See the examples below. Have the students make up their own examples. (Standard 9)

Fig. 9.11.

Ehrenstein Grids

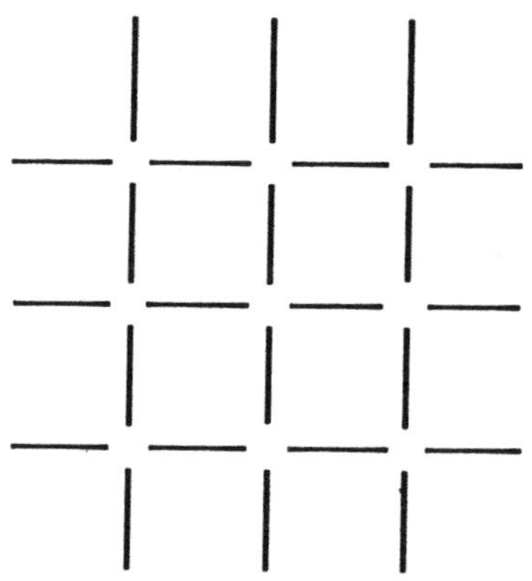

Fig. 9.12.

Kanizsa Triangle

3. On pp. 42-43, the artist uses eight steps to change the pattern of lines and shapes from a fish into a king's head. The students may want to try transforming one object into another in a number of related steps. (*Thirteen* by Remy Charlip and Jerry Joyner has many examples of this.)

Have students try the ten pennies problem below. By moving only three pennies, make the arrangement point in the opposite direction.

Fig. 9.13.

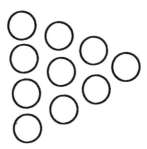

4. Another example of this type of pattern is How Many Moves. (See fig. 9.14.) Give students a copy of the worksheet and have them predict how many moves it will take to have pennies exchange places, and then try it.

5. Our brain has a tendency to want to complete patterns. Create a nonsense squiggle on a piece of paper. Give students a copy of the squiggle and ask them to make a picture from it. Have them share their finished products to see the different results that emerged from the same initial stimuli. Discuss how our own experiences shape the patterns we perceive.

   The television and board game of Concentration also illustrates our attempts to complete patterns. You may want to have students play this game.

6. The rectangle on p. 49 in *Visual Magic* seems to change shape. Ask students to try to draw this picture to discover the relationship of the lines that make this illusion. Have the students design their own illusions. (Standard 9)

Fig. 9.14. How Many Moves.

Can you predict the number of moves it would take to exchange five cubes on each side?

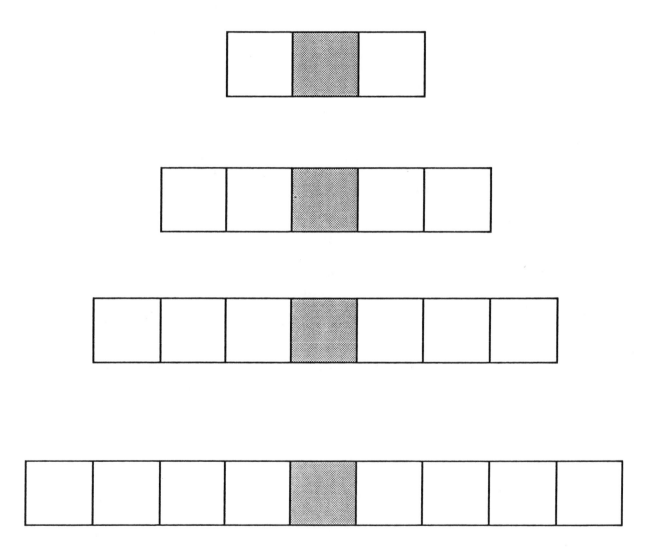

Directions: Put a penny heads up on the left side and a penny tails up on the right side. Pennies may move toward the other side one space or jump one space at a time but may never move backwards. Have the students predict how many moves it will take to have the pennies exchange places.

7. Toward the end of the book, the author includes a drawing by M. C. Escher. Escher created repetitive patterns in his work. An example of similar figures receding toward the center and diminishing in size is shown below. Using graph paper, have the students create their own repetitive design. (Standard 9)

Fig. 9.15.

8. Escher explained his drawings in terms of "regular division of the plane." An illustration he used is reproduced below. Have students try to draw one of these. (Standard 9)

Fig. 9.16

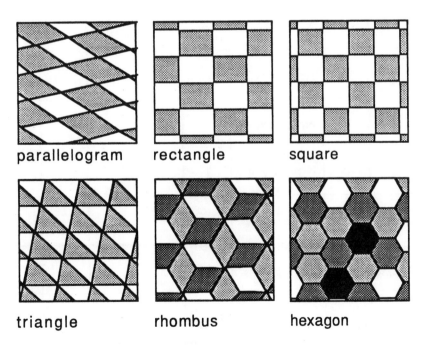

9. Escher's illustration of squares looks very much like a checkerboard. A checkerboard contains interesting patterns to explore. Have students estimate the total number of squares in an 8 x 8 square checkerboard. (See fig. 9.17). Make sure they include the 1 x 1 squares, 2 x 2 squares, 3 x 3 squares, and so on.

Fig. 9.17.

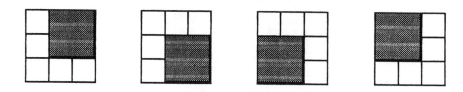

Have students complete the chart in figure 9.18 showing the number of squares in various size checkerboards. Encourage students to draw pictures such as shown above to help them figure this out. Discuss patterns. (Standard 9)

Fig. 9.18.

Size of Checkerboard

	1 by 1	2 by 2	3 by 3	4 by 4	5 by 5	6 by 6	7 by 7	8 by 8
# of 8 by 8 squares	None	None	None	None	None	None	None	
# of 7 by 7 squares	None	None	None	None	None	None	**1**	
# of 6 by 6 squares	None	None	None	None	None			
# of 5 by 5 squares	None	None	None	None				
# of 4 by 4 squares	None	None	None	**1**				
# of 3 by 3 squares	None	None						
# of 2 by 2 squares	None							
# of 1 by 1 squares	**1**	**4**		**16**		**36**		
Total number of squares	**1**							

A Clue in Code
Marilyn Singer
(New York: Harper & Row, 1985)

When the class trip money disappears from Mrs. Corfein's room, Sam and Dave Bean, twin detectives, try to solve the mystery. Sam recovers a paper airplane with a coded message written on it. Their friend, Rita O'Toole, helps them decipher the message which eventually leads them to the person who took the money.

Activities

1. When Sam, Dave, and Rita initially try to decipher the note, they use an alphabet substitution code. Rita explains how to substitute each letter for the letter that precedes it in the alphabet. Another code substitutes each letter for the letter that follows it in the alphabet. Explain to the students how to use a number substitution code. (A = 26, B = 25, C = 24, and so on.) Divide into pairs and have each student write a message using this substitution code. Have partners exchange their messages and decode.

2. The message Sam, Dave, and Rita try to decipher could have been written in many ways. Explain to the students the difference between codes and ciphers. (According to Paul B. Janeczko, author of *Loads of Codes and Secret Ciphers*, "A *code* is a word or a group of letters that stands for another word or group of words.... In a *cipher*, on the other hand, each letter or number in the message represents another letter of what is called the *plaintext*".) What Sam, Dave, and Rita discussed was really a cipher, as are the other examples we will use.

One such cipher uses times to arrive at letters by adding the numerals for each time and matching the sum to its letter position in the alphabet. Again, A = 1, B = 2, C = 3, and so on. For example: 7:45 = 7 + 4 + 5 = 16 = P, and 12:58 = 12 + 5 + 8 = 25 = Y. (Double digit numbers before the colon should be added as a double digit; those after the colon should be added as separate single digit numerals.) Have the students decipher the following: 12:29, 4:04, 1:00, 9:11   1:00   1:01, 4:59, 1:00, 5:22, 6:35. Have students use this system to encipher their own messages. (Standard 8) (From *More Codes for Kids*, © 1979 by Burton Albert, Jr. Reprinted by permission of McIntosh and Otis, Inc.)

3. Another cipher that may interest students looks something like computer feedback from a satellite. When they come to a >, have them look at the numeral that follows it. The numeral indicates the number of jumps forward needed to reach the code letter. A < and the numeral that follows it indicate the number of jumps backward. EARTH could be written as follows:

6 – M3 > 2REC – 54 + CA < 168XPH > 3BKR + 6T < 10 – 4BHY < 26 – D

(From *More Codes for Kids*, © 1979 by Burton Albert, Jr. Reprinted by permission of McIntosh and Otis, Inc.)

Have students decipher this message and then encipher their own.

> 2 MIN < 1 + B3 > 22T > 1RU – P + 6 < 5D < 1 + OE < 15 > 2QR

4. The previous ciphers have all included the key. Discuss with the students how they can use patterns to decipher a message without a key. Work with the message:

IAAP IA WP PDA YKNJAN KB JEJPD WJZ IWEJ WP OARAJ PKIKNNKS JECDP.
XNEJC AOYWLA LHWJO WJZ YKZA XKKG.

(Reprinted with the permission of Macmillan Publishing Company from *Loads of Codes and Secret Ciphers* by Paul B. Janeczko. Text © 1984 Paul B. Janeczko.)

First, it would be helpful to know the frequency list for English. (They may remember this from the chapter on statistics and probability. It is E, T, A, O, N, I, S, R, H, L, D, C, U, F, P, M, W, Y, B, G, V, K, Q, X, J, Z.) The next step is to make a frequency chart, tallying the number of times a letter appears in the cipher. In this example, A occurs most frequently; therefore, A may really be E. Have them replace the As with Es. Do any words look familiar? PDA might be THE. Write T for every P and H for every D. Continue. Eventually, the students should see the following:

W		Z	A		D			I	J			P						.
a	b	c	d	e	f	g	h	i	j	k	l	m	n	o	p	q	r	s	t	u	v	w	x	y	z

This appears to be a cipher that starts at e, runs to the end of the alphabet, and then ends at d.

Have the students study the following patterns to decipher:

a. MAX MBFX YHK RHNK XLVTIX BL GHP. EXTOX TM LXOXG. YHEEHP KHNMX MH MAX LXT VAXVDIHBGM.

(Answer: The time for your escape is now. Leave at seven. Follow route to the sea checkpoint.) (Reprinted with the permission of Macmillan Publishing Company from *Loads of Codes and Secret Ciphers* by Paul B. Janeczko. Text © 1984 Paul B. Janeczko.)

b. QCF QSJBW NBYY IF FJSYL. LVP JSF QV IF BW HJS VWF RFJQ WBWF. GFUJSQ JQ GJNW.

(Answer: The train will be early. You are to be in car one, seat nine. Depart at dawn.)

(Reprinted with the permission of Macmillan Publishing Company from *Loads of Codes and Secret Ciphers* by Paul B. Janeczko. Text © 1984 Paul B. Janeczko.)

c.

3-10-22	6-22-18-20	16-15-20-22-16-8	7-20	10-8-11-15
20-21-15	26-21-10-4-15	12-16-10-25-15-11-20	23-18	23-8
13-7-8-19-15-16	23-17	3-10-22	18-20-7-3	7-26-7-3
11-7-4-4	6-15	7-8-3	20-23-6-15	

(Answer: You must return at once. The whole project is in danger if you stay away. Call me any time.)

(Reprinted with the permission of Macmillan Publishing Company from *Loads of Codes and Secret Ciphers* by Paul B. Janeczko. Text © 1984 Paul B. Janeczko.)

5. So far, we have discussed how to use codes and ciphers to keep a message secret. What if we wanted to communicate with someone who spoke another language or was from a different planet? How would we use patterns to help others understand? Discuss this with the students and brainstorm possible ways to use patterns to communicate.

Have the students research how NASA has dealt with this issue and what diagrams and words it has sent on unmanned missions. The students might also want to research the type of messages SETI (Search for Extraterrestial Intelligence) has sent out. Ask students why mathematics is often used for this.

RELATED BOOKS AND REFERENCES

PATTERN BOOKS

Anglund, Joan Walsh. *A Friend Is Someone Who Likes You.* San Diego, Calif.: Harcourt Brace Jovanovich, 1958. (K-3)

Charlip, Remy. *Fortunately.* New York: Four Winds Press, 1964. (K-3)

Emberley, Barbara. *Drummer Hoff.* Englewood Cliffs, N.J.: Prentice-Hall, 1967. (K-3)

Joslin, Sesyle. *What Do You Say, Dear?* New York: Harper & Row, 1986. (4-6)

Kellogg, Steven. *Can I Keep Him?* New York: Dial Books for Young Readers, 1971. (4-6)

Low, Joseph. *What If...?* New York: Atheneum, 1976. (4-6)

Martin, Bill, Jr., and Eric Carle. *Brown Bear, Brown Bear, What Do You See?* New York: Henry Holt, 1983. (K-3)

_____. *Polar Bear, Polar Bear, What Do You Hear?* New York: Henry Holt, 1991. (K-3)

Mizumura, Kazue. *If I Were a Cricket...* New York: Thomas Y. Crowell, 1973. (4-6)

O'Neill, Mary. *Hailstones and Halibut Bones.* Garden City, N.Y.: Doubleday, 1961. (4-6)

Silverstein, Shel. *Who Wants a Cheap Rhinoceros?* New York: Macmillan, 1983. (4-6)

Viorst, Judith. *If I Were in Charge of the World and Other Worries.* New York: Atheneum, 1984. (4-6)

Zolotow, Charlotte. *If It Weren't for You.* New York: Harper & Row, 1966. (K-3)

_____. *Someday.* New York: Harper & Row, 1965. (K-3)

POETRY PATTERNS

Atwood, Ann. *My Own Rhythm: An Approach to Haiku.* New York: Charles Scribner's Sons, 1973. (4-6)

Bayley, Nicola. *One Old Oxford Ox.* New York: Atheneum, 1977. (K-3)

Brewton, Sara, and John E. Brewton. *Laughable Limericks.* New York: Thomas Y. Crowell, 1965. (4-6)

Cassedy, Sylvia, and Kunihiro Suetake. *Birds, Frogs, and Moonlight.* Garden City, N.Y.: Doubleday, 1967. (K-3)

Ciardi, John. *The Hopeful Trout and Other Limericks.* Boston: Houghton Mifflin, 1989. (K-3)

Corbett, Scott. *The Mysterious Zetabet.* Boston: Little, Brown, 1979. (K-3)

Rosenbloom, Joseph. *World's Toughest Tongue Twisters.* New York: Sterling, 1986. (K-3)

Ryan, Margaret. *How to Read and Write Poems.* New York: Franklin Watts, 1991. (4-6)

SECRET CODES

Albert, Burton, Jr. *Codes for Kids.* Chicago: Albert Whitman, 1976. (4-6)

Fletcher, Helen Jill. *Secret Codes.* New York: Franklin Watts, 1980. (K-3)

Janeczko, Paul B. *Loads of Codes and Secret Ciphers.* New York: Macmillan, 1984. (4-6)

Peterson, John. *How to Write Codes and Send Secret Messages.* New York: Four Winds Press, 1970. (K-3)

VISUAL PATTERNS

Gardner, Beau. *The Look Again, and Again, and Again, and Again Book.* New York: Lothrop, Lee & Shepard, 1984. (K-3)

_____. *The Turn About, Think About, and Look About Book.* New York: Lothrop, Lee & Shepard, 1980. (K-3)

Gardner, Robert. *Experimenting with Illusions.* New York: Franklin Watts, 1990. (4-6)

Shaw, Charles G. *It Looked Like Spilt Milk.* New York: Harper & Row, 1947. (K-3)

Simon, Seymour. *The Optical Illusion Book.* New York: William Morrow, 1984. (4-6)

Ziebel, Peter. *Look Closer!* New York: Clarion Books, 1989. (K-3)

MISCELLANEOUS

Burns, Marilyn. *The Book of Think*. Boston: Little, Brown, 1976. (4-6)

Charosh, Mannis. *Mathematical Games for One or Two*. New York: Thomas Y. Crowell, 1972. (K-3)

ADULT REFERENCES

Charlip, Remy, and Jerry Joyner. *Thirteen*. New York: Parents Magazine Press, 1975.

Espy, Willard R. *A Children's Almanac of Words at Play*. New York: Clarkson N. Potter, 1982.

Holt, Michael. *Math Puzzles and Games*. New York: Walker, 1977.

Schattschneider, Doris. *Visions of Symmetry: Notebooks, Periodic Drawings, and Related Work of M. C. Escher*. New York: W. H. Freeman, 1990.

Stenmark, Jean Kerr, Virginia Thompson, and Ruth Cossey. *Family Math*. Berkeley, Calif.: the Regents, University of California, 1986.

Whimby, Arthur, and Jack Lochhead. *Problem Solving and Comprehension*. Hillsdale, N.J.: Lawrence Erlbaum Associates, 1986.

Traditional Patterns of Teaching Mathematics with Changes Suggested by the NCTM Standards

Traditionally, some would suggest, mathematics teaching in the United States begins with the introduction of mathematics facts (adding, subtracting, multiplying, and dividing), and the application of mathematics principles are taught once these mathematics facts have been mastered. This approach has driven much of the scope and sequences we have seen in the student's graded textbooks. To an even larger extent this concept has driven the teaching our students have received in most classrooms. Most textbooks contain more information about math facts and computational procedures than practice with real-life situations. However, much of this information is found in extra activities or at the later stages of the textbook. Most teachers only try these extra activities or later chapters in the textbook "if there is enough time at the end of the year."

INCORPORATING THE STANDARDS INTO THE TRADITIONAL MATHEMATICS SCOPE AND SEQUENCE

The NCTM Standards are not intended to define individual courses or class sequences. Rather, they describe experiences to be included within the mathematics curriculum. A quick way to notice the difference is to recognize that the standards can be divided into two parts—the process components and the content components. The process components include problem solving, communication, reasoning, connections, and estimation. The content components include number sense and numeration, concepts of whole number operations, whole number computation, geometry and spatial sense, measurement, statistics and probability, fractions and decimals, and patterns and relationships. To help clarify these content areas, it is sometimes helpful to group them into four core experiences.

1. Use of Numbers

    a. Number Sense and Numeration

    b. Concepts of Whole Number Operations

    c. Whole Number Computation

    d. Fractions and Decimals

2. Geometry and Measurement

3. Patterns

4. Statistics and Probability

    a. Collecting Data

    b. Representing Data

    c. Interpreting Data

CONTENT TRADITIONALLY COVERED IN GRADES K-6 AND SUGGESTED CHANGES

KINDERGARTEN

Processes

- Children must be active learners

- Assist the children to realize the mathematics they already know

- Relationship of math to children's daily lives

- View the technology touching the children's lives

Use of Numbers

- Counting to 20 and writing numbers to 9

- Estimating and counting objects to 20

- Comparing two sets of objects

- Understanding ordinal numbers such as first, second, third

- Understanding vocabulary such as about, near, between, less, and more

- Consider parts and whole objects

Geometry and Measurement

- Comparing long vs. short, tall vs. short, large vs. small, and heavy vs. light

- Estimating measurements

- Recognizing and classifying simple shapes

- Recognizing colors

- Developing money awareness

- Developing beginning time and calendar awareness

Patterns

- Recognizing simple patterns
- Predicting pattern extensions
- Developing new patterns
- Focusing on regular events, shapes, designs, and sets of numbers

Statistics and Probability

- Making simple bar graphs relating to events in the children's lives
- Discussing data which connects to the children's lives
- Collecting, organizing, describing, and displaying data

FIRST GRADE

Processes

- Children must be active learners
- Discuss mathematics as it is connected to the daily lives of the children including other subject areas
- Learn strategies to solve and share mathematics situations using manipulatives, drawing pictures, and through discussion
- View and use technology that naturally touches the children's lives

Use of Numbers

- Counting, recognizing, and ordering numbers through 100
- Estimating numbers and objects to develop strong intuitive sense about number relationships using mental and calculator practice
- Skip-counting by 2, 5, and 10
- Using ordinal numbers such as first, second, tenth, etc.
- Developing place value and order concept for 1s, 10s, and 100s; using manipulatives, base ten blocks, play money, etc.
- Developing the concept of part (fractional) value such as halves, thirds, and fourths
- Learning basic adding and subtracting skills up to $9 + 9 = 18$ and $18 - 9 = 9$ using mental, paper and pencil, and calculator skills (these skills should be taught only after the children see the usefulness for these skills)
- Two-digit addition and subtraction without regrouping

Geometry and Measurement

- Draw, make, identify, and verbalize descriptions of triangles, circles, squares, and rectangles as they relate to the children's worlds, and learn vocabulary
- Introduce geometry visualization skills such as observing space and figures in space

- Use appearances to identify, compare, name, and operate on geometric figures
- Tell time to the hour and half hour
- Use calendars to recognize days, weeks, and months
- Use money to develop relative relationships among pennies, nickels, dimes, and quarters
- Estimate lengths and measures using standard, metric, and nonstandard measures

Patterns

- Recognize repeating numeric and geometric patterns
- Predict pattern extensions
- Focus on regularities and irregularities in events, shapes, designs, and sets of numbers

Statistics and Probability

- Make and interpret simple bar, line, line plot, and circle graphs representing data common to the children's lives
- Collect, organize, describe, and display data with which the children are familiar

SECOND GRADE

Processes

- Children must be active learners
- Discuss mathematics as it is connected to the daily lives of the children including other subject areas
- Practice strategies to solve and share mathematics situations using manipulatives, drawing pictures, and discussion
- View and use technology that naturally touches the children's lives

Use of Numbers

- Reading, writing, ordering numbers and their place values through 1,000. Practice to 10,000
- Skip-counting by 2, 5, and 10; practice others
- Introducing odd and even numbers
- Working with halves, thirds, and quarters
- Working with decimals of .5, .25, .75, using money to represent values
- Using ordinal numbers first ... tenth
- Understanding symbols $>$ and $<$
- Two-digit adding and subtracting skills with and without regrouping (carrying and borrowing)
- Introducing multiplication and division concepts
- Practicing estimation skills and exact answer skills using mental, paper and pencil, and calculator techniques

Geometry and Measurement

- Draw, make, identify, and verbalize descriptions of triangles, circles, squares, and rectangles as they relate to the children's worlds and learn vocabulary

- Introduce geometry visualization skills such as observing space and figures in space

- Use appearances to identify, compare, name, and operate on geometric figures

- Introduce "key problems" connected with geometry visualization skills such as incomplete concepts, orientation, and overlapping figures

- Informally recognize lines of symmetry

- Practice measuring length, area, and weight using standard and nonstandard units. Use inches, feet, yards, centimeters, meters, pounds, kilograms, quarts, and liters

- Tell time to the nearest minute

- Make change using coins and bills to solve real problems

- Understand the calendar using days, weeks, months to find dates

Patterns

- Recognize repeating numeric and geometric patterns including missing elements

- Predict pattern extensions

- Focus on regularities and irregularities in events, shapes, designs, and sets of numbers

Statistics and Probability

- Make and interpret simple bar, line, line plot, and circle graphs representing data common to the children's lives

- Collect, organize, analyze, and interpret numerical data with which the children are familiar

- Analyze uncertain situations; describe anticipated outcomes using manipulatives

THIRD GRADE

Processes

- Children must be active learners

- Discuss mathematics as it is connected to the daily lives of children including other subject areas

- Practice strategies to solve and share mathematics situations, involving more than one step, using manipulatives, drawing pictures, and through discussion

- View and use technology which naturally touches the children's lives

Use of Numbers

- Reading, writing, ordering numbers and their place values through 10,000; practice beyond 10,000

- Skip-counting by numbers 2 ... 10; practice others

- Name and compare fractions such as ½ and ¼ and relationships of fractions with whole numbers

- Work with decimals of .5, .25, .75 and terms such as tenths and hundredths, using money to represent values

- Understand symbols $>$ and $<$

- Four-digit adding and subtracting skills with and without regrouping (carrying and borrowing)

- Multiplication and division concepts—multiply two digits by one digit and divide with one divisor into two or three dividends (paper and pencil, and calculator)

- Practice estimation skills and exact answer skills using mental, paper and pencil, and calculator techniques

Geometry and Measurement

- Draw, make, identify, and verbalize descriptions of triangles, circles, squares, trapezoids, rectangles, and three-dimensional objects such as cubes and cylinders as they relate to children's worlds and learn vocabulary and spatial relationships

- Introduce geometry visualization skills such as observing space and figures in space—use active methods such as drawing, cutting, folding, acting out...

- Introduce "key problems" connected with geometry visualization skills such as incomplete concepts, orientation, and overlapping figures

- Recognize lines of symmetry, reflections, and translations

- Understand the concept of parallel and perpendicular lines

- Practice measuring length, area, and weight using standard and nonstandard units. Use inches, feet, yards, centimeters, decimeters, meters, pounds, ounces, grams, kilograms, cups, pints, quarts, liters, and Celsius and Fahrenheit

- Understand terms such as perimeter, square, volume

Patterns

- Recognize repeating numeric and geometric patterns including missing elements

- Predict pattern extensions—puzzles

- Focus on regularities and irregularities in events, shapes, designs, and sets of numbers

Statistics and Probability

- Make and interpret simple bar, line, line plot, and circle graphs representing data common to children's lives

- Collect, organize, analyze, and interpret numerical data with which the children are familiar

- Analyze uncertain situations; describe anticipated outcomes using manipulatives

- Understand the concepts of chance and averaging

FOURTH GRADE

- Students must be active learners
- Discuss mathematics as it is connected to the daily lives of students including other subject areas
- Practice strategies to solve and share mathematics situations, involving more than one step, using manipulatives, drawing pictures, and through discussion
- Practice solving complex problems in groups
- View and use technology that naturally touches the students' lives

Use of Numbers

- Learn about special terms such as multiples, prime, factors, percentages, and square numbers
- Recognize relationships of equivalent fractions
- Name and compare fractions such as ½ and ¼ and relationships of fractions with whole numbers
- Work with decimals of .5, .25, .75 and terms such as tenths and hundredths, using money to represent values
- Four-digit adding and subtracting skills with and without regrouping (carrying and borrowing)
- Multiplication and division concepts—multiply two digits by two digits and divide with two divisors into two or three dividends (paper and pencil, and calculator)
- Practice estimation skills and exact answer skills using mental, paper and pencil, and calculator techniques

Geometry and Measurement

- Discover properties of figures through analysis by using active methods such as cutting, folding, measuring…
- Move from visualization, through trial and error, to analysis
- Understand parallel and perpendicular lines by using a ruler and protractor
- Discover properties of parallelograms and triangles such as right angle and congruency
- Practice measuring length, area, and weight using standard and nonstandard units. Use inches, feet, yards, centimeters, decimeters, meters, pounds, ounces, grams, kilograms, cups, pints, quarts, liters, and Celsius and Fahrenheit
- Discover methods to determine perimeter, square, and volume

Patterns

- Recognize repeating numeric and geometric patterns including missing elements
- Predict pattern extensions—puzzles
- Focus on regularities and irregularities in events, shapes, designs, and sets of numbers
- Discover naming and uses for single and four-quadrant grids

Statistics and Probability

- Make and interpret simple bar, line, line plot, stem and leaf, and circle graphs representing data common to students' lives

- Collect, organize, analyze, and interpret numerical data with which students are familiar

- Analyze uncertain situations; describe anticipated outcomes using manipulatives and sampling data

- Understand the concepts of chance and averaging using coins, dice, cards and other real-life data and manipulatives

FIFTH GRADE

Processes

- Students must be active learners

- Understand mathematics as it is connected to the daily lives of students including other subject areas

- Practice strategies to solve and share mathematics situations, involving more than one step, using manipulatives, drawing pictures, and through discussion

- Practice solving complex problems in groups

- View and use technology that naturally touches students' lives

Use of Numbers

- Learn about special terms such as multiples, prime, factors, percentages, square and cubic numbers, common multiples and divisors, composite numbers...

- Discover fractional meanings for comparisons, equivalence, reducing, mixed numbers, and improper fractions

- Name and compare common fractions and the relationships of fractions with whole numbers

- Compute percentages and relate to decimals and fractions

- Understand purpose for ratio and proportion

- Discover value and understanding of scientific notation for use with paper and pencil, and calculator

- Practice estimation skills and exact answer skills using mental, paper and pencil, and calculator techniques

Geometry and Measurement

- Discover properties of figures through analysis by using active methods such as cutting, folding, measuring...

- Develop an understanding of the special forms of triangles and parallelograms and the factors that make them special

- Understand parallel and perpendicular lines by using a ruler and protractor to draw the figures

- Discover properties of parallelograms and triangles such as bi-sectors, right angles, and congruency
- Learn the properties of a circle such as area, radius, diameter, cord, circumference, and Pi
- Practice measuring length, area, and weight using standard and nonstandard units. Use inches, feet, yards, centimeters, decimeters, meters, pounds, ounces, grams, kilograms, cups, pints, quarts, liters, mass, and Celsius and Fahrenheit
- Discover methods to determine perimeter, square, and volume

Patterns

- Recognize repeating numeric and geometric patterns including missing elements
- Predict pattern extensions — puzzles
- Focus on regularities and irregularities in events, shapes, designs, and sets of numbers
- Discover naming and uses for single and four-quadrant grids

Statistics and Probability

- Make and interpret bar, line, line plot, stem and leaf, and circle graphs representing data common to students' lives
- Collect, organize, analyze, and interpret numerical data with which students are familiar
- Analyze uncertain situations; describe anticipated outcomes using manipulatives
- Understand the concepts of change and averaging using coins, dice, cards, and other real-life data and manipulatives
- Develop an understanding of statistical methods such as mean, median, and mode
- Develop extensive graphing abilities

SIXTH GRADE

Processes

- Students must be active learners
- Understand mathematics as it is connected to the daily lives of students including other subject areas
- Practice strategies to solve and share mathematics situations, involving more than one step, using manipulatives, drawing pictures, and through discussion
- Practice solving complex problems in groups
- View and use technology that naturally touches students' lives

Use of Numbers

- Develop beginning algebraic relationships such as equivalencies and letter and number substitutions

- Use special terms such as multiples, prime, factors, percentages, and square and cubic numbers, common multiples and divisors, composite numbers...

- Discover fractional meanings for comparisons, equivalence, reducing, mixed numbers, and improper fractions

- Compute percentages and relate them to decimals and fractions

- Understand purpose for ratio and proportion

- Discover value and understanding of scientific notation for use with paper and pencil, and calculator

- Practice estimation skills and exact answer skills using mental, paper/pencil, and calculator techniques

Geometry and Measurement

- Begin developing geometry skills of informal deduction; interrelate properties within and between figures and follow informal arguments such as what else can be concluded from given data

- Understand parallel and perpendicular lines by using a ruler and protractor

- Discover properties of parallelograms and triangles such as bi-sectors, right angles, and congruency

- Learn the properties of a circle such as area, radius, diameter, cord, circumference, and Pi

- Practice measuring length, area, weight, and temperature using standard and nonstandard units

- Discover methods to determine perimeter, square, and volume

Patterns

- Recognize repeating numeric and geometric patterns including missing elements

- Predict pattern extensions based on incomplete data

- Focus on regularities and irregularities in events, shapes, designs and sets of numbers

- Discover naming and uses for single and four-quadrant grids

Statistics and Probability

- Make and interpret simple bar, line, line plot, stem and leaf, and circle graphs representing data common to students' lives

- Develop extensive graphing abilities and determine most appropriate method for desired information

- Collect, organize, analyze, and interpret numerical data with which students are familiar

- Analyze uncertain situations; describe anticipated outcomes using manipulatives

- Understand the concepts of chance and averaging using coins, dice, cards and other real-life data and manipulatives, such as sum of numbers, on a given set of number cubes

- Develop an understanding of statistical methods such as mean, median, and mode

Index

A, My Name Is Alice (Bayer), 176
"Across the United States on Wheels," 44 (fig.)
Adams, Laurie
    Alice and the Boa Constrictor, 159-60
Addend, 38
Addition, 38-40, 203, 204, 206, 207
    Annie's One to Ten (Owen), 41-42
    Counting Wildflowers (McMillan), 39-40
    So Many Cats (de Regniers), 40-41
Adler, David A.
    Roman Numerals, 22-23
Alexander, Who Used to Be Rich Last Sunday (Viorst),
    51-52
Alice and the Boa Constrictor (Adams and Coudert),
    159-60
Angles, 63, 208-9, 210
    Grandfather Tang's Story (Tompert), 72-75
Annie's One to Ten (Owen), 41-42
Anno, Masaichiro
    Anno's Mysterious Multiplying Jar, 52
Anno, Mitsumasa
    Anno's Math Games III, 68-71
    Anno's Mysterious Multiplying Jar, 52
Anno's Math Games III (Anno), 68-71
Anno's Mysterious Multiplying Jar (Anno and Anno), 52
Area, 97, 205, 206, 207, 209, 210
    Pezzettino (Lionni), 101-2
"Area Measurement Data Collection Sheet," 26 (fig.)
Around the World in Eighty Days (Verne), 116-18
Arthur's Funny Money (Hoban), 155-57
Asch, Frank
    Popcorn, 48-50
"Average Outside Temperature," 137 (fig.)
Averages, 11, 17-19, 21, 23-24, 124, 132, 206, 208, 209,
    210. *See also* Standard 6
    Averages (Srivastava), 129-30
    Miss Pickerell and the Weather Satellite
        (MacGregor and Pantell), 134-36, 137
    What Do You Mean by "Average"?, (James and
        Barkin), 133-34
Averages (Srivastava), 129-30

Barkin, Carol
    What Do You Mean by "Average"?, 133-34

Base systems, 11, 21
    How to Count Like a Martian (St. John), 33-34
    One Wide River to Cross (Emberley), 17-19
Bayer, Jane
    A, My Name is Alice, 176
Becoming a Nation of Readers: The Report of the
    Commission on Reading, 3
The Boy with Square Eyes (Snape and Snape), 77-81
Brown, Jeff
    Flat Stanley, 67-68
Bunches and Bunches of Bunnies (Mathews), 45-47

Calendar, 97, 107 (fig.), 204, 205
    The Day That Monday Ran Away (Heit), 105-7
    Diary of a Church Mouse (Oakley), 108-9
Carle, Eric
    The Grouchy Ladybug, 98-99
Carlson, Nancy
    Harriet's Halloween Candy, 23-24
The Case of the Stolen Code Book (Rinkoff), 181-82
Charosh, Mannis
    Number Ideas Through Pictures, 178
"Check Register," 29 (fig.)
Checkerboard patterns, 194 (figs.)
Ciphers, 182 (fig.)
    A Clue in Code (Singer), 195-97
"Class Birthdays," 127 (fig.)
A Clue in Code (Singer), 195-97
Codes, 182 (fig.)
    The Case of the Stolen Code Book (Rinkoff), 181-82
    A Clue in Code (Singer), 195-97
Cole, Joanna
    The Magic School Bus at the Waterworks, 169-71
    The Magic School Bus Inside the Earth, 112-14
    The Magic School Bus Inside the Human Body,
        114-15
    The Magic School Bus Lost in the Solar System,
        56-57
Communication. *See* Standard 2: Mathematics as
    Communication
Conford, Ellen
    What's Cooking, Jenny Archer?, 161-62
Connections. *See* Standard 4: Mathematical Connections
Content components. *See* Standards 6 through 13

"Coordinate Graphing," 30 (fig.)
Coudert, Allison
    Alice and the Boa Constrictor, 159-60
Counting, 11, 202, 203, 204, 206
    One Watermelon Seed (Lottridge), 16-17
    One Wide River to Cross (Emberley), 17-19
    10 Bears in My Bed (Mack), 12
Counting Wildflowers (McMillan), 39-40
Cubes, 27 (fig.)
Cushman, Jean
    Do You Wanna Bet?, 136-43

The Day That Monday Ran Away (Heit), 105-7
de la Luz Krahn, Maria
    The Life of Numbers, 14-15
de Regniers, Beatrice Schenk
    So Many Cats, 40-41
Decimals, 204, 206, 207, 208, 210. *See also* Standard
    12: Fractions and Decimals
Dennis, J. Richard
    Fractions Are Parts of Things, 151-52
Diary of a Church Mouse (Oakley), 108-9
"Dice Toss," 142 (fig.)
Division, 38-39, 204, 206, 207
    The Doorbell Rang (Hutchins), 47-48
Do You Wanna Bet?, (Cushman), 136-43
Dollars and Cents for Harriet (Maestro and Maestro),
    150-51
The Doorbell Rang (Hutchins), 47-48
Dots, 153 (fig.)
Dr. Seuss
    The Shape of Me and Other Stuff, 64-65

"Ehrenstein Grids," 190 (fig.)
8,000 Stones (Wolkstein), 109-10, 111
Emberley, Barbara
    One Wide River to Cross, 17-19
Ernst, Lisa Campbell
    Sam Johnson and the Blue Ribbon Quilt, 179-81
Escher, M. C., 182, 193 (figs.)
    Visual Magic (Thomson), 190-194
Estimation. *See* Standard 5: Estimation
Even numbers. *See* numbers

Factor, 38
"Favorite Pets," 156 (figs.)
Fibonacci sequence, 182, 187
    Sea Witches (Robertson and Gal), 185-89
Flat Stanley (Brown), 67-68
Fleet-Footed Florence (Sachs), 126
Fractions, 153 (fig.), 154 (fig.), 171 (fig.), 203, 204,
    206, 207, 208, 210. *See also* Standard 12:
    Fractions and Decimals
    Fractions Are Parts of Things (Dennis), 151-52
Fractions Are Parts of Things (Dennis), 151-52
Froman, Robert
    Less Than Nothing Is Really Something, 28-30
    Rubber Bands, Baseballs, and Doughnuts, 88-90

Gal, Laszlo
    Sea Witches, 185-89
Gator Pie (Mathews), 149-50
Geometry. *See also* Standard 9: Geometry and Spatial
    Sense
    patterns, 74-75 (figs.)
Giganti, Paul
    How Many Snails?, 15-16
Goldreich, Esther
    What Can She Be? An Architect, 87-88
Goldreich, Gloria
    What Can She Be? An Architect, 87-88
Grandfather Tang's Story (Tompert), 72-75
Graphs, 21, 180-81 (figs.), 203, 204, 205, 206, 208, 209,
    210
    The Day That Monday Ran Away (Heit), 105-7
    Harriet's Halloween Candy (Carlson), 23-24
    Henry's Pennies (McNamara), 152, 155, 156
    Less Than Nothing Is Really Something (Froman),
        28-30
    Moira's Birthday (Munsch), 127-29
The Great Take-Away (Mathews), 42-43
The Grouchy Ladybug (Carle), 98-99

Harold & Chester in Hot Fudge (Howe), 157-58
Harriet Goes to the Circus (Maestro and Maestro), 13-14
Harriet's Halloween Candy (Carlson), 23-24
Heavy Is a Hippopotamus (Schlein), 103-5
Heit, Robert
    The Day That Monday Ran Away, 105-7
Henry's Pennies (McNamara), 152, 155, 156
Hoban, Lillian
    Arthur's Funny Money, 155-57
How Big Is a Foot? (Myller), 99-101
How Did Numbers Begin? (Sitomer and Sitomer), 21-22
"How Many Moves," 192 (fig.)
How Many Snails (Giganti), 15-16
How Much Is a Million? (Schwartz), 53-56
"How to build a balance scale," 111 (fig.)
How to Count Like a Martian (St. John), 33-34
Howe, James
    Harold & Chester in Hot Fudge, 157-58
"Hundred Chart," 18 (fig.)
Hutchins, Pat
    The Doorbell Rang, 47-48

If You Made a Million (Schwartz), 163-65
Interest, 164 (fig.)

James, Elizabeth
    What Do You Mean by "Average"?, 133-34
Jason and the Money Tree (Levitin), 165-66

"Kanizsa Triangle," 190 (fig.)
Kirigami, 76, 206, 207, 208
    Paper John (Small), 76-77
Klevin, Jill Ross
    The Turtle Street Trading Co., 167-69

Krahn, Fernando
  The Life of Numbers, 14-15

Laithwaite, Eric
  Shape: The Purpose of Forms, 83-86
Less Than Nothing Is Really Something (Froman), 28-30
Levitin, Sonia
  Jason and the Money Tree, 165-66
The Life of Numbers (Krahn and de la Luz Krahn), 14-15
Linear measurement, 97, 100 (fig.), 202, 204, 205, 206,
    207, 209, 210
  How Big Is a Foot? (Myller), 99-101
"Linear measurement data collection sheet," 100 (fig.)
Linn, Charles F.
  Probability, 131-32
Lionni, Leo
  Pezzettino, 101-2
Lottridge, Celia Barker
  One Watermelon Seed, 16-17

MacGregor, Ellen
  Miss Pickerell and the Weather Satellite, 134-36, 137
Mack, Stan
  10 Bears in My Bed, 12
Maestro, Betsy
  Dollars and Cents for Harriet, 150-51
  Harriet Goes to the Circus, 13-14
Maestro, Giulio
  Dollars and Cents for Harriet, 150-51
  Harriet Goes to the Circus, 13-14
The Magic School Bus at the Waterworks (Cole), 169-71
The Magic School Bus Inside the Earth (Cole), 112-14
The Magic School Bus Inside the Human Body (Cole),
    114-15
The Magic School Bus Lost in the Solar System (Cole),
    56-57
"Magic Square," 27 (fig.)
Mathematical connections. *See* Standard 4:
    Mathematical Connections
Mathematics
  communication. *See* Standard 2: Mathematics as
      Communication
  problem solving. *See* Standard 1: Mathematics as
      Problem Solving
  reasoning. *See* Standard 3: Mathematics as
      Reasoning
Mathematics education, overview, 1-6
  calculator use, 6
  essentials of education, 2
  historical perspective, 1-2
  integration into language arts, 5
  NCTM curriculum and evaluation standards, 3
  preschool, 4-5
  reading, role of, 2-3
  rote learning, 3-4
Mathews, Louise
  Bunches and Bunches of Bunnies, 45-47
  Gator Pie, 149-150
  The Great Take-Away, 42-43

"Maze," 71 (fig.)
McMillan, Bruce
  Counting Wildflowers, 39-40
McNamara, Louise
  Henry's Pennies, 152, 155, 156
Measurement. *See* Standard 10: Measurement
Merrill, Jean
  The Toothpaste Millionaire, 57-60
Million Dollar Jeans (Roy), 144-45
Miss Pickerell and the Weather Satellite (MacGregor
    and Pantell), 134-36, 137
Mode, bar graph, 130 (fig.)
Moira's Birthday (Munsch), 127-29
Money, 39, 48, 148, 158, 204, 205, 207
  Alexander, Who Used to Be Rich Last Sunday
      (Viorst), 51-52
  Alice and the Boa Constrictor (Adams and
      Coudert), 159-60
  Arthur's Funny Money (Hoban), 155-57
  Dollars and Cents for Harriet (Maestro and
      Maestro), 150-51
  Henry's Pennies (McNamara), 152, 155, 156
  If You Made a Million (Schwartz), 163-65
  Jason and the Money Tree (Levitin), 165-66
  Penelope Gets Wheels (Peterson), 43-45
  The Toothpaste Millionaire (Merrill), 57-60
  The Turtle Street Trading Co. (Klevin), 167-69
  What's Cooking, Jenny Archer? (Conford), 161-62
Mori, Tuyosi
  Socrates and the Three Little Pigs, 145-46
Multiple, 38
Multiplication, 38, 204, 206, 207
  Bunches and Bunches of Bunnies (Mathews), 45-47
  Number Families (Srivastava), 31-32
Munsch, Robert
  Moira's Birthday, 127-29
Myller, Rolf
  How Big Is a Foot?, 99-101

National Council of Teachers of Mathematics (NCTM)
    Standards. *See* specific standard numbers
National Institute of Education
  *Becoming a Nation of Readers: The Report of the
      Commission on Reading,* 3
NCTM Standards. *See also* specific standard numbers
Negative numbers, 21
  Less Than Nothing Is Really Something (Froman),
      28-30
Netts, 84
  monoclinic, 85 (fig.)
  orthorhombic, 86 (fig.)
Number Families (Srivastava), 31-32
Number Ideas Through Pictures (Charosh), 178
"# of Children x Height," 54 (fig.)
Number patterns, 175-76, 177 (fig.), 182-89, 202, 203,
    204, 205, 206, 207, 209, 210
  Sea Witches (Robertson and Gal), 185-89
  Some Things Go Together (Zolotow), 175-76, 177 (fig.)
  Too Hot to Hoot (Terban), 183-84

Number sense and numeration. *See* Standard 6: Number Sense and Numeration
Numeration. *See* Standard 6: Number Sense and Numeration
Numbers, 175, 204
    Number Families (Srivastava), 31-32
    Number Ideas Through Pictures (Charosh), 178

Oakley, Graham
    Diary of a Church Mouse, 108-9
Odd numbers. *See* numbers
One Watermelon Seed (Lottridge), 16-17
One Wide River to Cross (Emberley), 17-19
Origami, 76, 206, 207, 208
    Paper John (Small), 76-77
Owen, Annie
    Annie's One to Ten, 41-42

Paine, Penelope Colville
    Time for Horatio, 110-12
Palindromes, 182
    Too Hot to Hoot (Terban), 183-84
Pantell, Dora
    Miss Pickerell and the Weather Satellite, 134-36, 137
Paper John (Small), 76-77
Pascal's Triangle, 182, 187-88 (figs.)
    Sea Witches (Robertson and Gal), 185-89
"Pattern sequences," 186 (fig.)
Patterns and relationships. *See* Standard 13: Patterns and Relationships
Penelope Gets Wheels (Peterson), 43-45
Peterson, Esther Allen
    Penelope Gets Wheels, 43-45
Pezzettino (Lionni), 101-2
"Picture clock," 98 (fig.)
Place value, 11
    One Wide River to Cross (Emberley), 17-19
    Zero. Is It Something? Is It Nothing? (Zaslavsky), 19-20
Popcorn (Asch), 48-50
Probability, 206, 208. *See also* Standard 11: Statistics and Probability
Probability (Linn), 131-32
Problem solving. *See* Standard 1: Mathematics as Problem Solving
Process components, Standards 1 through 5, 7-9
Product, 38
"Proportional drawing," 79 (fig.)
"Paper puzzles," 78 (fig.)

Quotient, 38

Razzell, Arthur G.
    This Is 4: The Idea of a Number, 24-28
Reasoning. *See* Standard 3: Mathematics as Reasoning
Relationships. *See* Standard 13: Patterns and Relationships
Rinkoff, Barbara
    The Case of the Stolen Code Book, 181-82

Robertson, Joanne
    Sea Witches, 185-89
Rogers, Paul
    The Shapes Game, 65-66
Roman numerals, 22-23
Roman Numerals (Adler), 22-23
Roy, Ron
    Million Dollar Jeans, 144-45
Rubber Bands, Baseballs, and Doughnuts (Froman), 88-90

Sachs, Marilyn
    Fleet-Footed Florence, 126
Sam Johnson and the Blue Ribbon Quilt (Ernst), 179-81
Scaling
    What Can She Be? An Architect (Goldreich and Goldreich), 87-88
Schlein, Miriam
    Heavy Is a Hippopotamus, 103-5
Schwartz, David M.
    How Much Is a Million?, 53-56
    If You Made a Million, 163-65
Sea Witches (Robertson and Gal), 185-89
"Search for Fractional Wholes," 154 (fig.), 171 (fig.)
"Seasons Birthday Bar Graph," 128 (fig.)
Shape: The Purpose of Forms (Laithwaite), 83-86
The Shape of Me and Other Stuff (Dr. Seuss), 64-65
Shapes, 63, 203-4, 205, 206, 207, 209, 210
    Shape: The Purpose of Forms (Laithwaite), 83-86
    The Shape of Me and Other Stuff (Dr. Seuss), 64-65
    The Shapes Game (Rogers), 65-66
The Shapes Game (Rogers), 65-66
Singer, Marilyn
    A Clue in Code, 195-97
Sitomer, Harry
    How Did Numbers Begin?, 21-22
    Spirals, 82-83
    What Is Symmetry?, 66-67
Sitomer, Mindel
    How Did Numbers Begin?, 21-22
    Spirals, 82-83
    What Is Symmetry?, 66-67
Small, David
    Paper John, 76-77
Snape, Charles
    The Boy with Square Eyes, 77-81
Snape, Juliet
    The Boy with Square Eyes, 77-81
So Many Cats (de Regniers), 40-41
Socrates and the Three Little Pigs (Mori), 145-46
Solomon Grundy, Born on Oneday (Weiss), 189-90
Some Things Go Together (Zolotow), 175-76, 177 (fig.)
Space, Shapes, and Sizes (Srivastava), 102-3
Spatial relationships
    Anno's Math Games III, (Anno), 68-71
Spirals (Sitomer and Sitomer), 82-83
Spinners, 141 (fig.)
"Sprouts," 90 (fig.)
"Squaring up," 81 (fig.)

Srivastava, Jane Jonas
  Averages, 129-30
  Number Families, 31-32
  Space, Shapes, and Sizes, 102-3
  Statistics, 125
St. John, Glory
  How To Count Like a Martian, 33-34
Standard 1: Mathematics as Problem Solving, 7, 201, 202
Standard 2: Mathematics as Communication, 8, 201
Standard 3: Mathematics as Reasoning, 8, 201
Standard 4: Mathematical Connections, 9, 201
Standard 5: Estimation, 9, 201, 207, 208, 210
Standard 6: Number Sense and Numeration, 11-34, 201
  "Area Measurement Data Collection Sheet," 26 (fig.)
  averages, 11, 17-19, 21, 23-24, 208
  base systems, 11, 17-19, 21, 33-34
  "Check Register," 29 (fig.)
  "Coordinate Graphing," 30 (fig.)
  counting, 11, 12, 16-19, 202, 203, 204, 206
  cubes, 27 (fig.)
  definition of, 11
  graphs, 21, 23-24, 28-30, 203
  Harriet Goes to the Circus (Maestro and Maestro), 13-14
  Harriet's Halloween Candy (Carlson), 23-24
  How Did Numbers Begin? (Sitomer and Sitomer), 21-22
  How Many Snails? (Giganti), 15-16
  How to Count Like a Martian (St. John), 33-34
  "Hundred Chart," 18 (fig.)
  Less Than Nothing Is Really Something (Froman), 28-30
  The Life of Numbers (Krahn and de la Luz Krahn), 14-15
  "Magic Square," 27 (fig.)
  negative numbers, 28-30
  Number Families (Srivastava), 31-32
  odd and even numbers, 31-32, 204
  One Watermelon Seed (Lottridge), 16-17
  One Wide River to Cross (Emberley), 17-19
  place value, 11, 17-20
  Roman Numerals (Adler), 22-23
  10 Bears in My Bed (Mack), 12
  This Is 4: The Idea of a Number (Razzell and Watts), 24-28
  Zero. Is It Something? Is It Nothing? (Zaslavsky), 19-20
Standards 7 and 8: Concepts of Whole-Number Operations and Whole-Number Computation, 38-60, 201
  "Across the United States on Wheels," 44 (fig.)
  addition, 39-40, 203, 204, 206, 207
  Alexander, Who Used to Be Rich Last Sunday (Viorst), 51-52
  Annie's One to Ten (Owen), 41-42
  Anno's Mysterious Multiplying Jar (Anno and Anno), 52
  Bunches and Bunches of Bunnies (Mathews), 45-47
  Counting Wildflowers (McMillan), 39-40

  definitions, 38-39
  division, 47-48, 204, 206, 207
  The Doorbell Rang (Hutchins), 47-48
  The Great Take-Away (Mathews), 42-43
  How Much Is a Million? (Schwartz), 53-56
  The Magic School Bus Lost in the Solar System (Cole), 56-57
  money, 39, 48, 57-60
  multiplication, 38, 45-47, 204, 206, 207
  "# of Children x Height," 54 (fig.)
  Penelope Gets Wheels (Peterson), 43-45
  Popcorn (Asch), 48-50
  So Many Cats (de Regniers), 40-41
  subtraction, 38, 39-40, 42-45, 203, 204, 206, 207
  The Toothpaste Millionaire (Merrill), 57-60
Standard 9: Geometry and Spatial Sense, 63-90, 202
  angles, 63, 72-75, 208-9, 210
  Anno's Math Games III (Anno), 68-71
  The Boy with Square Eyes (Snape and Snape), 77-81
  definition, 63
  Flat Stanley (Brown), 67-68
  geometry patterns, 74-75 (figs.)
  Grandfather Tang's Story (Tompert), 72-75
  kirigami, 76, 77, 206, 207, 208
  "Maze," 71 (fig.)
  netts, 85-86 (figs.)
  origami, 76, 206, 207, 208
  Paper John (Small), 76-77
  "Proportional drawing," 79 (fig.)
  "Paper puzzles," 78 (fig.)
  Rubber Bands, Baseballs, and Doughnuts (Froman), 88-90
  scaling, 87-88
  Shape: The Purpose of Forms (Laithwaite), 83-86
  The Shape of Me and Other Stuff (Dr. Seuss), 64-65
  shapes, 63-66, 203-4, 205, 206, 207, 209, 210
  The Shapes Game (Rogers), 65-66
  spatial relationships, 68-71
  Spirals (Sitomer and Sitomer), 82-83
  "Sprouts," 90 (fig.)
  "Squaring up," 81 (fig.)
  symmetry, 63, 66-67, 76-77, 83-86, 205, 206
  tangram, making your own, 73 (fig.)
  topology, 68-71, 76, 88-90
  "Triangle Design," 70 (fig.)
  What Can She Be? An Architect (Goldreich and Goldreich), 87-88
  What Is Symmetry? (Sitomer and Sitomer), 66-67
Standard 10: Measurement, 97-118, 202
  area, 97, 101-2, 205, 206, 207, 209, 210
  Around the World in Eighty Days (Verne), 116-18
  calendar, 97, 105-9, 107 (fig.), 204, 205
  The Day That Monday Ran Away (Heit), 105-7
  definition, 97
  Diary of a Church Mouse (Oakley), 108-9
  8,000 Stones (Wolkstein), 109-10, 111
  graphs, 105-7, 127-29, 152, 155, 156, 203, 204, 205, 206, 208, 209, 210
  The Grouchy Ladybug (Carle), 98-99

Standard 10: Measurement (continued)
  Heavy Is a Hippopotamus (Schlein), 103-5
  How Big Is a Foot? (Myller), 99-101
  "How to build a balance scale," 111 (fig.)
  linear measurement, 97, 99-101, 100 (fig.), 202, 204, 205, 206, 207, 209, 210
  The Magic School Bus Inside the Earth (Cole), 112-14
  The Magic School Bus Inside the Human Body (Cole), 114-15
  Pezzettino (Lionni), 101-2
  Space, Shapes, and Sizes (Srivastava), 102-3
  temperature, 108, 112-15, 207, 209, 210
  time, 97, 98-99, 204, 205
  Time for Horatio (Paine), 110-12
  volume, 97, 102-3, 108, 114-15, 207, 209, 210
  weight, 97, 103-5, 108, 109-10, 111, 205, 206, 207, 209, 210
Standard 11: Statistics and Probability, 124-46, 202
  "Average Outside Temperature," 137 (fig.)
  averages, 124, 129-30, 132-36, 206, 208, 209, 210
  Averages (Srivastava), 129-30
  "Class Birthdays," 127 (fig.)
  definition, 124
  "Dice Toss," 142 (fig.)
  Do You Wanna Bet? (Cushman), 136-43
  Fleet-Footed Florence (Sachs), 126
  Million Dollar Jeans (Roy), 144-45
  Miss Pickerell and the Weather Satellite (MacGregor and Pantell), 134-36, 137
  mode, bar graph, 130 (fig.)
  Moira's Birthday (Munsch), 127-29
  probability, 124, 131-32, 134-43, 206, 208
  Probability (Linn), 131-32
  "Seasons Birthday Bar Graph," 128 (fig.)
  Socrates and the Three Little Pigs (Mori), 145-46
  spinners, 141 (fig.)
  Statistics (Srivastava), 125
  What Do You Mean by "Average"? (James and Barkin), 133-34
Standard 12: Fractions and Decimals, 148-71, 201-2
  Alice and the Boa Constrictor (Adams and Coudert), 159-60
  Arthur's Funny Money (Hoban), 155-57
  decimals, 148-51, 152, 155, 157-62, 204, 206, 207, 208, 210
  definition, 148
  Dollars and Cents for Harriet (Maestro and Maestro), 150-51
  dots, 153 (fig.)
  "Favorite Pets," 156 (figs.)
  fractions, 148-50, 151-52, 153-54, 157-60, 169-71, 203, 204, 206, 207, 208, 210
  Fractions Are Parts of Things (Dennis), 151-52, 153-54, 171
  Gator Pie (Mathews), 149-50
  graphs, 148, 152, 155, 156
  Harold & Chester in Hot Fudge (Howe), 157-58
  Henry's Pennies (McNamara), 152, 155, 156

  If You Made a Million (Schwartz), 163-65
  interest, 164 (fig.)
  Jason and the Money Tree (Levitin), 165-66
  The Magic School Bus at the Waterworks (Cole), 169-71
  money, 148, 150-51, 152, 155, 157-66, 204, 207
  "Search for Fractional Wholes," 154 (fig.), 171 (fig.)
  The Turtle Street Trading Co. (Klevin), 167-69
  What's Cooking, Jenny Archer? (Conford), 161-62
Standard 13: Patterns and Relationships, 175-97, 202
  A, My Name Is Alice (Bayer), 176
  The Case of the Stolen Code Book (Rinkoff), 181-82
  checkerboard patterns, 194 (figs.)
  A Clue in Code (Singer), 195-97
  definition, 175
  "Ehrenstein Grids," 190 (fig.)
  Escher, M. C., 182, 193-94 (figs.)
  Fibonacci sequence, 182, 187
  graphs, 180-81 (figs.)
  "How Many Moves," 192 (fig.)
  "Kanizsa Triangle," 190 (fig.)
  Number Ideas Through Pictures (Charosh), 178
  number patterns, 175-76, 177 (fig.), 182-89, 202, 203, 204, 205, 206, 207, 209, 210
  numbers, 175, 178, 204
  palindromes, 182, 183-84
  Pascal's Triangle, 182, 187-88 (figs.)
  "Pattern sequences," 186 (fig.)
  Sam Johnson and the Blue Ribbon Quilt (Ernst), 179-81
  Sea Witches (Robertson and Gal), 185-89
  Solomon Grundy, Born on Oneday (Weiss), 189-90
  Some Things Go Together (Zolotow), 175-76, 177 (fig.)
  temperature, 189 (fig.)
  Too Hot to Hoot (Terban), 183-84
  Visual Magic (Thomson), 190-94
  visual patterns, 175, 179-81, 202, 203, 204, 205, 206, 207, 208, 209, 210
  "0-99 chart," 184 (fig.)
Statistics. See Standard 11: Statistics and Probability
Statistics (Srivastava), 125
Subtraction, 38, 203, 204, 206, 207
  Annie's One to Ten (Owen), 41-42
  Counting Wildflowers (McMillan), 39-40
  The Great Take-Away (Mathews), 42-43
  Penelope Gets Wheels (Peterson), 43-45
Sum difference, 38
Symmetry, 63, 205, 206
  Paper John (Small), 76-77
  Shape: The Purpose of Forms (Laithwaite), 83-86
  What Is Symmetry? (Sitomer and Sitomer), 66-67

Tangram, making your own, 73 (fig.)
Temperature, 97, 108, 189 (fig.), 207, 209, 210
  The Magic School Bus Inside the Earth (Cole), 112-14
  The Magic School Bus Inside the Human Body (Cole), 114-15

10 Bears in My Bed (Mack), 12
Terban, Marvin
   Too Hot to Hoot, 183-84
This Is 4: The Idea of a Number (Razzell and Watts),
   24-28
Thomson, David
   Visual Magic, 190-94
Time, 97, 98 (fig.), 204, 205
   The Grouchy Ladybug (Carle), 98-99
Time for Horatio (Paine), 110-12
Tompert, Ann
   Grandfather Tang's Story, 72-75
Too Hot to Hoot (Terban), 183-84
The Toothpaste Millionaire (Merrill), 57-60
Topology, 76
   Anno's Math Games III (Anno), 68-71
   Rubber Bands, Baseballs, and Doughnuts
      (Froman), 88-90
"Triangle Design," 70 (fig.)
The Turtle Street Trading Co. (Klevin), 167-69

Verne, Jules
   Around the World in Eighty Days, 116-18
Viorst, Judith
   Alexander, Who Used to Be Rich Last Sunday,
      51-52
Visual patterns, 175, 202, 203, 204, 205, 206, 207, 208,
   209, 210
   Sam Johnson and the Blue Ribbon Quilt (Ernst),
      179-81

Volume, 97, 108, 205, 206, 207, 209, 210
   The Magic School Bus Inside the Human Body
      (Cole), 114-15
   Space, Shapes, and Sizes (Srivastava), 102-3

Watts, K. G. O.
   This Is 4: The Idea of a Number, 24-28
Weight, 97, 108, 205, 206, 207, 209, 210
   8,000 Stones (Wolkstein), 109-10, 111
   Heavy Is a Hippopotamus (Schlein), 103-5
Weiss, Malcolm E.
   Solomon Grundy, Born on Oneday, 189-90
What Can She Be? An Architect (Goldreich and
   Goldreich), 87-88
What Do You Mean by "Average"? (James and Barkin),
   133-34
What Is Symmetry? (Sitomer and Sitomer), 66-67
What's Cooking, Jenny Archer? (Conford), 161-62
Whole-number computation. *See* Standard 8:
   Whole-Number Computation
Whole-number operations. *See* Standard 7:
   Whole-Number Operations
Wolkstein, Diane
   8,000 Stones, 109-10, 111
Zaslavsky, Claudia
   Zero. Is It Something? Is It Nothing?, 19-20
Zero. Is It Something? Is It Nothing? (Zaslavsky), 19-20
"0-99 chart," 184 (fig.)
Zolotow, Charlotte
   Some Things Go Together, 175-76, 177 (fig.)

About the Authors

Kathryn L. Braddon has been a reading specialist for more than 20 years with the Manchester-Shortsville Central School District. She is a member of the International Reading Association (IRA) and local reading council, the Association of Math Teachers of New York State (AMTNYS), and Delta Kappa Gamma. Mrs. Braddon is a contributing editor for *Helping Children Learn* newspaper and an author of activities soon to be published that will accompany multicultural children's literature. She is a winner of nine Teacher Resource Center minigrants and a noted conference speaker.

Nancy J. Hall began her career as a pre-first teacher in New York in 1977. Since then, she has worked with students from preschool through college level in both public and private schools. She has experience with children considered to be handicapped, average, and gifted in the regular classroom, pull-out programs, and in a laboratory school. She has served as Executive Director of Connections, a nonprofit organization designed to work with girls and women in math and science, and in 1988 received an award for excellence in teaching from the University of Northern Colorado. Ms. Hall has been active in designing curricula for 15 years and was selected to serve on the Colorado State Task Force on Elementary Curriculum. She is employed as an Instructional Designer at Red Rocks Community College in Lakewood, Colorado. Ms. Hall is married and lives in the mountains outside of Denver.

Dale Taylor is a K-5 school principal and the K-12 District Curriculum Director for the East Grand Forks, Minnesota Public Schools. In addition, he teaches at the University of North Dakota in the Center for Teaching and Learning and serves as the chairperson of the Advisory Councils for the Academies of the Deaf and Blind in Faribault, Minnesota. As a current member of the Minnesota "PRIME" committee, a group working within the Minnesota Council of Teachers of Mathematics, Mr. Taylor is responsible for providing inservice opportunities on the NCTM Standards to the teachers in northwestern Minnesota. He is married and has two sons.